CW00760503

Finding Mangan

Finding Mangan

The Lives and Afterlives of Ireland's National Poet

Bridget Hourican

GILL BOOKS

Gill Books
Hume Avenue
Park West
Dublin 12
www.gillbooks.ie

Gill Books is an imprint of M.H. Gill and Co.

9780717194834

Designed by Bartek Janczak
Print origination by Dexal Design
Edited by Djinn von Noorden
Proofread by Sally Vince
Printed and bound by L&C Printing, Poland
This book is typeset in Minion Pro.

For permission to reproduce poetry, the author and publisher gratefully
acknowledge the following:

© Bloodaxe Books; Faber & Faber

The paper used in this book comes from the wood pulp
of sustainably managed forests.

A CIP catalogue record for this book is available from the
British Library.

5 4 3 2 1

For Frank

Contents

I fell through that pit abysmal

I first heard of James Clarence Mangan – or at least his name first floated free from the morass of Irish poets before Yeats – in the early hours of Monday, 4 August 2008, in a bar called McGruders on Thomas Street, in the Liberties. It was a bank holiday weekend and my friends and I had hatched an ambitious plan to get wasted away from our usual haunts. McGruders sounded promising: recently opened with a very young owner rumoured to be from a family with 'connections'.

We arrived late on the Sunday night to find that McGruders had the tatty, hopeful, makeshift air of a squat – rooms spiralling into other rooms and out to courtyards hung with bobbing lanterns – but there was hardly anyone around. Dublin sweeps clean for the August bank holiday and we'd got it wrong: the flotsam wasn't washing up here. But we'd come this far and the people, if few, weren't dull: a mix of street locals and art students from the college up the road. Our drug hopes centred on a long, tall boy who greeted us like long-lost friends and was clearly off his head. He kept hitting his phone first on his head and then off the table, until it finally smashed, to his great astonishment. But whatever he was on, what he sold us didn't work. We were retreating into stoical irony when at about midnight everything changed: Shane MacGowan arrived with a girl who had the kind of technicolour looks that make everyone else look like they're in black and white. My friends John and Trevor went to chat her up and came back to report that she was thrillingly rude to them, 'She's like a bad orphan.'

Everything became suddenly clear. John looked hard at a fat young man, who was wandering round wearing nothing but runners, a pair of small billowing shorts like a nappy and a sign round his neck reading 'Say No to Drugs' and announced with calm certitude: 'He has the drugs.' McGruders' very young owner, who had long, dirty-blond Californian beach-boy hair, looked at Shane, tossed his surfer locks, and uttered the magic words, 'Lock-in,' changing the bar in an instance from sparse to intimate. We pushed three tables together and the owner set down three defiant ashtrays – it had been four years since the smoking ban.

The Bad Orphan picked up a guitar, stood on a chair and began belting out Van Morrison's 'Gloria'. She had an explosive voice, loud and rough like Janis or Tina, and the atmosphere exploded. I sat down beside Shane. Beside me, young men formed a polite, informal line. They had something urgent to impart. One after another they whispered, 'Shane, man, you saved my life,' in low, heartfelt tones. Some of them proffered track marks on their arms, in pride, solidarity or regret, I wasn't sure which. Shane didn't say much. He just nodded, without expression and without vanity, obliterating the hierarchy of star and fan. If that sounds like I'm romanticising addiction, I can't imagine anyone else of his level of fame being so down – the word is precise – with his fans.

He had this book of Irish poetry on him with a shiny green and gold cover, the kind of thing that's sold in tourist shops beside leprechaun hats and bodhráns – a totally naff design, which, in his possession, became more hip than a chic Faber cover. The young men seized on the book as another way in. 'An Irish Airman Foresees his Death!' said one triumphantly, like a dog returning a stick. He got the nod, but I knew he knew, and maybe Shane knew he knew, that Shane had long pronounced this his favourite Yeats poem. Another guy, who said he was from Limerick, announced that he would now read a poem. The Bad Orphan was still belting out songs, and everyone had got stuck into insistent conversations, so only Shane and I paid any attention to the reading, which was as well because the guy couldn't read poetry. He kept stressing the wrong word. It was like someone singing off-key in karaoke and I had to stop myself giggling. At the end Shane said humorously, distinctly, and enigmatically: 'That is the Munster way of saying verse.'

When I woke up some twenty hours later in Trevor's spare room – with Trevor politely knocking on the door to inform me my family was going spare trying to reach me (my phone had died) – I had throbbing through my mind like one of those insistent refrains from a dream 'A Vision of Connaught in the 13th Century', and I saw myself back squinting at a page of Shane's book trying to read this Mangan poem, which Shane had said was his favourite, but finding that the print was jumping around because of the MDMA and because I only had one contact lens in, being too inept to insert the other. At this memory I sat up in blind panic, afraid that I'd passed out with the lens still in (I hadn't).

Over the next few days, between apologies and Alka-Seltzers, I started going through my Irish poetry anthologies. They are a desultory collection, most of them with Yeats as the starting point, but in an early edition of the *Penguin Book of Irish Verse* (1970), edited by Brendan Kennelly, I found a whole heap of Mangan. In fact, unusually, maybe uniquely, in a book spanning from the eighth to the late twentieth century, Mangan gets by far the largest selection of any poet (Kennelly explains in his intro that Yeats is 'already widely available in paperback'). Here I found the poem that Shane said was his favourite, 'A Vision of Connaught in the Thirteenth Century'. To my hungover jittery eyes, it was wonderful (and is still wonderful). Here is the first stanza:

> I walked entranced
> Through a land of Morn;
> The sun, with wondrous excess of light,
> Shone down and glanced
> Over seas of corn
> And lustrous gardens aleft and right.
> Even in the clime
> Of resplendent Spain
> Beams no such sun upon such a land;
> But it was the time,
> 'Twas in the reign,
> Of Cáhal Mór of the Wine-red Hand.

This has ease and grace and simplicity, achieved by the bare, restricted palette. A few consonantal variations (-an/-un/-on) carry the stanza so that any new sound enters with force: 'excess' is excess, 'Beams' beams out. The second stanza has similarly restricted sounds, but the third starts to get diffuse in menace, and the fourth is overloaded by exclamation marks and the 'aghast', portentous vocabulary of H.P. Lovecraft. The final stanza is redeemed when the sun that beamed over the first verse makes a brief effective return:

> I again walked forth;
> But lo! the sky
> Showed fleckt with blood, and an alien sun
> Glared from the north

The 'alien' is pivotal: it picks up the consonantal n's and the 'seas of corn' from the first stanza, transporting us to Keats and Ruth 'in tears amid the alien corn'. From this initial reading, I gained a view of Mangan as a writer of fits and starts – Yeats called them 'electric shocks' – who hits astonishing notes but cannot sustain them.

Six weeks after this night, Lehman Brothers collapsed, precipitating the worst global recession since the 1930s. McGruders closed shortly afterwards, though the sign remained up for years and was included in a mordant website called Dublin Ghost Signs:

When I started to read more about Mangan and discovered the morbid glamour of his life, which as much as his verse has kept his reputation if not alive then at least undead, I began to think there was something significant and fitting about my first encounter with him. That this Baudelaire of the Dublin Liberties – an alcoholic, opium addict, dandy* and writer of strange, exotic, esoteric verses

---

*Dandy seems a mocking term for Mangan's attire, which was more tramp than Beau Brummell, but I think his insistence on specific flamboyant garments (cloak, coat, steepled hat, umbrella, shaded spectacles) leading to the creation of a distinctive look comes out of the same motivation as the dandy's: to set himself apart in the crowd.

– should burst his way through a drink and drug binge during a Liberties lock-in with our own *poète maudit*, Shane MacGowan, seemed almost too good to be true. And other minor notes from the night seemed to resonate with tropes in Mangan's life and work: the attention-seeking costumes of the art students recalled his famously eccentric attire; my jittery, myopic eyes referenced the mysterious blinding that he describes in one of his memoirs; the 'lock-in' recalled that the Liberties was, for most of Mangan's life, a place apart, outside Dublin city jurisdiction and running its own lawcourts until 1840. The collapse of Lehman Brothers and the subsequent recession recalled the deflation and depression after the Napoleonic Wars, which bankrupted his father, while the subsequent closure of McGruders evoked all the closures and demolitions in the Liberties during his lifetime.

This may all seem like bogus retrospective validation – a faith-based search for clues and meaning once you've settled the outcome – but it's not entirely specious. Symbols, tropes and motifs in Mangan's life and work perpetually feed his myth and, as I would discover, people's 'encounters' with him frequently acquire a mysterious, uncanny significance.

*

It was sometime later that I was asked by an academic press to write a brief biography of an Irish writer of my choice for their *Life and Times* series. I was considering George Bernard Shaw because I find his love letters so intriguing – such dazzlingly incisive wit, but what was he deploying it for if he didn't want to sleep with these women? – but I don't love the plays and the thought of his terrifying longevity and productivity (ninety-four sentient years, thirty-seven volumes of collected works, *a quarter of a million letters*) began to panic me. It was then, perhaps, that the image of Mangan returned as the dangerously seductive negation of Shaw: dead at forty-six, just six volumes of collected works (which includes his correspondence), scant biographical sources and an aura of romantic dissolution, which is the thrilling antithesis to Shaw's teetotal efficiency.

I signed a contract that gave me, I think, six or seven months to deliver, which seemed feasible for the brief wordcount requested. I began by efficiently dividing his life into three distinct parts to make it manageable, and to mark his progression from plain James Mangan (1803–30) to Clarence Mangan (1831–45) to the National Poet (1846–9). In Part One, he is the son of a bankrupt Liberties grocer who is apprenticed aged fifteen as a scrivener (legal clerk) to support his family and builds up a small reputation among a tiny coterie as the author of pseudonymous 'wordplay' poems in almanacs. In Part Two, he inserts 'Clarence' into his name and begins publishing translations of German Romantics and Oriental poets in popular and literary journals, to the awe and amazement of his contemporaries, and in about 1840 he adopts his signature look of coat, cloak and hat and becomes a Dublin street character. By Part Three, he is going nowhere fast as a barfly and opium addict who sleeps rough and torments friends and colleagues with begging letters. When the Famine breaks out, his condition mirrors the condition of the country and yet, before succumbing to malnutrition and cholera on 20 June 1849, he manages to produce the handful of masterpieces including 'Siberia', 'My Dark Rosaleen' and 'O'Hussey's Ode to the Maguire', which are the greatest artistic response to the Famine and guarantee his fame well into the twentieth century.

Even at this preliminary stage, when my grasp of the historical period was rudimentary, I could see that the facts of this 'shilling life' hardly added up. I didn't know anything then of the tradition of dualism in Mangan scholarship but I already felt that I was dealing with two Mangans: the poor Liberties Catholic whose family is bankrupted and who ends up on the streets himself, a depressingly familiar tale; and the literary star, master of all languages and illustrious contributor to erudite journals, a dazzling tale even for a Protestant university graduate and an almost impossible one for a Catholic autodidact of that period. And I didn't see how either of these Mangans – plain James or esoteric Clarence – could have become the National Poet during the Famine. At first these disconnects were the puzzles I needed to keep me interested but Mangan didn't respond in the usual way to inquiry and research. Instead of resolving the dilemmas, he kept fissuring and dividing. Yes, the poems are (mostly) short but they are also slippery and dissembling and when you try to nail their meaning, they sliver off like mercury. And, instead of speeding up the narrative, the scantness of the biographical sources exposed the gaps and threw up more questions. It seemed dishonest to present as fact information which I had begun to suspect was somewhere between speculative and actively falsified.

I might have managed these difficulties had I kept the detachment and distance necessary to produce the brief, adroit biography that was being asked of me, but somewhere between weighing up his memoirs (which may not be memories) and his 'love' poems (which may not be about being in love) and possibly on that very first night in McGruders, I lost any sense of detachment. The image that I would eventually build up of Mangan is that of a parasite, who in life wormed his way into other people's poems and fed off them and was now worming his way into me.

Mangan was under my skin, a neural itch which for the longest time I didn't know how to allay. I was too immersed to write a distilled life and there was no call for a comprehensive biography, since he had been subjected to one in 1999 and no new haul of papers had emerged to justify going again, and anyway you can't aspire to comprehensiveness when there are more gaps than sources.

This suited me fine. Faced with the exhaustive and exhausting amassing of information endemic to so many biographies, I always begin to feel like I've strayed into one of those Borges short stories about infinity – like the 'The Book of Sand', which has neither beginning nor end, or 'The Library of Babel' that contains every coherent book ever written or that might ever be written, or the series of rooms, corridors and courtyards that run unendingly into each other in 'The House of Asterion' – and since these are images and metaphors of a monstrous plenitude that is impossible to achieve and vertiginous to contemplate, they seem to carry a moral, like a latter-day Aesop's fable, that the pursuit of the infinite will send you mad, even as it takes you further from your subject – who will recede into the distance in proportion to the amount of information you are heaping on them.

I also hold this fantasy of omniscience – that you can contain the totality of a life between two covers – responsible for the tone of impartial detachment that is always creeping into biographies. A biography is subjective narrative, a compilation of often unreliable memories and suspect facts, selected and shaped by one person, the biographer. But instead of admitting to their unreliability and instability, as novelists do, biographers aspire to a model of impersonal objectivity: they absent themselves from the narrative and affect to marshal the data with the disinterest of a software program so as to create the reassuring impression that here is the life, exactly how it happened, as empirical and indisputable as, say, an encyclopaedic entry on the lifecycle of an earthworm.

In fact, not only is every human life mysterious and unverifiable in itself (though perhaps that is also true of earthworms) but in choosing what material to focus on and how to present it, biographers can't avoid bringing all their own cultural assumptions, prejudices and upbringing – all their personality and everything that has ever happened to them – to their understanding and analysis of the subject, and eventually they will get called out on this. When I first read Richard Ellmann's biography of Wilde I thought it was great, but years later I read an essay by Colm Tóibín in which he sarcastically quotes this sentence from Ellmann: 'Since neither Wilde nor Douglas practised or expected sexual fidelity, money was the stamp and seal of their love' and that sent me back to the biography, which, sure enough, I now saw was judgmental and latently homophobic although Ellmann would have indignantly denied this, and none of the reviewers picked up on it when it was published in 1988. In the fifteen years between its publication and Tóibín's essay, public opinion had shifted radically and exposed Ellmann not as a virulent homophobe, but as marked by the prejudices of his time.

God knows what solecisms and anachronisms I would make about Mangan on which the future would judge me harshly – maybe something related to his addictions, homelessness or sexual squeamishness, or maybe to something else entirely (it is hard to say what the future will fixate on). Whatever it turned out to be, I felt that aspiring to an assured tone of impartial detachment would make me a hostage to fortune, but injecting hesitancy and subjectivity would signal my awareness that I know this isn't the life as it happened, but merely as I am configuring it (*I* being only human). The quickest and easiest way to do this is to break the third wall and enter the text, but when I began explaining to a friend, who used to run a bookshop, the kind of book I was hoping to write, which in homage to Hunter S. Thompson I was terming 'gonzo biography', he said rather wearily, 'Oh right, I know the type of thing, *Mangan and Me*' and then looked at me sympathetically and said, 'It's always women being made to write these confessional biographies; I think it's really unfair.' I was taken aback since I hadn't realised that's what I was writing – that in order to be published, I was having to expose myself in just the way, my friend's sympathy seemed to imply, that women have always had to strip in order to earn their living. But when I began looking into it, I saw that he was right – there are any number of these books and they are mostly written by women who do rather spill out their hearts and minds and pudenda. And maybe they are being exploited; or maybe they are just the social media generation, wholly comfortable with sharing and self-exposure; or maybe they have the same bitter compulsion of Gwen John, Frida Kahlo, Sylvia Plath, Kathy Acker and all the other auto fixated avenging viragos, to bring themselves into focus, to get people to look, in furious reaction to centuries of the culture of *not* looking, blurring or soft-focusing women out. But whichever it is, this was another model of biography I had to reject because I don't have the nerve to strip and if I did, I wouldn't choose Mangan as my seven veils. To quote him quoting someone else: 'I cannot do so if I would, and I know that I would not if I could.'

He references this in his slithery memoir in which he says he *won't* be 'laying bare [his] own delinquencies without cloak or equivocation' but he also *won't* be joining those who have 'published their autobiographies without directly revealing themselves'. This escape from what he calls the 'models' of autobiography available to him, and his way of defining himself through what he won't do rather than what he *will*, is entirely characteristic, and when I found myself knocking down perfectly serviceable models of biography, I felt he must have infected me. My list of the lives I didn't want to write kept growing: not a Distilled Life, not Comprehensive, not Impartial & Detached, not Confessional, not Fictionalised (because if you get it wrong, which I would, it resembles a botched resuscitation where the patient is alive but horribly altered) and not Docu-Drama/Re-enactment because the scene-setting involves intrusive speculation into characters' thoughts about which I am phobic and the more I came to know about Mangan, the more opaque he became and the more he seemed to tremble at the edge of dissolution. I was terrified that I would handle him the wrong way and he would crumble into dust, like those bodies or artefacts buried for centuries in the bog or at sea which disintegrate on contact with air.

It was terrible to be piling up the corpses of the books that I didn't want to write and could not have written had I wanted to. One of the Manganistas I met on my travels told me that he wrote his MA on Mangan in 'gobbledy-gook *Finnegans Wake* type language' and while this wasn't immediately intuitive – because Mangan wrote perfectly grammatical if sometimes contorted English – I could see exactly how, writing on Mangan, you might end up in late Joyce, amid the wreckage of language, trying to find a form to fit the subject. The fact that quite possibly there is no perfect form is no disincentive because, as in the search for love, the ideal is so entrancing that we persist through all our terrible attempts at it, telling ourselves optimistically that every failure gets us closer to success, and that deciding what we don't want is crucial in getting us to what we do want.

Researching Mangan in the early days, I got used to the blank stares of my friends and contemporaries when I mentioned whom I was working on (and the hint of panic in their eyes that I would start explaining him to them), as well as to the distant light of recognition that would come over the faces of those schooled before the mid-1970s, when Mangan was taken off the syllabus. Frequently they would dredge something up: an elderly journalist recited 'The Woman of Three Cows' for me with great zest; a retired civil servant quoted the lines from Yeats's 'To Ireland in the Coming Times' ('Nor may I less be counted one / With Davis, Mangan, Ferguson'), and an artist mentioned the medley in Thin Lizzy's last album *My Black Rose* ('My Dark Rosaleen is the only colleen'). At a Christmas fair in the Point, when I stopped at a stall to haggle over a Harry

Kernoff lithograph of Mangan, a man in a hat appeared out of the crowd and began imparting the most abstruse information; and a retired barrister told me that when he was a junior counsel defending a petty criminal who was an alcoholic and drug addict, the case came up against a judge known for his love of nineteenth-century poetry, so the barrister took a chance. 'My lord,' he said (this was when you still addressed judges like that) 'my client has a weakness but he is fighting it. "He fell through that pit abysmal, the gulf and grave of Maginn and Burns, and pawned his soul for the Devil's dismal stock of returns."' – 'But yet redeemed it,' capped the judge and, very pleased with himself for finishing the quote and, thinking sympathetically of the poor genius who wrote it, went on to bestow a light sentence.

From these encounters I got a hazy sense of continuum, of Mangan's lingering presence in Irish culture, a piece of flotsam that keeps coming back on the tide. And then I met Frank.

It was on our second or third date, which means it was November 2011, that I brought up Mangan. We were pushing our bikes across the Ha'penny Bridge, which means that we must have just eaten in Terra Madre, a tiny Italian on the quays with which Frank was then enamoured, although within six months he would ditch it as suddenly and cheerfully as he had first taken it up, leaving its proprietor, who was besotted with Frank like all restaurateurs, bereft. The date was as thrilling and awkward as all early dates when something is happening, made more so by the age difference and by Frank's refusal, or inability, to chat me up in any of the usual ways while, at the watery level of his intuition, taking me in with a completeness that I would have found unnerving had I, or he, been conscious of it. Into the thrill and awkwardness, I threw the name of Mangan, expecting some kind of recognition but unprepared for the immediate happy and calmly unsurprised 'Oh, good,' as if Mangan were the obvious and indeed the only choice for me. He began to talk about Joyce's love of Mangan and I was aware of having passed some kind of a test, though I had yet to experience his passionate fulminations against people's research choices, by which he judged them, the way others might judge on taste in music or film. In time I would come to see my choice of Mangan as having an eerie perfection: if I had consciously sought a subject to bind me to Frank, I could not have chosen better. This isn't because of a shared love of the poems – Frank claimed to be tone deaf on poetry – but because of his understanding of Mangan as a particularly subtle nationalist whose ironic rejection of *The Nation's* rugged Irish exceptionalism prefigures and feeds into Joyce's pillorying of the Gaelic League and Irish Ireland. It was amazing to me that Frank, who could not have quoted one line of Mangan's, had the strongest sense of him as a lurker in Irish history, whose enigmatic presence in the narrative helps determine its course, and who must therefore be worth the considerable difficulty involved in tracking him down and 'solving' him.

*

When I was reviewing books – which I liked but eventually gave up because it was driving me to gush or spite, with a kind of weary irony as default – I began to notice that if a book was any good, or even if sufficient work had gone into it, then it contained its own critique: a passage which pinpointed more devastatingly than any critic could what the book was actually about (as opposed to what it claimed to be about) and where, within its own terms, it was failing. I felt these critiques were always unconscious, an eruption of the author's despairing awareness that the book is going in a direction they hadn't intended and is resisting their efforts of control.

In D. J. O'Donoghue's biography of Mangan, this self-critique comes towards the end. Published in 1897, his was the first full-length biography and within the severe constraints – Mangan left no archive or direct descendants – it is meticulously researched, but there is a sense as you read it, of his skittish subject getting away from him and his tools of pedantry and punctiliousness being unequal to the task of cracking someone so witty, subtle and enigmatic. The moment you realise – and that he himself realises – that he is trying to pick up water with a fork comes towards the end when he relates an anecdote told by William Carleton, author of *Traits of the Irish Peasantry* and Mangan's most famous literary contemporary:

[Mangan] was invited to a social party at the hospitable house of Mrs Hutton of Summerhill. Mangan, rather to the astonishment of his friends, accepted the invitation and when Carleton arrived was known to be in the house, but not with the party assembled. The novelist was asked to fetch Mangan out of a room to which he had retreated. 'We cannot induce him to come into the drawing room,' said the hostess. Carleton – who knew Mangan and his ways very well, and who was in some sort a boon companion of his, though Mangan had no moral sympathy with his coarser nature, and hardly one single point in common with him – asked 'Is there any whiskey about?' 'Yes,' said Mrs Hutton, 'the butler will show you the supper-room and you will find a decanter of whiskey on the side board there.' Carleton proceeded to look for the poet, whom he eventually found hidden under cloaks, coats and wraps in one of the rooms. 'What are you doing there?' queried Carleton. 'Seeking an opportunity of escape,' faltered the poet, 'I had no right to come here – I don't know why I did come.' 'Well,' said the novelist, 'come and have a nip of something that will put courage and life in you.' He gave Mangan a glassful of whiskey, and took one himself, and after a while the timid poet allowed his captor to introduce him to the hostess and her guests, whom he soon delighted by his brilliant talk, but whom he also gladly left.

This story, with its gratuitous swipe at Carleton's coarseness and its suggestion that he was deploying the situation to get himself whiskey, is obviously not how Carleton told it. O'Donoghue lets it hang as a tragicomic anecdote of Mangan's social anxiety and alcoholism and doesn't comment on the startling particularity of the Man in the Cloak (one of Mangan's pseudonyms) hiding under more cloaks and coats. His overt concern is to position Mangan as 'moral' and 'brilliant', and Carleton as his opposite, and in the process, he turns Mangan into victim and quarry. The story is unpleasant as well as funny because of its atmosphere of bullying. The use of the impersonal sets them up as archetypes – worldly novelist and sensitive poet – but since this is O'Donoghue's account, not Carleton's, it doesn't strike us as a tale about novelists and poets, but about biographers and their subjects.

The job of the biographer is to 'capture' the subject. Sometimes the subject co-operates and yields up their papers and access to their contacts, or their descendants do, and the biography is then designated as 'official' or 'authorised', but at other times co-operation is refused and the unauthorised biographer is forced to stalk the subject through libraries and other people's archives and correspondences, wrinkling them out of hiding places, and cajoling/threatening friends and descendants. Under normal circumstances, this behaviour would be considered aggressively intrusive but the biographer is presuming on a kind of social contract: by becoming famous, the subject is taken to have agreed to the spotlight and to an audience, just as Mangan in accepting the invitation to the party is taken to have agreed to entertain the guests. The biographer claims to have an affinity with (to be a 'boon companion' of) the subject, but in truth they have 'hardly one single point in common' – under no circumstances would the brilliant subject ever do the drudge work of a biographer, and biographers (of poets in particular) know only too well that their literary style is much 'coarser' than their subject's. The previous year O'Donoghue had in fact published a biography of Carleton, who had proved an easy subject with a straightforward autobiography, extensive correspondence, and cooperative daughters. O'Donoghue is conscious of having had to chase Mangan down and dislikes being made to feel so coarse, rapacious and worldly compared to his elusive subject. To distance himself from the process, he transposes these traits onto Carleton, against whom he appears to hold a grudge. (That it is Mangan, the recalcitrant subject, whom O'Donoghue values and praises, should be no surprise to anyone familiar with the parable of the prodigal son.)

The anecdote ends with Mangan's escape; he 'gladly leaves'. This is O'Donoghue wryly acknowledging that for all his diligence in tracking down sources and interviewing survivors, he has not in fact succeeded in 'capturing' Mangan. He has not been able to describe, analyse or explain him. His biography has uncovered much new information and yet Mangan remains as he would say of himself 'unknown', 'inurned', 'unbeheld' and 'unbribable'. You don't blame O'Donoghue for being unable to hold down his frustrating subject but the passage fizzes with things unexplored and its author's painful if unarticulated awareness of his own failure.

The passage serves as a critique of biography in general and its crass methods of stalking, trapping and bribing which cannot hope to reveal the truth of a subject any more than a coarse social approach like Carleton's can hope to relax the morbidly sensitive, but the passage is also particular to Mangan. His presence in the anecdote is evanescent, transient and *fleeting* – which is to say exactly the quality that led him in 1831, when he was twenty-eight years old, to adopt the pseudonym of 'Clarence'. He liked to quote the description of the Duke of Clarence in Shakespeare's *Richard III*, from which he took the pseudonym – 'Clarence is come / false, fleeting, perjur'd Clarence' – and there is nothing haphazard about him alighting on these three adjectives which openly admit that the name he is writing under is *false* (something his contemporaries, who referred to him routinely as Clarence, tended to forget) and that as a translator he is also false, as in deliberately or carelessly inaccurate, as well as *perjur'd*, in that he ascribes translations to the wrong author and will pass off his own work as someone else's ('fathering upon other authors the offspring of my own brain'), and that his footprint on his own life is *fleeting* – he left no archive and made only the faintest imprint on the usual biographical sources.

Absence means omission but there is something palpable, almost aggressive, about Mangan's absences. I'm reminded of the eerie little nursery rhyme I used to recite to frighten and thrill myself as I went upstairs to bed in the long, thin, shadowy house we lived in until I was eight: 'Yesterday, upon the stair / I met a man who wasn't there / He wasn't there again today / I wish that man would go away.' (The house and the poem were like an Edward Gorey sketch.) This exactly describes Mangan at the party – he's there but not there, present in the house but absent from the party, which makes everyone uneasy; they wish this man, who isn't there, would go away.

Once you are alerted to the peculiar quality of his absences, you begin to see them as pervasive: Mangan is transitory or absent from his childhood and youth, from his paternal heritage, from the places he lived, from his sexuality, from six years of his life, from his love affair(s), from the revolutionary struggle he claims to support, from his archive and from his own creativity (he can only access his imagination by way of someone else's through translation) and after a while these myriad absences begin to swirl, coalesce and dissolve into each other to suggest the nullifying absences of Bret Easton Ellis's teens electing to 'Disappear Here' so that they become, like the title of the book, less than zero, and the virtuoso absences of Houdini, and the mutely unbending absence of Bartleby the Scrivener ('I prefer not to'), and the paradoxical absences of ghosts (a ghost being a 'presence' which denotes an absence), and the mournful absences that echo around refugees forced to flee their homelands, and the vicious absences (or absenting) perpetuated through apartheid, gerrymandering, 'extraordinary rendition' and all the ways that states contrive to remove or isolate people they don't want.

I think that all these things play into Mangan's absences, and if you factor them all in, maybe you get an explanation for the existence of someone so improbable. When I grasped just how often and how ingeniously he absents himself, and how many hiding places and exits he avails of, I began to understand why I kept discarding different models of biography: I was pre-empting his escape from them. It is difficult, maybe impossible, to engage with someone who is constantly flitting off so it's not surprising that Mangan's biographers and critics have tried to give him a more definite outline, to render him as a distinctive character, to put shape and form on shadow and blur. The shapes they have given him – the Melancholic, the Nationalist, the Romantic, the Joker, the Postmodernist – are now part of who he is because if he still exists, or subsists, in the national memory/psyche, it is through the renderings of his critics and interpreters. Tracking these renderings is part of what I want to do in this book – not so much *Mangan and Me* but *Mangan, Me and Them* – but first I would like to try and hover in his absences, in the spaces he created before his brilliant interpreters arrived to fill them in.

Part One: The lives

Maybe I dreamt it

Mangan made three attempts (that we know of) to tell the story of his early life: in a letter to an editor, at the instigation of his confessor, and as an article for a journal. None of these versions was published in his lifetime and when they did appear, they weren't believed.

All three versions tell the same story, with variations, focusing on his early life from childhood to early adulthood. Among Manganistas, it is the second version, written in autumn 1848, that has iconic status: because it's the longest and strangest and because the manuscript is extant; you can visit it in the Royal Irish Academy, where it sits isolated in a box, not part of an archive because Mangan didn't leave papers. There are no handwritten drafts of poems tracking the false starts and crossings-out on the way to the final draft, and there are only thirty-one letters in manuscript, mostly short and begging.

In this wasteland, the longer memoir appears as a relict whose improbable survival from a period of wreckage and devastation is a kind of miracle. When I made the pilgrimage to the Royal Irish Academy for a viewing, it didn't disappoint. Everything about this manuscript is entrancingly strange. Inscribed in a small, oblong music book, the text flows between the staves in different colours – dark brown, blue, black, and light brown, though the colours are now mostly faded. I wondered if the different colours had some significance, like dark brown for depression, blue for candour, black for rage. The text is a pleasure to read, well-spaced out and written in the exquisitely legible copperplate of the trained scrivener. Only a few words and phrases are crossed out and only a few inserted later; either he composed with remarkable ease and fluency, or this is a clean copy, put together from earlier scrawled drafts.

We can date the composition of this memoir with some accuracy to autumn 1848 when Mangan was forty-five (though he looked at least six years older and thought he was six years younger). His addict's behaviour – sleeping rough, changing lodgings, cadging loans, forgetting to eat – had become endemic since the death of his mother two years earlier and the list of his sufferings in 1848 has a Job-like relentlessness. At the beginning of the year, he was living in 'a miserable back room destitute of every comfort, a porter bottle doing duty for a candlestick, and a blanketless pallet for a bed and writing table'; in May he was admitted to St Vincent's charity hospital 'to find rest and healing' and touched the nuns' hearts by exclaiming, 'Oh! the luxury of clean sheets.' After about a month, he discharged himself – the nuns wouldn't let him drink – only to find himself in Richmond Surgical Hospital a few mornings later, 'bruised and disfigured by a fall of nearly fifteen feet, into the foundation of a house, then recently sunk. This occurred in the nighttime when he was utterly unconscious of his whereabouts; and his escape from mortal accident seemed almost miraculous.' Irish public life at the time was similarly destitute, bruised, disfigured, sunk, etc. The Famine was in its third year and unrelenting and the nationalist movement to which Mangan was affiliated, Young Ireland, had suffered a series of seismic shocks: in May the sentencing to transportation of John Mitchel, founder of the radical paper *United Irishman* and an editor and encourager of Mangan's; in early July the arrest for sedition of Charles Gavan Duffy, editor of *The Nation* and one of Mangan's closest friends (which is not to say very close); in late July the comprehensive failure of the skirmish known grandiloquently as the Young Ireland Rebellion and colloquially as the Battle of Widow McCormack's Cabbage Patch; in August the arrest of the rebellion leaders, and in October their sentencing to death (later changed to transportation).

It seems remarkable Mangan could write anything at all in this personal and national apocalypse, let alone write well, but it's part of his aberrancy that in youth, when Auden says poets should be 'exploding like bombs', he was circumspect and stifled, while at the chaotic end of his life he was fecund and inventive. In 1848 he published eight essays and thirty-six poems and wrote many more that weren't published till after his death, including 'The Nameless One', which was Yeats's favourite of his poems and reads as a kind of companion piece to the memoir. Both texts follow the same trajectory from boyhood's 'drear night-hour' to 'want, and sickness, and houseless nights' but where the poem is assured and poised, its images of waste and want juxtaposed against invigorating images of flow ('one whose veins ran lightning'), the memoir is unfiltered and does not seek balance.

After an introductory flurry in which Mangan gives several contradictory reasons for why he is writing the memoir, he embarks on his story. We learn that he learnt, very young, to take refuge in books and solitude to escape his father, who is the memoir's most menacing and most memorable character, a kind of monster to whom not one, but three zoomorphic images attach themselves: he treats his children 'habitually as a huntsman would treat refractory hounds'; his proud boast is that they 'would run into a mouse-hole to shun him'; and he is a 'boa-constrictor *without his alimentative propensities*'.*

The young Mangan does his best to fold into his books and succeeds in being ignored until a family crisis erupts: the father, being recklessly spendthrift, goes bankrupt. Casting around for succour, his eye falls on his eldest son whom he drags from his books and solitary ramblings with a characteristically bestial verb – could he not 'behoof himself on behalf of his kindred?' Without the defence, if also without the consent, of his passive mother, the adolescent Mangan is apprenticed to a scrivener, so that his meagre wages can support the family.

From this catastrophe, he never recovers. As he lurches from one crisis to the next, the text takes on a cyclical nightmarish quality, caught in a pattern of office–breakdown–recovery–return to office. The office hours are impossibly onerous – 'from early morning till near midnight' – and the rooms are confining, 'pestiferous', and inhabited by 'coarse, uncultivated, semi-savage' co-workers who, like the father, take on serpentine traits so that the narrator feels 'as if shut up in a cavern with serpents and scorpions'. The nervous breakdowns occasioned by the offices are acute – his 'voice of agony' cries 'into some interminable chasm' – and mental torment soon becomes physically manifest: his body wastes away and he is confined to bed, 'a ruined soul in a wasted frame'. Removal from the office, together with exercise and his 'almost miraculously recuperative power' affects a cure – 'I arose, as it were, out of myself … I felt as if I could feast upon air and thought alone.' But recovery means return to the office and the whole bloody business starts again, with new torments – during his second bout in hospital he's placed in bed with a leprous boy who

---

*Mangan's enigmatic italics which suggest that his father squeezes victims to death not because he's hungry but because he can, or that his father manifests the terrifying squeezing capacity but doesn't act on it.

infects him with leprosy, though his family fails to notice either the infection or its subsequent miraculous cure.

The nightmare cycle breaks thanks to a 'chance encounter' on a ramble round the countryside of Rathfarnham. Significantly, it's the first time he gets out to open air and when he meets a young man – nameless, like almost everyone in the memoir – he embarks on the memoir's first recorded conversation (elsewhere people in authority talk at him). The exchange is even humorous, though on the gloomy subject of predestination. Inevitably, Mangan takes the dark view that the 'majority of mankind will be irrevocably consigned to eternal misery'. The optimistic young man starts pleading for 'the goodness, the justice of God' but Mangan brusquely interrupts him: '"Stop," said I, "What do you[—]"'.

And here the tale does stop on its unfinished question since it's the last page of the music book and there is no more space left to write. Remarkably, this open ending creates a 'commodius vicus' back to the start: inside the front cover is a note in different handwriting which reads: 'This fragment was written at my instance by poor Mangan. While composing it, he lodged in Fishamble Street. The remnant of the biography never came into my possession; and I fear the author either lost or destroyed it. – C.P.M., SS. Michael and John's, June 23rd, 1849.'

The date is three days after Mangan's death; 'C.P.M.' is Fr Charles Patrick Meehan, curate of St Michael and John's church in the Liberties, and the 'remnant' he refers to is the missing sequel to the memoir, which we surmise must start mid-sentence like *Finnegans Wake*, completing the question: 'What do you[—]'

*

Reading between the staves in the soft gloom of the Academy, my first thought was 'misery memoir': the relentless solipsism, the terrible childhood, the histrionic and evidently fabricated sequences, the hint of release in the final scene … all this seemed terribly familiar. At the same time, the feel of it was strange, not like anything I had read before, madder than a misery memoir but smoother. Something about it seems to touch a nerve in readers. The nineteenth century rose in a wave to denounce and deny it.

Its first reader, Fr Meehan, the man who commissioned it, was affronted. Among all its bizarre claims, he chose to go to battle over a description of a 'tottering old fragment' of a house in Chancery Lane, to which, Mangan wrote, the family moved after the father's bankruptcy. The description is certainly lurid:

> These dens, one of which was over the other, were mutually connected by means of a steep and almost perpendicular ladder … the place of the [window] being supplied, not very elegantly, by a huge chasm in the bare and broken brick wall. In the upper apartment which served as our sleeping-room, the spiders and beetles had established an almost undisputed right of occupancy; while the winds and rains blew in on all sides, and whistled and howled through the winter nights like the voices of unquiet spirits.

This ruined tower, straight out of the Tarot, complete with chasms, beasts and ghosts, is a Mangan trope, resonating with all the ruined Teutonic and Gaelic towers in his poems. It whistles and howls for attention, and Meehan didn't disappoint. He told Mangan stiffly that he 'did not think it a faithful picture' – Mangan apparently replied that he 'dreamt it' and offered to 'destroy the performance' but Meehan preferred that Mangan 'leave it as a souvenir' in his possession.

Within a year of offering up this 'souvenir', Mangan was dead from cholera and malnutrition, on 20 June 1849. A few months later, a shorter memoir found its way into the press – the account that Mangan had written in about 1845 in a letter, or series of letters, to his editor on the *Dublin University Magazine*. It tells, more briefly and less strangely, the same tale of neglect and misery as the longer memoir, making similar claims about the father's improvidence, the long hours labouring in the scriveners' offices, and the 'disgusting obscenities and horrible blasphemies' of his co-workers. It breathes the same atmosphere of claustrophobia and paranoia – 'My mother and father held me by chains of iron. I dared not move or breathe but by their permission. They seemed to watch my every action, and to wish to dive into my very thoughts' – but comes across less unhinged than the longer memoir since there are no outlandish anecdotes. Even so, a reader, signing himself 'D.C.' in a letter to *The Nation* (13 October 1849) reacted with a mixture of pedantry and outrage. After furiously querying Mangan's claims about the hours that scriveners worked, their rate of pay, and the behaviour of his co-workers in the office, D.C. (who has never been identified*) goes into full denial: 'I have too much respect for the memory of Clarence Mangan, as a literary man, to wish wantonly to cast a slur upon his character – it is my firm conviction that the autobiographical confession is a forgery upon the man and I know it to be a lie in itself.' (Mangan would have loved this: an exact iteration of *false perjur'd Clarence*.)

A year later, Mangan's final version of his life appeared in *The Irishman*. He had written it in his last months, in the third person, as an apparent obituary of 'poor Mangan!' by 'a medical man' signing himself 'E.W.' It is a tour de force of irony – Mangan, taking refuge behind a pseudonym, has found his way back to poise and detachment. Maybe he had to disgorge the pain before he could turn his habitual mocking irony on his own life, or maybe

---

*I think 'D.C.' was a scrivener – he seems personally outraged by Mangan's slurs on the trade and he knows the solicitors' offices where Mangan worked, which wasn't common knowledge – and I think he was a pious Catholic: he emphasises that two of Mangan's co-workers were future Catholic bishops (again not common knowledge) so couldn't have perpetuated 'obscenities and blasphemies', and he blames Mangan's drinking on Trinity College (the university of the Protestant ascendancy) although Mangan didn't start working in Trinity till 1842 and his boozing had begun decades earlier, as all Dublin knew.

he achieves detachment because this version was written explicitly for publication. Where the earlier versions read like howls into the void, the article plays up ironically to an audience presumed to be enjoying the joke of the author dissociating from himself. Although it contains a new, impossible anecdote – sent out aged five by a 'hair-brained [sic] girl' to buy a ballad, 'poor Mangan' gets soaking wet and is left near blind for the next eight years – nobody wrote in to take issue.

Thirty-two years later, the public finally got a chance to read the long memoir written in the music book, when it was published in the *Irish Monthly* in 1882 – not because Meehan had decided enough time had lapsed, but because it had gone out of his possession. The editor's note explains that:

A kind friend showed me an old oblong book ruled for music, containing two or three chapters of what proved to be a life of the poet Mangan written by himself. ... Fr Meehan, who knows not how the manuscript escaped his keeping, has with characteristic generosity, placed it at our disposal. We trust it will be followed in these pages by some original particulars concerning this very gifted man, who is not to be judged by this fragmentary confession of one of his dark hours, which draws too dark a picture of himself and his father.

However, the plea didn't work: Mangan was judged. Apparently, a generation wasn't enough time to soften the reaction to his craziness. *The Freeman's Journal* was censorious: 'From its beginning to its sudden conclusion, the reader cannot get rid of the impression that the fancies, ideas and imaginings are much exaggerated, much over excited' (17 August 1883). Yeats anguished that it 'was full of terrible, untrue things that [Mangan] believed'. Meehan now went public, giving his account of how the memoir came to be written, including his challenge to Mangan over the description of Chancery Lane and his final dismissive verdict that the memoir was 'the merest *rêve d'une vie*, with here and there some filaments of reality'.

This combination of dismay, dismissiveness, pedantry and infantilising reached its apogee with O'Donoghue's biography in 1897. O'Donoghue doesn't know what to do with the memoir. He needs it for his account of Mangan's childhood – without the memoir, the childhood is a desert – so can't dismiss it outright but it is anathema to his neat and orderly mind. He tiptoes around the outlandish claims, hastily dismissing the leprosy tale as 'of course, purely imaginary'* and is happiest fact-checking dates and metrics. He reports back meticulously that Mangan was seventeen in 1820, not eleven; that Chancery Lane was a 'respectable' street in 1818 and housed Mangan's first employer; that scriveners worked reasonable hours and had four months off in the summer; that among Mangan's supposedly blasphemous co-workers was another almanac poet who befriended him and two future archbishops who 'esteemed him highly'.

These corrections confirm our sense of the memoir as a kind of distorting mirror where office hours swell, respectable houses crumble to ruins, children shrink into mouse holes, future archbishops are hissing scorpions, and the narrator is stripped of everything that we know Mangan possessed at the time – friends, early publishing success and good looks. But O'Donoghue's attempt to have it both ways – correcting Mangan on details but accepting his unsubstantiated claims on, for instance, his father's profligacy and cruelty – isn't very satisfying. It's as if he has seized upon the different coloured inks as an excuse to compartmentalise and

---

*The leprosy sequence cannot be accurate because hospitals didn't allow bed-sharing between patients and leprosy sores were unmistakeable and incurable.

subdivide the narrative – Mangan is here (blue ink?) in his right mind and telling the truth, and here (black ink?) out of his mind and delusional – but the memoir doesn't read like that. It reads as weird but cohesive, its distortions pervasive, not partial.

And then the twentieth century began. In February 1902 a twenty-year-old undergraduate, James Joyce, radically reassessed the memoir in an extraordinary lecture on Mangan to his college debating society:

> In a moment of frenzy [Mangan] breaks silence, and we read how his associates dishonoured his person with their slime and venom, and how he lived as a child amid coarseness and misery and that all whom he met were demons out of the pit and that his father was a human boa-constrictor. … They who think such a terrible tale is the figment of a disordered brain do not know how keenly a sensitive boy suffers from contact with a gross nature. When someone told him that the account which he had given of his early life, so full of things which were, indeed the beginnings of sorrows, was wildly overstated, and partly false, he answered – 'Maybe I dreamed it.' … One whose nature is so sensitive cannot forget his dreams in a secure, strenuous life.

The originality and subversion of these insights don't really hit you unless you know what has come before; then you realise that Joyce has taken on a half-century of outrage and confusion. He leapfrogs over the older generation in grasping that a narrative may be unstable and farfetched but that doesn't make the narrator necessarily insane or a liar – since trauma is frequently repressed and unrecoverable by memory, it may manifest in strange images and metaphors which seek to convey the depth rather than the facts of suffering, and to remain true to the spirit rather than the letter of an abusive childhood. This is startlingly modern, as is his grasp of the exquisite irony of Mangan's response when he is accused of making it up. Joyce turns the tables on Meehan (whom he doesn't bother naming), implicitly mocking him for his failure to realise that for romantic poets, dreams, not reason, are the way to truth.

As so often with Mangan, the optics are almost too good to be true – there is a kind of perfection, which belongs more to fiction than to life, in it being the young Joyce who strikes the chord that sounds the new century. Freud's *Interpretation of Dreams* had been published three years earlier in an edition of 600 copies, which didn't sell out and which Joyce certainly knew nothing about, but the ripples were starting, the age of psychoanalysis was on its way, and Joyce is foreshadowing twentieth-century understanding of memory and trauma and of dreams as no longer random vagaries, but desperate signals from our unconscious; not untethered imaginings, but scrambled clues to our most hidden desires.

Joyce appeared to have settled the question of the memoir. Entering the scene in the 1970s and 80s, the great Mangan scholars Jacques Chuto and David Lloyd have no quarrel with the nineteenth century's view of the memoir as exaggerated, wild and imaginary but this doesn't bother them; it fits just fine with their understanding of Mangan. Chuto points out that the memoir tells us more about Mangan's miserable life in the late 1840s, when he was writing it, than it does about the 1810s and 20s when it is set, while Lloyd terms it 'a fiction' and 'a representation of psychosis'. They are not saying quite the same thing (they never are) – Chuto's Mangan is prey to the subjectivity of memory, while Lloyd's Mangan is detachedly portraying himself having a psychotic episode – but they are Joycean in their willingness to let the memoir exist in a liminal zone, as something both true and untrue.

Chuto and Lloyd looked like having the last word but in 1999 Ellen Shannon-Mangan, an American academic married to a man who claimed kinship with Mangan, published the longest and most comprehensive biography to date. Hers is biography as chivalric tale and, in her rush to rescue Mangan from his perceived detractors, she demands a retrial of the memoirs: Mangan is a 'courageous witness to the abuse he suffered' and his confessions aren't delusional or even figurative. With the energy of a crusading lawyer in a Hollywood movie, she sets to work challenging long-accepted evidence: some of the houses in Chancery Lane in 1818 *may* have been fleapits; certain scriveners' apprentices *may* have worked unfeasibly long hours; the co-workers in at least one of his offices *might* have been sneering; some hospitals *might* have allowed bed-sharing.

Her efforts are earnest, moving and frequently unintentionally hilarious. Trying to construct a candid memoir from phantasmagoria, to make lucidity out of convolution, involves her in conjecture and presumption, which derives from a premise – of Mangan's guileless sincerity – which is so evidently *false*, so counter to who he is and who he continually tells us he is, that you are left bemused as to how she has spent so long in his company without grasping what his editors on *The Comet* (12 January 1833) understood immediately: that he is 'a mystifier, a humbugger of the first water'.

It is easy to scoff at Shannon-Mangan, but weirdly it turns out that, like Joyce, she was also ahead of her time and heralding a sea change in the new century. When the #metoo movement launched, the airwaves were alight with people 'speaking their truth' and begging us to 'believe victims' who are 'witness to their own suffering'. This is the exact language of Shannon-Mangan and, hearing it, I realised that while I had been patronisingly dismissing her as unsophisticated and unable to grasp the idea of unstable narration, she had leapt forward to intuit that it is an outrage and an abuse even, to ask proof from victims who have found the courage to speak out.

The question of Mangan's memoir has not, as I had thought, been settled. It has not gone away. It can still be deployed in the seemingly unending debate around memory and trauma, truth and fiction. To borrow Fr Meehan's excuse to the *Irish Monthly* for losing the memoir (which echoes the last line of Carleton's tale when Mangan 'gladly leaves'): it is a text that continually 'escapes its keeping'.

The lost childhood of
James Mangan

The memoirs might occupy us less – and their accuracy be easier to assess – if there was more to go on, but Mangan's ur-absence is from his childhood and youth. He was baptised James Mangan on 2 May 1803 in Rosemary Lane Chapel in the Liberties; twenty-eight years later, on 4 December 1831, the initials J.C.M. appeared in a new journal, *The Comet*, in the first known use of his pseudonym 'Clarence', which he was soon to make famous. Between these two baptisms, the religious and the literary, is a void.

I made a list of the extant sources for the twenty-eight years from 1803 to 1831:

- Parish records of Rosemary Lane Chapel
- Wilson's Dublin Street Directories
- Numerous poems in *Grant's* and *New Ladies* almanacs 1818–26
- Four poems, published between 1826 and 1830 in *Robins Dublin* and *London Magazine*, *The Friend*, *Dublin Monthly Magazine*, *Dublin Literary Gazette*
- A short note, undated, written between 1822 and 1826

- A silhouette portrait, with taken 'at the age of 19 years' inscribed on the back
- The recollections of a few relatives and acquaintances (recorded after his death)

This is fabulously scant. All the usual biographical portals are closed: there is no surviving contemporary correspondence to, from, or about the young Mangan or his family, no school reports, no diaries (either his own or other people's), no mentions in local journals or newspapers, no surviving homes that might be visited, no toys, drawings, books, *things*. Their absence calls attention to the process by which such stuff is generally preserved. Who saves it? Proud parents? Meticulous institutions? The anxious child who grows into a neurotic adult? In the game of preservation, it clearly helps to stay in one place, to go to good schools that keep records, to have gregarious and loving (or at least dutiful) parents who monitor your progress and build the kind of social connections that yield letters, anecdotes and recollections.

Only four recollections recalling Mangan in young adulthood are extant and only one (a poem) is by a friend; the others are from country relatives who knew him slightly (if at all) and an acquaintance who worked with him briefly in a solicitor's office. Mangan lived all his life in the same neighbourhood and he was famous in his lifetime; when he died, newspapers and publishers were hungry for reminiscences of him and within months of his death, the publisher John O'Daly, who was bringing out an anthology which included some Mangan translations, was questioning people for a biographical article, and two decades later the author and publican John McCall began researching for a biography. Why did so little come to light? Mangan's early life is as occluded as Shakespeare's, but this wasn't sixteenth-century rural Stratford. It was the start of the age of data retrieval and storage, when governments were beginning the process of tracking their citizens through censuses, surveys, catalogues and statistical inquiries, and writers, galvanised by Boswell's *Life of Johnson* (1791), were extending the possibilities of biography.

When I read biographies, my main interest is the early years. At an impressionable age I read Graham Greene's essay 'The Lost Childhood', which quotes a line from Æ of all people* – 'In the lost childhood of Judas, Christ was betrayed' – which greatly appealed to me because it conveys, in an image of arresting strangeness (we never think of Judas as a child), Wordsworth's truism that 'the child is father to the man' and that the key to adult intention lies in childhood. I've always assumed that my interest in stalking the subject through childhood was a quest for that intention, but since I've chosen to write the life of someone whose childhood is a void, I wonder now if what attracted me to Æ's quote wasn't the excitement of understanding Judas' betrayal, but the mystery of the loss. All we can glean from the surviving sources on Mangan are a few dates, addresses and unsubstantiated recollections.

His parents, James Mangan and Catherine Smith, met in Dublin and married in Rosemary Lane Chapel in the Liberties in 1798, both having come to the capital a few years earlier, his father from Shanagolden, Co. Limerick, where he may have worked as a hedge teacher, and his mother from a prosperous family farm in Kiltale, Dunsany, Co. Meath. Catherine was sent to Dublin to help an aunt, Mary Farrell, run a grocers in 3 Fishamble Street and on the aunt's death, she inherited the business. On their marriage, James took over the shop. Their first child, William, was born in 1799 and must have died before 1806 when a second William was

---

*Surprising because you don't expect to find Æ – the pseudonym of George Russell (1867–1935), poet, novelist, painter, publisher, nationalist – mentioned outside Ireland. He only survives today through his famous contemporaries, e.g. his walk-on part in Joyce's *Ulysses*, when Dedalus, having borrowed money from him, remarks: 'A.E.I.O.U.'

baptised, but his death isn't recorded in the parish register and he went unmentioned until the 1980s when his parish baptism record was unearthed. Patrick Smith, a cousin who remained in Kiltale, recalled, in a note to Mangan's first biographer John McCall, a daughter 'who died from the effects of a scald' and this may be how the first William died, his gender reassigned, since a mystery seems to have attached to the daughter from the start. Mangan refers in two versions of his memoirs to a sister 'driven from home' by his father, but a cousin, Mrs Coffey 'had no recollection of a sister' and there is no baptism cert and no one has been able to find out anything about her. The early biographers took Mangan at his word and supplied him with a sister, but Joyce picked up on the obfuscation – in his short story 'Araby', the boy narrator is in love with 'Mangan's sister', who is never named.

James was baptised in Rosemary Lane chapel on 2 May 1803, the eldest of three surviving brothers (John was born in 1804) and was educated in the small schools round the Liberties set up by the Jesuits during the Penal era to educate working-class men and boys. For eight years, from ages seven to fifteen, Mangan was a Jesuit boy, taught to declaim poetry and to decline Latin and French verbs and possibly also Spanish and Italian. In later life, when he was working in the Ordnance Survey, his knowledge of Latin was queried, but the subtlety and convolution of his thinking, which attracted (and irritated) another Jesuit boy, James Joyce, could be termed Jesuitical. The only story he ever told about his schooldays, in the long memoir, reveals a precocious subtlety: his neat definition of the word parenthesis ('I should suppose a *parenthesis* to be something included in a sentence – but which might be omitted from the sentence without injury to the meaning of a sentence') excited his teachers' praise. One of them, after conversing with him, apparently declared presciently: 'You will be a rattling fellow, my boy – but see and take care of yourself!'

The uneasiness of that parting shot suggests that Mangan's fragility and peculiarity – always the first things anyone remarks about him – were already evident in childhood. I can't remember now at what stage of my research I began diagnosing him. It wasn't at the beginning when he appeared as a marvellously dissolute romantic – an opium-eater like De Quincey and Coleridge! a *poète maudit* like Baudelaire! a dabbler in Eastern exotica like Byron and Moore! – and I took his cloaking and hatting as another romantic pose, a kind of inverse take on the dandy; and his gloom and depression, if not as an outright pose, then something he accentuated to conform with romantic tropes.

But as I read on, something began to shift. Maybe it was the description his interlocutors have left of his monologues (never conversations) or when I began to notice that his letters are never dialogues (he never asks his correspondents how they are doing or how the kids are or what they think of the latest scandal), which led me to the understanding, which made me sad, that he had no intimates. Or maybe when I read his paranoid letter to his editor, 'My mother and father … seemed to watch my every action, and to wish to dive into my very thoughts.' Or maybe when I realised that his long memoir reads like one of Freud's case histories. Whatever the stimulus, I know that by the time I read Terence Brown's essay making the case that Mangan was bipolar, I'd already come to the view that he wasn't just eccentric, he had a condition which must be somewhere described in the psychiatrists' bible, the *Diagnostic and Statistical Manual of Mental Disorders* (DSMMD).

I did my best to resist diagnosing him because I'm not a psychiatrist and even if I were I would have to respect the Goldwater Rule whereby psychiatrists agree not to give their professional opinion of public figures whom they haven't personally examined and which I think historians should also sign up to because you can't take seriously books that retrospectively diagnose historical figures with conditions that weren't classified or described until the mid-twentieth century. But when it comes to Mangan, any sense of professionalism deserts me. I would read these lines: 'I arose, as it were out of myself … I felt as though I could feast upon air and thought alone' and exclaim, as Terence Brown did, 'bipolar! manic!' and I'd read his auto-description of 'the adamantine barrier that levered me from a communion with mankind' – and collate it with his monologues to conclude 'autism', and I'd go further, atomising his condition into the most rarefied phobias and syndromes: I think he had gymnophobia (fear of nudity) and aphenphosmphobia (fear of being touched) and scopophobia (fear of being stared at) and depersonalisation-derealisation disorder ('detachment from one's surroundings, perceiving the world as foggy, dreamlike/surreal, or visually distorted) and strangest of all, I think he had Cottard's Syndrome: I think he thought he was a ghost and that's how he came up with this extraordinary line: 'So meagre am I, no lathe is like me / Death for his shadowy stillness cannot see me.'

I could go on but throughout my research I found I could not stop making lists of e.g. his favourite words, his neologisms, the places he lived, the books he read, his methods of taking cover, and these gave me the kind of satisfaction you get from ticking tasks off to-do lists, and that the great botanists and entomologists of the Enlightenment must have got from distilling plants and insects down to their Latin names and chief characteristics, but while I don't despise the organising tendency in general, I do recognise that cataloguing Mangan is pinning a butterfly to a slide. And when I found myself breaking him down to an assembly part of mental disorders, I had a sudden flash of our descendants laughing at the 300+ disorders of the *DSMMD* the way we laugh at medieval doctors for the four humours. The mind is a vortex, not a grid, and you can't explain Mangan through lists and diagnoses, but since we're here in his unmapped childhood with the priest's warning ringing in our ears – 'see and take care of yourself!' – maybe we can say that there was *something* about Mangan and whatever it was, it manifested early.

In 1811 or 1812, James Mangan senior, in the sarcastic words of his brother-in-law John Smith 'considered himself rather encumbered by the care of shopkeeping so invited my brother, Patt (at that time in London) to join him in trade, which my brother accepted.' Patt Smith's name now appears in *Wilson's Directory* as the proprietor of 3 Fishamble Street and, according to John Smith, Mangan senior 'removed to another neighbourhood and left his young son, the late J.C.M., with my brother who reared him and kept him in school until he was 14 or 15 years'. Mangan never mentions being reared by his uncle, which is no proof either way. His first biographer, John McCall, suggests that Mangan senior now 'opened up as a vintner near the Old Bleeding Horse pub on Camden St and commenced to speculate in building and de-possessing houses in that neighbourhood and in Kilmainham, with a view to letting them in tenements'. *Wilson's* records Mangan & Langson as wine merchants in Greek Street in 1813 and 1814 and at Lower Ormond Quay in 1815–16; this could be Mangan's father, although the addresses aren't that near the Bleeding Horse.

'Mangan & Langston' disappear from *Wilson's* in 1817, which is significant because around this time Mangan senior seems to have gone bankrupt. John Smith claimed that he was of 'a reckless disposition' and Patrick Smith elaborated that 'he used to give sprees and balls and when he could not entertain [people] as he wished in his own house he used to bring them to hotels' and that 'owing to the two gents he got to conduct his business, and his own extravagance, he failed'. (Mangan goes between the two explanations: in his impersonal memoir, his father is 'robbed by those around him' but in the letter to his publisher he claims 'My father was a merchant of this city and ruined himself by speculation. He had a princely soul, but no prudence,' and in his longer memoir, 'his great and besetting sin was improvidence'.)

Around 1818, Mangan left school. He would always claim, with considerable bitterness, that his bankrupt father removed him early to put him to work to support the family, but in his uncle's (and everyone else's) estimation, 'fourteen or fifteen' was the usual age to 'be kept' in school and it is hard to think what other options there would have been for the son of a bankrupt Catholic grocer in 1818. The sympathetic priests don't seem to have spoken up for him, but what could they have proposed? His temperament wasn't suited to the priesthood, even if the Church had been in a position to recruit in Ireland in the 1810s, which it wasn't. And while Trinity College had started accepting Catholics in 1793, this didn't extend to supporting them financially. The impoverished sons of Protestant clergymen got grants ('sizarships') and exceptional students could win foundation scholarships, but these weren't open to Catholics who, if they were admitted to Trinity, had to pay their own way; Thomas Moore was also the son of a Catholic grocer but, crucially, a rich grocer.

Mangan, very aware of his connection to Moore, wrote in his long memoir: 'I share with an illustrious townsman of my own the honour, or the disreputability – as it may be considered – of having been born the son of a grocer.' Maybe he built his adolescent dreams on following in Moore's glittering footsteps; maybe part of his father's 'reckless extravagance' was promising to send him to Trinity. Instead, he was torn from his books and apprenticed as a scrivener in a solicitor's firm at just the time that he was launching as a poet. In 1818 he had two poems published in *Grant's* and *New Ladies* almanacs and he soon became a prolific contributor, under various pseudonyms. His almanac poems are precocious and suggest a preoccupation with death, a neurotic sense of entrapment, a witty sense of humour and (like every other young poet of the time) the strong influence of Byron. In 1826 both almanacs folded and a deep silence descends until 1831 when he turns up in a new journal, *The Comet*, under the name by which he will become famous: 'Clarence'. His public career now starts up, and with it, the sources: as Clarence Mangan, he corresponded with well-known men who kept some of his letters and wrote about him in their memoirs, and he gained a national profile so that his doings were tracked in the press. There is never a lot, but after 1831 it becomes possible to flesh out his life.

*

The story of Mangan's youth, assembled from the brief surviving sources, is obviously *fleeting* and riddled with gaps. Is it also *false* and *perjur'd*? Beyond the obvious – the existence of the sister is either falsified or elided – what I find striking is the asymmetry: all the sources are from the maternal side of the family. From the Mangans, there is nothing, which means that the only things we know about the father's background – that he came from Shanagolden and may have worked as a hedge-school teacher – we know from his in-laws. The pattern of Smith presence and Mangan absence continues through the historical record: the Smith trail of obituaries, wills, estates and land deeds is extensive and points to the clan's exceptional caution, stability, clannishness and financial acuity. When Mangan's uncle John Smith died, aged ninety-three, on the Meath homestead, his obituary notice (*The Nation*, 12 February 1859) approved his 'constant exercises of strict probity in the discharge of the important duties of a substantial farmer' and John's nephew, Michael Smith, a Dublin provision merchant, left an estate worth £6,000 in 1862. After taking over the Fishamble grocery from Mangan's father, the Smiths held on to it for seven decades as part of a network of family businesses round Dublin.* For the centenary of Mangan's death in 1949, Kiltale produced a host of Smith descendants, including a famous hurler and a farmer living on the original homestead who apparently owned a painting of Mangan (like the remnant of memoir, it has disappeared). In the 1980s Shannon-Mangan found the Meath farm still remaining in Smith family hands, which, for Ireland, shows astonishing fixity of tenure.

The contrast with the Mangans is acute: a *Limerick Leader* journalist went to Shanagolden for the centenary and reported back glumly that 'one hundred years is a short time in the life of any village yet to-day no one in Shanagolden knows the place where James Mangan [senior] was born. The majority are indifferent, and the few that care contend amongst themselves as to the exact place.' (*LL*, 18 June 1949).† Nobody has been able to provide James Mangan with parents or siblings; the nearest relation anyone can suggest is Denis Mangan, 'said to be a cousin of the poet', who doubled his acreage during the Famine and married his daughter to the wealthiest man in north Kerry. Their son was the 1916 hero The Rahilly, and after the Rising the family was eager to claim Mangan – in 1971 Jacques Chuto met a descendant named James Clarence Mangan O'Rahilly but no one has ever firmed up that tenuous 'said to be'. Apparently a 'quarter of the Catholic population of Shanagolden was lost in the Famine' – this may include Mangan's more direct relatives.

Mangan was heir to two oppositional forces. He displays nothing of the rooted, clannish, thrifty Smiths and everything of

---

*Patt Smith and his son Michael Smith owned the Fishamble store between 1811 and 1854 (letting it out for some of those years), after which it was owned by the McNally family until 1887 – the McNallys, also from Kiltale, had married into the Smiths. Michael Smith's sister married John Plunkett, who became manager and foreman of Michael's bacon curing business in Copper Alley.

†In his 2003 history of Shanagolden, local historian Thomas Culhane claimed that 'the Mangan residence is alleged to have stood where the grotto is now sited and adjacent to the library' but he doesn't say who alleged this, and in a minutely detailed account of local doings he has nothing to say about James Mangan's direct family, though he mentions a few possible cousins.

the opaque, feckless, absent Mangans. The portrayal in the memoir of his father as a snake devouring his children gestures to the myth of Cronus/Saturn swallowing his children after he has castrated his father, Uranus. Mangan senior is the Cronus figure who has cut off his roots completely and who psychologically swallows his children so that they fail to prosper or procreate. Mangan perpetuated this inheritance of loss by altering his name so decisively that his contemporaries referred to him as Clarence as if it were his patronymic. When he began his desultory study of Irish in the 1840s, he must have been delighted to discover that 'gan' is Irish for 'less' or 'without': his name had loss stitched into it.

But within the marriage, the roles are reversed: it is the Smith mother who is absent, and the Mangan father present. The only recorded physical description of Catherine, from her niece, Mrs Coffey, shows the usual Smith preoccupation with respectability: 'Mangan's mother was a nice staid respectable looking old woman, wore a quilted cap and was always neat and tidy in her appearance.' Just one other attribute distinguishes Catherine: her silence. In his memoirs, Mangan writes of the terrible moment when his father demands that he leave school and start work: 'Could I not behoof myself in support of the family? If my excellent mother thought so, she said nothing.' And later, recounting one of his nervous breakdowns, he recalls that 'the wretched depression of my spirits could not escape the notice of my mother, but she passed no remark on it'. If he seems to be aching for his mother to speak, then according to his cousin Patrick Smith, he was part of the silencing: 'The two brothers [James and William] were so odd in cheer that their mother could not speak to them when in certain moods.' Catherine Mangan is a woman silenced by her husband and sons and ignored by her brothers and nephew (the sole description of her comes from the only female relative on record). She is so effaced that it takes an effort to recall that she brought to the marriage the thriving grocer's store, the prosperous farm in Meath and the solid mercantile connections in Dublin and London; she should have been the dominant, or at least an equal, partner.

James Mangan, who arrives into the story without wealth, family or connections, made himself felt. He is the only character to emerge strongly from the Smith testimonies: there is a throughline from John Smith's magnificently sarcastic 'he considered himself rather encumbered by the care of shopkeeping' to Mrs Coffey's description three decades later of the uncle she had known in his old age: 'a fine old blustering sort of a fellow'. He presents as the opposite to Mangan whereas Catherine is very like her cloaked, Bartleby-esque son. In a complicated manoeuvre, Mangan seems to have drawn down loss and absence from both parents.

Mangan's problematic memoirs aside, the Smiths are the only witnesses we have to the homelife of James and Catherine, and they are suspiciously defensive, always shrilly insistent on James' fecklessness, an attitude that seems to have got baked in down the generations. Denis Plunkett, son of a Smith cousin, wrote into the *Evening Telegraph* (1 May 1909) to protest that Mangan 'was a frequent visitor and welcome guest in my mother's comfortable house, where he could have constantly stayed'. When a great-grand-nephew was questioned about his famous ancestor in 1949, his main concern was to insist that Mangan 'wouldn't have had to sleep in Dublin's doorways had he cared to come the Kiltale way. The Smiths were a snug family, and they took a great pride in the lad's poetry'. This is contradicted by a line in John Smith's letter to John O'Daly, which admits that 'Mangan was the sole support of his parents,' suggesting that the Smiths weren't so very 'snug' about looking after Catherine and her children. And although the Smiths spread their businesses across the extended family for generations, none of the three Mangan boys entered their uncles' or cousins' businesses (John also became a scrivener and William was apprenticed to a cabinet maker).

Mangan barely mentions his cousins in his correspondence, and when he does, it's negative. In a letter to Gavan Duffy in 1847, he admits staying with the Plunketts but doesn't acknowledge them as relatives, and his description of their hospitality would have outraged poor Denis had he seen the letter:

For some days and nights I wandered the streets, dependent upon chance and charity … I had some melancholy consolation in thinking that I should be found dead of hunger somewhere about the suburbs of the city. And found at length I was, nearly in truth at the point of death, by one who did not know me, but who kindly assisted my fainting steps to a place to which I had just recollection enough to direct him – the classical locality of Copper Alley. There Mr Plunkett, the factor of my cousin Michael Smyth [*sic*], gave me a bed (a rug upon straw) in a barrel-loft, for two or three nights, and sent me up a cup of tea at intervals. GOD bless him.

This was Denis's mother's 'comfortable house'! Mangan goes on to describe calling on Michael Smith in Dublin:

I then waited on my cousin himself – he who now owns the house that ought to be mine – and just said, 'Michael, I am going down to your father's – your family have often solicited me to pay them a visit – I will now test their sincerity.' He coldly told me that I would be welcome – and I set off – and paid my last maravedi for a seat in the Caravan. And so, here I am – with the fresh breezes of Heaven blowing about me – with rivers of the purest spring water to drink – but with nothing, positively nothing to eat, excepting eggs, which I direct to be boiled very hard to compensate for the absence of bread.

This is funny, or at least tragicomic – the starving poet in the middle of Black '47, the worst year of the Famine, overdosing on eggs! – but the tone is sour. It's not just that he contradicts the Smiths' accounts of hospitality (Mangan was quite capable of protecting his self-image as a lonely outcast by eliding previous visits to the farm and turning the gold of his aunt's 'comfortable house' into the straw of a stranger's 'barrel-loft'), it's the resentment and sarcasm ('I will now test their sincerity') running through his lines that suggests a rift, or at least, strain between the two families. Mangan doesn't usually reach for sarcasm, and he generally liked to gush over his benefactors in the manner of a Gaelic poet praising his patrons.

There seems something dark and unsayable behind the Smiths' defensiveness and Mangan's sourness. Maybe the Smiths lent James senior money and then cut him loose as a bad investment but when their peculiar nephew became famous, they had to counter the suggestion of negligence, so took care to paint a black picture of the father. Or maybe the Smiths were ashamed of their sister's marriage and unwilling to tell the world how bad Mangan's childhood had been because of an omertà around mentioning domestic abuse – see the outraged public reaction when Mangan's confessions were finally published.

Just one line on James Mangan not written by his son or his in-laws survives for the record: a note in John O'Daly's papers scribbled on a certificate for Prospect [Glasnevin] Cemetery: 'James Mangan erected this Stone to the Memory of his son John Mangan who died 4 May 1835.' In this wreckage of a family where nobody gets commemorated, there is something moving in this act of fond and upright paternity, the only moment on record where we catch James Mangan behaving like a normal, loving father and spending his money with propriety. But it is not enough to save him. His essential quality of oppressiveness is too indelibly conveyed by the terse language of his in-laws and the feverish images of his son, who throughout his life could never write the word 'father' without alarm bells going off.

*

His biographers' efforts to assemble Mangan's childhood through parish registers, street directories, cemetery certificates and compromised recollections allows us to trace a narrative of impoverishment and resentment. But the youthful Mangan remains unreachable: in the absence of diaries, letters and anecdotes, we don't know what it felt like for the boy. As a homeless addict in his forties, he remembered it all as terrible, but shortly before his thirtieth birthday, when he was emerging from obscurity to national fame, he wrote a poem, 'To Childhood', in which he yearns after the 'enchantment' and 'crystal joy' of those 'golden hours' when 'Life was new and Hope was young.' After a fairly pedestrian opening, which could be the work of any young Romantic, the reader is suddenly submerged in the third stanza into a shimmering shifting world of contrasting light and shade in 'lines so good that they could not have been written by anyone but Mangan' as Joyce would put it. The 'thy' is childhood:

I see thy willow-darkened stream,
Thy sunny lake, thy sunless grove,
Before me glassed
In many a dimly-gorgeous dream,
And wake to love, to doubly love
The magic Past!
Or Fiction lifts her dazzling wand,
And lo! her buried wonders rise
On Slumber's view,
Till all Arabia's genii-land
Shines out, the mimic Paradise
Thy pencil drew!

Everything in this world is a mirage: the reader falls through multiple refracting layers without ever finding solid ground. There are no foundations: nostalgia is built on a magic, not an actual, past; fiction arises out of sleep, not life; religion is a representation drawn by an effaceable pencil, not a pen. And when I try to analyse what the lines might mean, I find myself falling through explanations which similarly refuse to 'land'. The mirage could be personal (Mangan revealing that he has no happy childhood to remember) or a critique of romanticism (Mangan exposing as a fantasy the romantic myth of childhood) or a critique of nostalgia in general. I liked these explanations – Clarence says childhood is *false* – but I couldn't quite land it because the lines are sheer joy to read and how could Mangan convey joy so convincingly if he hadn't felt it himself? And when do you feel joy like that except in childhood? If he is sounding the true note of joy to tell us that joy is a mirage, then the form disrupts the message, which is a very Manganese explanation, but maybe what he is conveying via shift and shimmer isn't mirage, but transience. Maybe the lines aren't an ironic commentary on our tendency to romanticise the past but an attempt to describe the reality of joy as something we move through fleetingly and can never retain although we spend all our lives trying, by creating simulacrums of it in dreams, art and religion.

This is a lot to be contained in one short stanza and the explanation left me dazzled and dizzy and not knowing much more about what Mangan's childhood was actually like, except that perhaps there is no *actually*, and not only with Mangan, and not only for lack of sources, but with all of us, everywhere: our childhoods are 'gone in the wind' (to borrow another Mangan phrase, which may have given Margaret Mitchell the title to her repulsive bestseller).

Tick-tick, tick-tick! –
Not a sound save Time's

In January 2015 I moved to the Tenters, the area southwest of St Patrick's Cathedral, bounded by the South Circular Road, Cork Street and Newmarket Square. Frank and I had broken up a few months earlier. In four months, we would be back together and in five and a half years we would be married, but I didn't know that then, and I was heartbroken.

The neighbourhood wasn't one I had ever spent any time in and in my first weeks I was bewildered by the meander of small streets turning into each other and was constantly getting lost, not helped by my tendency to leave home without my glasses. I had never minded wandering round in a haze, even in unknown foreign cities where I didn't speak the language, but now I was feeling unmoored. I had got used to regarding Frank as the fixed pole by which I oriented myself: physically fixed in that he would root himself to his desk with wine and cigars to write Joyce for hours, and emotionally fixed since he was always himself no matter the company, his conversation invariably high even with very small children, and temporally fixed through the Kantian dependability of his routine. I knew his bakery, grocery and bookshops, his barber, tailor and dry cleaners, the café, wine bar and restaurant currently in favour, and I knew at what times in the day or week he would call into each of these. I had had my place in this pleasing pattern, and now, excluded from it, I seemed to have lost all direction.

Thus, it was that I was some days or weeks wandering this way and that before I realised that the street continuous with my own was called Clarence Mangan Road. Naturally I took this as A Sign but as I walked up and down the wide, cheerful, tree-lined street of semi-detached pebble-dash houses and lovely pocket gardens, I felt that nowhere could be less Manganese* – e.g. less mournful, shadowy, layered and enigmatic. There was no hope, I was sure, of encountering his ghost. When I complained to my neighbour that he didn't belong here, but to the Liberties, she pointed out soothingly that the Liberties was 'full' (i.e. named long ago) and that 'they' (i.e. Dublin County Council) had done their best to 'house him' close to home.

This image of Mangan as a tough social-housing case driving the Council mad with his exquisite obduracy did get a laugh out of me but I couldn't get over my sense that 'they' had got it wrong, even when, after another week's peregrinations, I realised they had moved his friends, or at least colleagues, in beside him: Petrie, O'Donovan and O'Curry Roads, which bisect or run parallel to Clarence Mangan Road, commemorate the scholars George Petrie, John O'Donovan and Eugene O'Curry, who worked with Mangan on the Ordnance Survey in the late 1830s and early 40s. All these streets went up in the 1920s and 30s and I was moved that whoever had the naming of this signature social housing in the newly independent state had chosen to commemorate painstaking scholarship rather than military uprisings, though I did recognise that it was all coming from

---

*I prefer this adjective to 'Manganesque' since the element manganese on the periodic table is defined as 'a rare trace element' with contradictory attributes – 'hard yet very brittle, difficult to fuse but easy to oxidise'.

the same place, since the names of these nineteenth-century Gaelic revivalists, no less than the 1916 men, signalled the new state's pride in its past and aspirations for the future. There was a pioneering zeal to the invocation of these scholars but it is now tinged with mordant irony because the aspiration to Gaelicise the country didn't come off and, in fact, when I think of the way Irish was deployed in the newly independent Ireland, I'm reminded not of the semantic rigour of O'Donovan and O'Curry, but of the sly fudge of Mangan, who liked to give the impression that he could read and understand Irish when he really couldn't.

When I researched a bit more, I realised that it wasn't surprising I couldn't sense Mangan in the Tenters: I doubt he ever set foot there. When he was born the whole area was fields where, as the memorial tablet in Weavers Square has it, 'linen cloth was spread out on tenterhooks to bleach in the sun'. In Mangan's youth, the Tenter fields were still stiff with cloth and alive with workers but in 1824 the last remaining protective tariffs for Irish linen were removed, exposing the Liberties to competition from northern England, and the textile industry collapsed. The fields became wasteland before being re-purposed some decades later as market gardens. When the planners and architects of the newly independent state descended in the 1920s, they found a blank slate, which they used to lay out good-quality semi-detached, low-rise social housing, with gardens back and front, and generous allotments. My neighbours told me there was a rough patch in the 1980s when the building of high-rise apartment blocks collided with the heroin epidemic, but by the time I arrived the high-rises were being pulled down, and the junkies moved on, and the Council was selling off the social housing, and the whole area was hipsterfying faster than a London borough. Little girls with flying curls, named for characters in Victorian novels or the more rarefied Celtic myths, sped up and down on scooters while their parents piously scooped the poop of bichon frises. On Saturdays we compared baskets of knobbly organic vegetables from the market in Newmarket Square, where one week, in a state of helpless hungover disconnect, I bought an usually elongated duster made of ostrich feathers, its reach unnecessarily long for my small house, but which would do very well for Frank's, might even extend to his uppermost shelves where the undisturbed dust liked to form fine filmy layers over books and busts and candlesticks.

*

It was January weather, cold and wet, when I moved into the Tenters and the line I kept repeating as I wandered the streets was one from Verlaine, which has stuck in my head since school: *Il pleure dans mon coeur comme il pleut sur la ville*. It weeps in my heart like it weeps on the city. I found this satisfyingly mournful, with its assonance and homonyms and the way 'pleu' lands with the soft repetitive thud of a heartbeat. But it's a very self-conscious line. It invites you to observe yourself wandering around the city crying in the rain. You can't say this line without feeling sorry for yourself and by then I'd lived long enough with Mangan, and with Frank, to have developed the instinct to cut sentimentality with irony, to exclaim in a kind of parody of misery, 'O the rain, the weary, dreary rain / How it plashes on the windowsill!' Mangan loves that word *plash* – which starts like pleut but, instead of the dying fall, rises to a resounding splash – and in an early short story, he goes full plash in this mordant description of a courtyard:

> To the rere of the house extended a long and narrow court yard, partly overgrown with grass and melancholy-looking wild flowers, but flagged at the extremity, and bounded by a colossal wall. Down the entire length of this wall, which was connected with a ruined old building, descended a metal rain spout; and I derived a diseased gratification in listening in wet weather, to the cold,

bleak, heavy plash, plash, plash of the rain, as it fell from this spout on the flag beneath. I have sat nine hours consecutively at my back parlour window, with a cigar between my lips and a pitcher of pump water at my side, to hearken to this dismally monotonous echo.

Here is his signature mix of irony and agony. The story is about lost love, and the description in this passage is of the deeply depressed narrator sitting there counting down the drops, just as the narrator in a later poem counts down the clock ('Tick-tick, tick-tick! – Not a sound save Time's, / And the wind-gust, as it drives the rain'). But though immersed in the romantic poetry of despair, Mangan is hyper-alert to its self-indulgence, its tendency to wallow in its own misery, and he admits, what Verlaine will not, the 'diseased gratification' a poet takes in the pathetic fallacy of sitting among the ruins, crying in the rain.

The forlorn courtyard, at once exposed and enclosed, is as essential to the mood as the rain. Although it has the quality, like all Mangan's vistas, of a dreamscape, I think he was describing an archetypal house in the Liberties. Shortly after I moved into the Tenters, a friend moved into a tiny terraced house by St Audeon's church, and I liked to walk up to his via the backstreets. I would leave my house and amble down the cheerful tree-lined streets via the green in Oscar Square. At The Coombe (the road, not the hospital) I always had the sharpest sense of crossing over: the streets would abruptly narrow, the gardens disappear, the houses huddle together on terraces, the only visible greenery was what sprouted from chimney tops. Dark lanes would straggle into dead ends, overlooked by grimy windows soldered shut so tight you couldn't imagine them opening should you yell for help. Behind long walls connected to 'ruined old buildings', I could imagine Mangan's 'narrow court yards, partly overgrown'. On Meath Street,

Liberty Market was a jumble of soft toys and squat statues of the Buddha and sticks of incense and synthetic clothes and gummy sweets, none of it old or valuable or artisanal, everything made last year or last month, in Asia probably, and shipped over in job lots, and yet the market, like the Liberties, feels old, sullen with history.

Where the Tenters seemed to me to be constantly hearkening back to its recent bucolic condition of fields and market gardens, the Liberties is the longest-settled and most densely populated area of Dublin, extemporised over centuries, continually pulled down and remade, but at no point yielding space to gardens, parks, or semi-Ds, and perhaps it was lack of greenery which allowed the Liberties to stubbornly resist gentrification even during the Celtic Tiger when all of Dublin was being flipped, or so I hazarded until I realised that Stoneybatter just across the river is equally terraced, gardenless and treeless and it hipsterfied as fast as the Tenters, which suggests that the Liberties' resistance is something more than vegetative.

I'd never lived in the Liberties but from my earliest years in Dublin, as a student, I had the strongest sense of it. In college some brave boy would gather our money and head up to the Oliver Bond Flats to buy acid and sometimes he'd come back with tabs and sometimes he'd come back robbed, at which point a cynic would say knowingly that he was scamming us (a sour and pointless accusation since it couldn't be proved either way and if we weren't willing to take the risk ourselves, we should suck it up). And periodically over the years we would head up to drink in The Clock, or check out the end of year show in NCAD, or go to Hallowe'en parties in Taylor's Hall, or gigs in Vicar Street, where one night Chuck D of Public Enemy cracked us up because he kept saying 'Tiocfaidh ár Lá' with such joyful satisfaction that we realised he thought the phrase was 'Chuck D, Our Law'. And later, when I was working in *The Dubliner* and hanging out with my friend Tim in the brief time he also worked there, it was to Thomas Street we'd drive for him to score, so that over the years I had come to associate the Liberties with drugs, art, illegality and wild nights. It wasn't chance that we'd headed up here the night of the lock-in where I first met Mangan.

To get to my friend's house I had to pass through the network of dark alleys that press against the walls of St Audeon's church. Here hooded figures would scope me briefly before dismissing me as harmless and returning to their transactions. Late one night, on my way back home, I came upon a curly-haired Brazilian stumbling drunk through these alleys, his open-faced naivete and lack of English, no less than his absolute inebriation, marking him out like the trail of blood from a wounded animal that brings scavengers circling, so that I had no choice in all conscience but to walk him home, which meant, since he could neither gesture nor explain, letting him guide me the longest way round to get to a door within a hundred metres of where I'd found him.

*

It was in late February that I did my Mangan Walk of the Liberties. I knew I wouldn't run into Frank since the Liberties wasn't part of his dependable routine, except at 8 a.m., where he might cross the Liffey at Bridge Street, but that wasn't a risk because I would never do a Mangan walk early morning; Mangan's time is twilight or evening, when Frank would be crossing downriver at Parliament Street to take a left onto Dame Street and through to Wicklow Street to shop in Dunnes (butter, raspberries, blueberries, yoghurt) and Fallon & Byrne (cheese, boar burger) and The Corkscrew (wine, red), piling up purchases as he went, dangerously overloading his handlebars with such ludicrously heavy bags that I had got used to people I didn't know stopping me in the street to beg me to get him a basket or paniers, which I had done, but he wouldn't use them; they offended his aesthetic.

To prepare for my tour, I made one of my lists of all the addresses Mangan had lived, or at least stayed:*

- 3 Fishamble Street [1803–15]
- Chancery Lane [1815–c.29?]
- Charlemont St [c.1829–c.37?]
- 9 Peter Street [1837–c.46]
- 5 Richmond Street [1838]
- Johnson's Lane [1847]
- Glasnevin [June 1847]
- 151 Upper Abbey Street [1848]
- Fishamble Street [1848]
- Bride Street [1849]

And the addresses of the schools he attended:
- [Jesuit School], Saul's Court [1810–14]
- Michael Courtney's Academy, Derby Square [1814–16]
- Reverend Doyle's, Arran Quay [1816]
- William Browne, Chancery Lane [1817–18]

And the addresses of his work places, including the journals and newspapers he contributed to:
- Kenrick Solicitors, 6 York Street [1818–25]
- *Grant's* and *New Ladies* almanacs, Patrick Street [1818–26]
- Matthew Frank Solicitors, 28 Merrion Square North [1826–9]
- Thomas Leland Solicitors, 6 Fitzwilliam Square [1830–8]
- *The Comet*, 2 Church Lane [1831–3]
- *Dublin University Magazine* [1834–48]
- The Ordnance Survey, 21 Great Charles Street [1838–41]

---

*The addresses are culled from his correspondence; he may have addressed letters from friends' houses where he was staying.

- Trinity College Dublin, College Green [1841–6]
- *The Nation*, 12 Trinity Street [1842–4] and 4 D'Olier Street [1844–8]

He did most of his writing in pubs, so I added his known haunts:
- Bligh's, Patrick Street
- Widow MacDonagh's, Bride Street
- The Shades, College Green
- The Bleeding Horse, Camden Street

Then I got hold of a map of the old Liberties:

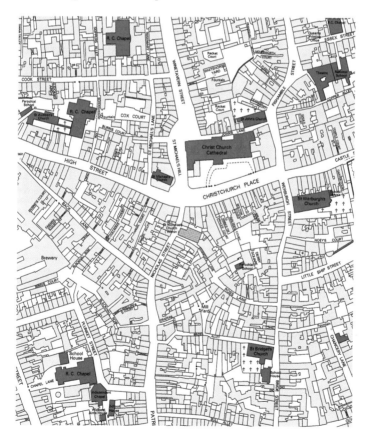

This map of the early nineteenth-century Liberties is still recognisable as the Liberties of today: Patrick Street and High Street have been widened and straightened and the once earthy street names are now anodyne – Skinner's Row is Christ Church Place, and Volunteer's Yard is Catherine Street, and Cuckold's Row is Brabazon Street and Crooked Staff is Ardee Street – and the lanes and alleys and dead ends, which cluster like broken veins in the old map, have been razed, their evocative names – Angel Alley, Dog & Duck Yard, Skipper's Lane – forgotten. But the routes that Mangan walked are the same: to get from Chancery Lane, where he lived, to Patrick Street, where he liked to drink, you still take a left onto Golden Lane and go across Bull Alley, or you turn onto Bride Street and go across Bride Alley (now Bride Road).

Just looking at his routes gives me claustrophobia. In childhood and at least once in adulthood, Mangan visited the family farm in Meath and as a young man he would take rambles up to Rathfarnham and maybe out to Monkstown, but these were brief escapades: he was born, schooled, lived, studied, worked, drank and died within a few streets in the inner city. We call Dickens a London novelist and Cavafy an Alexandrian poet and Pessoa a Lisbon poet, but they all got out, lived in other places, travelled to other countries. I can't think of another writer so tightly bound to such a small, tight place as Mangan. If Joyce, who lived at eighteen addresses across Dublin, from Bray to Drumcondra, is a Dublin writer, then that term is much too expansive for Mangan. He is a Liberties poet.

I began my walk where he began: at his birthplace. But I couldn't find it. I wasn't expecting to see the actual house or the original address. The building was demolished in the 1970s and the address was changed long before that: in 1885 part of Fishamble Street was subsumed into the newly created Lord Edward Street and Mangan's birthplace became 3 Lord Edward Street, and fifteen years later, it was renumbered 5. I was prepared for all that, but Lord

Edward Street starts on Dame Street and then turns a right angle and seems to disappear into Christ Church Place and I couldn't see any numbers. I googled for a bit and discovered that a barber's called Cut and Sew, near Dublin Castle, is 5 Lord Edward Street, but a pub called The Bull and Castle, round the corner from the barber's, is also 5–7 Lord Edward Street. I walked up and down between the two and decided, based on the old map, that it had to be the pub.

The Bull and Castle is a new build and it looks like its name, like a British gastropub, and not remotely Manganese, but I appreciated the astonishing continuity of the site: in the eighteenth and nineteenth centuries, a grocer's meant a wine, spirit and provisions merchant so Mangan was born over the pub, so to speak, and remarkably, a pub is what the site continued as almost uninterruptedly until today.* That people are still drinking where he was born seems a kind of memorial. A photo survives of the original building, showing the pub at street level. The image is grainy and blurry, and you can barely make out what W.F. Wakeman – a journalist who as an adolescent had worked with Mangan on the Ordnance Survey – noted in 1887: 'The most remarkable feature to be noticed at this house is a stone inserted in the front wall, under the window-sill of the second storey. On this stone is carved a shield with a coat of arms … the armorial bearings of the old Anglo-Irish family of Usher, well and sharply cut.'

The Ushers (or Usshers) provided Dublin with a King of Arms in the sixteenth century and a famous scholar, Archbishop Usher, in the seventeenth century, for whom a quay, a street and a library

---

*You can pursue the premises under different owners through Thom's Directory: until 1886 it was in the hands of Mangan's Smith relatives (they married into the Gowans and McNallys) and it was then successively: John Healy's Public House in 1887–1959; Tom Farrelly's pub in 1960; G. Donohue's in 1962–3, The Castle Inn in 1965–9 and again in 1973–2002. In the 1970s the owners of The Castle Inn knocked down the original house to create a purpose-built pub.

in Trinity College is named. That Mangan was born in the House of Usher caused huge excitement among American scholars in the early twentieth century when they were teasing out his uncanny resemblance to Edgar Allan Poe, who also died in 1849 (though six years younger); was also an alcoholic and opium addict; also suffered a difficult childhood and may also have died celibate (Poe married his very young, tubercular cousin but the marriage was probably unconsummated); was also a writer of poems and stories full of dead brides, petrification, exotic travel, storms, clouds, outcast heroes and 'insufferable gloom'; also uses the refrain 'Ollalu' ['Ulalume'] in a poem ; and in his story 'The Fall of the House of Usher', describes the house's inheritor, Roderick Usher, in exactly the terms that people described Mangan, right down to the 'cadaverousness of complexion', the 'eye large, liquid and luminous', the 'ghastly pallor', the 'silken hair' of 'wild gossamer texture', the 'nervous agitation' and the mysterious sister who disappears. In the story's last lines, the House cracks, the 'mighty walls rushing asunder' and the 'fragments' disappear into the lake. All of which suggests that, in order to be true to the romantic creed, which formed both men, Mangan's birthplace, the House of Usher, had to disappear (not that this excuses Dublin City Council allowing the demolition of this very early Georgian house with its association to two famous Dubliners).

From his disappeared birthplace I went in search of his baptismal place on Rosemary Lane, off Cook Street, five minutes' walk away. I knew I wouldn't find the actual 'chapel', because it was only ever a storehouse, appropriated for covert Catholic worship during the Penal era and it reverted to its original use in 1815, but not only was the storehouse-turned-chapel gone, I couldn't find any trace of Rosemary Lane or of the other three lanes, Chapel Yard, Skipper's Lane, Swan Alley, which, according to the old map, used to lead from Cook Street to the Liffey.

As I hovered at a locked gate peering in to see if it led to a buried lane, a car pulled up and a suited man got out to greet a dark figure and I got a glimpse, beneath the hoodie, of a face with the skin drawn so tight and the eyes so sunken that it was already a skull, and then the suit was back in his car and the skull had magically faded into the atmosphere in a way that I recognised, invisibility being the dealer's super power. That people are still scoring smack in the Liberties today seems like continuity, though Mangan wouldn't have had to arrange illicit meetings to feed his habit – you could get opium in laudanum, which was available in chemists without prescription, though if you wanted grains of opium, like De Quincey, that would have been trickier to source. But a stigma was attached to opiate use, even then, and Mangan and his defenders alternate between admitting and denying his addiction. In an 1836 essay he gaily claims to have 'repeatedly devoured stupendous quantities of opium' but in his impersonal memoir of 1849 he insists dourly that he 'never swallowed a grain of opium in his life and only on one occasion took – and only then as medicine – laudanum'. It is hard to prove anything from these contradictory statements except that he was happier in 1836 than in 1849.

I've argued it out with Jacques Chuto, the editor of the *Collected Works*, who is a much greater Mangan expert than me. Chuto thinks, on balance, that Mangan wasn't an opium addict, that it was all malicious gossip, but I respectfully disagree. I'm convinced that he was: because he had an addictive nature and was always short of money, and laudanum was cheaper than gin; because he was a self-conscious Romantic who quotes De Quincey and Coleridge on their opiate addictions; because he wrote a strange, lovely essay called 'A Sixty-Drop Dose of Laudanum' which dissolves into itself; because of his pallor, much commented on; because in the late 1830s a sensuality comes into his verse – 'Spring, like a spirit, floats everywhere / Shaking sweet spice showers loose from her hair' – which is the sensuality of the Orient, his new craze, but could also be the effect of opium, a drug that liquefies the senses; because he was shadowy, indirect, secretive and bad with money, and because his work is full of cyclical recurrences, which recall the cyclical patterns addicts fall into.

These cyclical patterns were now defining my tour. To get to his first school, I had to loop back to Fishamble Street, pausing at the corner at a pub called Copper Alley, which commemorates another razed alley of that name, where Mangan's cousin Michael Smith had his successful bacon-curing business, managed for him by other cousins, the Plunketts, who put Mangan up in their 'comfortable house' or, according to Mangan, their 'hayloft'. Taking a left onto Cow's Lane, a new pedestrian street created in the 1990s, I walked up and down looking for Saul's Court, the address of Mangan's first school, which Google maps suggested had been preserved in the name of a solicitors' firm. I couldn't find it, but I did see one building that Mangan knew: Smock Alley Theatre was closed down in 1787 and served as a whiskey store before being repurposed as St Michael and John's Church in 1815. It was deconsecrated in 1989 and is now a theatre again.

His next school, Michael Courtney's Academy, was in Derby Square, opposite St Werburgh's Church, which meant looping back past his birthplace. I couldn't get into St Werburgh's, where Lord Edward Fitzgerald is buried, either then or subsequently; I have always found it locked, which seems appropriate since Mangan probably never entered himself, it being Anglican. And there is no trace of the confusingly named Derby Square, which was more of an inner courtyard than a square. To reach it you passed through an 80 ft covered passageway, which Mangan spent two years or so, aged twelve and thirteen, burrowing through to get to school. Derby Square survived until the 1980s but is now an apartment block backing onto Jury's Hotel.

Mangan's final school was on a street opposite Derby Square, Chancery Lane, where the family moved in 1818. It's less than five minutes' walk from Fishamble Street but Mangan felt this as acute social slippage. How bad it was is a matter of debate among biographers – Shannon-Mangan would like to believe Mangan's lurid description of the house in the memoir, but *Wilson's Directory* confirms that in 1818 Chancery Lane housed the lawyers for whom it was named and that it can't have been anything like the slum that Mangan depicted. There is no way now of knowing since nothing remains of the house or school or of any building that isn't late twentieth century.

Mangan wasn't long in his last school before he was removed by his father to begin his apprenticeship in Kenrick's in York Street, a five-minute walk from his new home. To get there, you turn briefly onto Golden Lane, which in Mangan's time still housed goldsmiths but is now mostly apartment blocks, and take Whitefriar Street to York Street, a broad and handsome street now given over to large buildings (social housing blocks at one end and the Royal College of Surgeons at the other). There are no numbers to locate number 6 where Kenrick's solicitors stood, nor number 42 where, in 1824, Mangan saw the Gothic author Charles Maturin coming out of his house and followed him. Nor could I find a plaque to Maturin, author of one of the nineteenth century's most famous novels, *Melmoth the Wanderer*.

Looping back again, down Whitefriar Place, I took a left onto Peter Street where the Mangan family moved in 1837 and remained almost a decade. The Georgian houses are long gone, and the street today is dominated by four large buildings, including the former Adelaide Hospital, built 1858, which is now apartments. This helps locate where number 9 stood because Mangan's cousin Mrs Coffey told John McCall, with typical Smith insistence on bourgeois respectability, that the Mangan family lived in 'a fine furnished house, nearly opposite to the present Adelaide Hospital, and were most comfortably situated'.

'Nearly opposite' the former Adelaide Hospital is now a car park, built in 1967 as part of Jacob's biscuit factory (now gone) on what had been the grounds of St Peter's Church. I looked in vain for the commemorative plaque, which, I had read, had gone up when the church came down: 'From December 1711 this was the site of "French Peters", the church and cemetery of the non-conforming French Huguenots' but there is no trace of this plaque, the briefest reminder of the church that stood here for 250 years, and there is nothing now to tell anyone that French Huguenots' helped build the Liberties, and that the poet of death once lived beside a graveyard.

A boy drew up on a bike beside me and repeatedly shouted up to the flats above, a name something like 'Johhhnnn-Jo' on a long ululation, to no reply. He skirted towards the entrance of the flats, and following him with my eyes I saw, tucked discreetly into the alcove and sheltered from the wind, a small tent where someone was living and, in front of the flats' sliding doors, a large raggy soft toy, whether dispelled from the tent or tossed from a window, I wasn't sure.

Peter Street turns onto Bride Street where Mangan lived the last months of his life. By now I had looped nearly full circle, and I was back within a few minutes of Mangan's birthplace. He came home to write his memoirs and then to die. The number of his last 'hovel' hasn't been recorded but even if it had been, it couldn't be viewed since there isn't one Georgian building left on Bride Street. It was here that Dr William Wilde found the dying Mangan on 13 June 1849 and brought him, or had him brought, to the nearby Meath Hospital on Long Lane. I trailed in their steps and arrived to find that the Meath Primary Care Centre is still a hospital but a twentieth-century build. Standing in front of this site of Mangan's last abode, the phrase that had come to mind as I hovered in front of the phantom plaque to French Peter's – 'the ghost of a graveyard' – returned as an epitaph for the whole tour.

Walking back home through wet streets, I thought that of course Mangan was absent from the tour, and I had been crazy to think that I would find any trace of 'the man who wasn't there'. Mangan's Liberties were destroyed twice: through the civic altruism of the Guinnesses, who pulled down rotting tenements in the late nineteenth century to remake the area in cheerful Victorian red brick, and through the greed of property developers in the late twentieth century, who razed whole terraces to the ground and bulldozed through lanes, alleys and courtyards without, it seems, anyone much objecting.

I played with the idea of setting up a 'Mangan Tour of the Liberties' as a brilliant piece of theatrical irony. When someone in the group started complaining, as they surely would, that the tour was a non-event, a ramble around lanes and buildings that no longer exist, I would get sententious and point out that if there were anything to actually *see*, then the tour wouldn't be Manganese. I would take 'diseased gratification' in demonstrating that the only buildings surviving from Mangan's time are the places he couldn't go: the Anglican churches. I would stop by the few remaining boulders of the old city wall near Cook Street and tell them they must seek him in cracks and fissures, ruins and fragments, gaps and elisions.

Peripathetically recreating himself

In 1826 Mangan wrote a poem, untitled like all his poems for the almanacs, which takes the form of an ironic eulogy to an old ragman, 'a buyer of cast-off wares, old clothes and trumpery / Old hats, old shoes, old iron and old brass'. The narrator describes, first, the old man's funeral:

> I have reason to remember well
> The eve on which I assisted at his funeral
> The water spouts of the wide, blank, grey sky
> Were burst and flooded all the earth beneath –
> And I who had forgotten my umbrella
> Was absolutely lost for want of it,
> My hat especially being quite demolished!

Then his apparel:

> His dress was picturesque – his brown boots mounted
> Seven inches and a half beyond his knees;
> The skirts of his torn coat hung down in tatters;

> Round, and round, and round his throat and chin and mouth
> Was wound in many a fold his vast cravat.

Then his daily routine:

> Each day, and day by day, he wended forth,
> To prosecute the business of his calling,
> Which, for the most part, lay in crying: 'Howl Clew!'

And the stir he caused as he walked the streets:

> The passengers around him stopped entranced,
> And waggoners, and persons who sold fish,
> And men who carried sacks of cabbages,
> And other men who followed after wheelbarrows,
> And many more who had nought to do, but were
> Peripathetically recreating
> Themselves

Before ending up at the ragman's 'lone grave', on which the narrator promises to plant flowers and water them 'every morning with – a watering pot!'

The poem has a place name – the old man lives in 'a silent cellar, / Lying at the back of Ragamuffin Lane' – which I can't find on the old map, which doesn't mean it didn't exist colloquially; it has the ring of other Liberties place-names since elided, like Murdering Lane, Cuckold's Row and Cutthroat Lane, but equally, Mangan could have made it up. Either way, this is a Liberties poem: the ragman's appearance recalls a noted Liberties eccentric, Zozimus, the blind street bard or 'gleeman' whom Mangan would have seen declaiming demotic verse on the corner of Patrick Street, and whose 'long, coarse, dark description of a frieze-coat with cape' perhaps influenced Mangan's own later attire; and the fish, cabbage, barrows and wagons recall the Liberties' markets, which survive, sanitised, in Meath Street today.

I love this poem, which has never been anthologised or received any critical attention. I would give up most of Mangan's German translations for more of these 'waggoners and persons who sold fish' and for the way that the lines wind around, from the folds of the 'vast cravat', to the 'day, and day by day, he wended forth', to the men 'Peripathetically recreating / Themselves', which is one of those Mangan lines where the archaic collides with the postmodern. He is a good sixty years ahead of Wilde in focussing on the possibilities of self-invention and the idea of 'peripathetic recreation' is very twentieth-century avantgarde. The neologism ('pathetic' + 'peripatetic' = 'pathetic wanderer/ homeless itinerant') suggests reinventing yourself as a tramp or hobo, like Chaplin perhaps, or Beckett's characters, or the more unlucky of Ken Kesey's Merry Pranksters who took to the road to find enlightenment but ended up as acid casualties, or dead.

The passage is reflexive, doubling back on itself – the street loafers are performers 'peripathetically recreating themselves' and they are voyeurs looking at the literal embodiment of 'peripathetic recreation', the itinerant ragman – and this is typical of Mangan's sinuous irony, the way that he strikes a pose and simultaneously steps back to observe himself in the pose. The passage acquires a retrospective shimmer because it prefigures with ironic detachment and scary prescience Mangan's own 'peripathetic recreation' as the Man in the Cloak, condemned to wandering the Liberties in 'an eternity of peripateticalism' as he wrote in an 1841 essay in deliberate reference to the Wandering Jew and the Ancient Mariner, and a probably unconscious nod to his earlier poem.

I like to think of 'the Peripathetic' as Mangan's contribution to psychogeography, the now very modish discipline which explores the psychological experience of walking round a city (like me in the previous chapter, I guess). If you google 'psychogeography', you will be directed to Will Self, Ian Sinclair, the Lettrists, the Situationist Internationals, the Dadaists, Walter Benjamin, Dickens on his London night walks and sometimes De Quincey and Blake, although Edgar Allan Poe's 'Man in the Crowd', who directly inspired Baudelaire's flâneur, is generally credited as psychogeography's first archetype. Nobody mentions the Peripathetic although he predates Poe's Man in the Crowd by fourteen years and the flâneur by a few decades.

Presumably writers in earlier centuries walked around cities and wrote about it but apparently that wasn't psychogeography, which has to be a response to the industrial revolution and urban alienation. By their repudiation of gainful employment, private property and the nuclear family, both Mangan 'wending' through the Liberties in his beggar's tatters, and Baudelaire sauntering round Paris in his velvets and silks, reproach the capitalist model in a way that makes respectable citizens nervous. It's not surprising that Mangan gets no credit for his contribution to psychogeography because he is not as famous as Baudelaire or Poe, and he didn't plant his flag on the terrain. No sooner had he created the Peripathetic, than he disappeared him from his writings. He mentions Dublin/ the Liberties in just two poems, two short stories, a late essay and his memoirs. He wrote almost a thousand poems, and numerous stories and essays and he describes his city in just *six* of these and frequently only in passing. And it's not that he avoided writing about places and buildings; his work is crowded with Teutonic castles and Oriental minarets and medieval monasteries and Gaelic towers – he was happy to depict place and space, as long as it was exotic, distant or imaginary.

This put me in a terrible sulk, and I began mentally lecturing him for missing the opportunity to engage us, his twentieth- and twenty-first-century readers. We are children of street photography and Joyce's *Ulysses*, of Isherwood's 'I am a camera' and *objet trouvé* art, of cinéma-vérité and reality TV. Nothing is too humdrum for our attention (though some things are too rarefied). In his irony, metafiction and unreliable narration, Mangan can seem astonishingly postmodern, but his refusal to ground his aesthetics in the observed and mundane dates him to the pre-Joycean world that had yet to realise that the most interesting things are under the nose and that the future will celebrate those who record them minutely. I wouldn't mind but he was *of* the streets; he had a tramp's eye view of the city. He walked everywhere, pounding the streets 'each day and day by day', changing lodgings, slipping in and out of offices, scribbling in crowded taverns, but never, or rarely, scribbling down what he saw before him. When he did manage to get it down, on those six brief occasions, it is stunning: humorous and subtle, surreal and phantasmagorical, but grounded in the local and the actual. If he had sent the Peripathetic down those shadowy streets he might, I thought, be more famous.

He didn't though, and when I was done wringing my hands in a useless litany of would've, could've, should've, I turned to his contemporaries to see what they had to say about their city. I wanted descriptions of Dublin in the literally *rare* old times, between the Act of Union and the Famine, but I couldn't find anything. I found plenty of tales of rural Ireland (from e.g. William Carleton, Gerald Griffin, John & Michael Banim) and plenty of romantic tales and poems set in the distant past or in exotic locations (from e.g. Moore, Maturin and Mangan himself), including, as a kind of sub-genre, racy tales of bucks, gamblers and buccaneers in eighteenth-century Dublin, but I couldn't find anything set in contemporary Dublin and I couldn't find any images of it either. The elegance of Georgian Dublin inspired James Malton's prints in the 1790s and a century later, impoverished Dublin would inspire Walter Osbourne and

Rose Barton, but no early/mid nineteenth century artist (that I could find) took Dublin as their subject, or even as a backdrop.

Mangan was born, lived and died in a hiatus: a city that no one seemed to want to write about, read about, or paint. I had thought the echoing absence of the Liberties and Dublin from his work was another of his characteristic elisions, and it is, but when I realised that his contemporaries were similarly evasive about where they lived, I realised that the story is bigger than him.

*

The Dublin that Mangan was born into was not the city that his parents had moved to in the 1790s. They had arrived to a charged capital, whipped into revolutionary fervour. In 1782 the Irish parliament had gained the freedom to legislate and set its own parliamentary agenda for the first time in 300 years and reformist MPs had followed up by demanding the repeal of the penal laws, which for two hundred years had restricted Catholics professionally and electorally. By 1795 Catholics could buy land on a long-hold lease, serve in the armed forces, vote (but not sit in parliament) and enter the legal profession (but not the judiciary). Reform ignited ambition, as it tends to do. Emboldened by the French Revolution, the United Irishmen made common cause with France against England. The first French invasion was wrecked by bad weather in December 1796 and martial law was imposed across the country; the second invasion, in summer 1798, was reinforced by uprisings across Leinster, but was brutally suppressed. Less than two years later, Irish MPs were induced to vote for their own extinction through bribery and false promises – the Act of Union (1800) abolished the Irish parliament and placed Ireland under direct rule from Westminster. The promise that Union would be accompanied by Catholic emancipation (the removal of the ban on Catholics sitting in parliament and as judges) was dashed within weeks of the Act when George III came out against, and the Union began in bitterness and recrimination.

The Liberties were centre stage during the years of rebellion. It was in Tailors Guild Hall on Back Lane that the Dublin Society of United Irishmen first met in 1791 and two of the most prominent United Irishmen, Napper Tandy and Oliver Bond, were wealthy Liberties merchants. Bond was arrested, together with fourteen others, at a meeting at his home in Lower Bridge Street in March 1798 and two months later another leading United Irishman, Lord Edward FitzGerald, was surprised in his hiding place in the house of a feather merchant on 151 Thomas Street; he died in gaol from his wounds on 4 June 1798 and was buried in the crypt of St Werburgh's Church, which Mangan passed daily on his way to school.

Three years after the Act of Union, the Liberties had a final starring role. The last gasp of the United Irishmen came when Mangan was ten weeks old and within earshot of his cradle. On 23 July 1803 the 25-year-old Robert Emmet marched onto Thomas Street in his general's uniform, with an army of under 200 men, many of them Liberties' weavers and artisans, and most of them 'unduly fortified by the long wait in neighbouring taverns'. Things quickly fell into disarray and Emmet tried to call off the rebellion, but it had gone beyond his control. The lord chief justice, Lord Kilwarden, on his way to Dublin Castle, was dragged from his carriage, together with his son-in-law, a clergyman, and both were piked to death by the drunken mob.

Three months later, on 20 September 1803, a platform was erected close to the spot of Kilwarden's murder and to Lord Edward's arrest, outside St Catherine's Church on Thomas Street, in front of a large crowd that may have included Mangan's parents. After his body was cut from the scaffold, Emmet's handsome head was severed from the neck – the same head that just the day before had made the most eloquent speech in Irish history. Raising it to the crowd, the hangman intoned three times, 'This is the head of a traitor, Robert Emmet.' The corpse was disposed of secretly to prevent his grave becoming a rallying point for rebels. Emmet's friend Thomas Moore wrote a poem famous throughout the nineteenth century – 'O, breathe not his name! let it sleep in the shade / Where cold and unhonoured his relics are laid' – and the 'unremembered grave' became a trope in Mangan's poetry.

Mangan grew up in a city and a district reeling from bloodshed and betrayal and too riven by bitterness for further reform. The police force, doubled in size after Emmet's rebellion, patrolled the city, giving 'a military look throughout'. On Burgh's Corn Market, the heavily fortified barracks, 'each window [with] a sloping cover, from which soldiers can fire without being annoyed by the mob', loomed over Thomas Street, a constant reminder that the Liberties was not to be trusted.

Growing up Catholic in the Liberties in the early 1800s, Mangan still experienced his religion as something covert and suspicious. He worshipped in makeshift chapels down side streets (the Penal Laws prohibited Catholic churches from being built in stone or on main roads) and slipped under archways to attend stop-gap Jesuit schools run without state support. News from the Catholic Committee (the dogged group of lawyers and merchants fighting for Catholic rights) was always bad: of petitions rejected, meetings broken up, members arrested and imprisoned, editors and publishers prosecuted, gagged and jailed.

When he was twelve years, Mangan heard a remarkable sound: the bell toll of St Michael and John's, the church birthed on the site of the former Smock Alley Theatre. This was the first Catholic bell to ring in Dublin for 300 years and the city alderman initiated legal proceedings to silence it but backed down when the parish priest secured Daniel O'Connell as advocate. Mangan served as an altar boy in this church, but there were no more Catholic churches built in the Liberties for another two decades. Church-goers in the Liberties still talk about 'doing the seven chapels' – a reference to the area's seven Catholic churches, built in stone on main thoroughfares, that went up in the great spate of church-building that followed Catholic emancipation in 1829. These are still standing and not one of them existed in Mangan's youth. He was twenty-two before Dublin got a Catholic cathedral; twenty-six before O'Connell brought about emancipation, and twenty-eight before a national school system was set up to educate children of all faiths.

If politically the period of his youth was the sound of doors slamming shut, then economically it was a candle sputtering out. The Liberties was for centuries the mercantile and trading centre of Dublin, home to the city's weaving, brewing, distilling, tanning, gold, jewellery, printing and publishing trades and with its own courts of justice supplying jobs for lawyers, judges, clerks and scriveners. It was a teeming, overcrowded area where wealth jostled with poverty. The Reverend James Whitelaw's memorable description captures the area in 1798 just before Mangan was born:

> The streets are generally narrow, the houses crowded together; the rears of backyards of very small extent, and some without accommodation of any kind. Of these streets, a few are the residence of the upper-class of shopkeepers or others engaged in trade; but a greater proportion of them, with their numerous lanes and alleys are occupied by working manufacturers, by petty shopkeepers, by labouring poor and beggars, crowded together, to a degree distressing to humanity.

It was an area in decline, even before the Act of Union, but when Mangan was born, Golden Lane still housed the goldsmiths that

gave it its name; Skinner's Row was still an emporium of booksellers, jewellers and goldsmiths; wealthy merchants still lived in Thomas Street, Winetavern Street and High Street, and clerks and lawyers, serving the Liberties' courthouses, lived in Chancery Lane and Chambers Street. An early print of Robert Emmet's execution outside St Catherine's church shows a terrace of fine gabled brick houses, the distinctive 'Dutch Billies' built by Huguenot merchants in the seventeenth and eighteenth centuries – reminding us that in Mangan's youth, the Liberties looked like Amsterdam.

During the Union debates in the late 1790s, the anti-unionists had thundered dire warnings that the closing down of parliament would destroy Irish businesses through the removal of protections and exposure to direct competition from British products. Their warnings proved immediately justified for the printing and publishing trades, which promptly collapsed, and for the city's manufacturing economy, which, in the words of Dublin's historian, David Dickson, was 'hollowed out'. Dickson quotes the satirical journal the *Irish Magazine and Monthly Asylum for Neglected Biography*, in 1814: 'Dublin is now a city that has not built a ship or a sloop since the Union, a city that has not manufactured a cable, an anchor or an oar since the same fatal period, a city that has no intercourse beyond Liverpool or Whitehaven.'

But for some trades and industries, the anti-union argument looked, for a time anyway, like project fear. Brewing and distilling did just fine (though Guinness eventually cannibalised all the smaller brewers) and, crucially for the Liberties, Belfast linen-makers had negotiated protective tariffs for the Irish cotton industry, to remain in place until 1824. The Liberties mills availed of this to switch from silk and wool to cotton; it was less skilled work, meaning lower wages and lower prices, but it prolonged the survival of the Liberties' main industry for two decades. The wars with France, ongoing since 1793 and resurgent in 1803, helped by creating a market for Irish agricultural produce. There was money coming into the country; in 1812 Mangan's father had enough credit to speculate in property and open a vintners.

Then came the Battle of Waterloo in 1815. Following this victory, prices slumped with the annual average price per cwt of wheat falling from 17/6 in the period 1812–15 to 11/6 for 1821–5. Poor weather and a terrible harvest in 1816 turned 1817 into a famine year with attendant epidemics: typhus and relapsing fever spread through the country, infecting an estimated million and a half people and killing perhaps 65,000. Rural migrants crowded into the streets of Dublin and 25,000 people were admitted to the city's fever hospitals. There was a period of sharp deflation and the Bank of Ireland had to restrict credit in late 1819.

The recession almost destroyed the Guinness brewery, the most successful company in the Liberties, then over fifty years in business. It did destroy a high number of small businesses. By March 1817 the new lord lieutenant for Ireland, Robert Peel, was voicing his concern to the House of Commons, and by May there were so many crowded into the debtors' prisons that Peel's secretary warned him that unless something were done, 'some dreadful fever may be the consequence during the summer'. The date is significant – within the year, Mangan would be set to work to support his family. By 1821 the value of property had fallen '30 per cent in parts of Dublin, and in that part of it called the Liberty, it has, perhaps, fallen 50 per cent'.

It got worse. In 1824 the protective tariffs negotiated by the Belfast weavers were removed from cotton. The Liberties could not begin to compete with the mechanised mills of north England and by April 1826, '3,100 looms were idle and some 20,000 people were directly affected by collapse in employment'. Subscriptions were raised 'for the distressed weavers in the Liberties, great numbers of whom were starving'. In its annual report of 1826, the Sick and Indigent Roomkeepers Society noted the 'dreadful visitation of fever and other malignant disorders, the consequence of poverty and want which are principally from the stagnation of trade … particularly in the woollen, cotton and silk in that part of the city called the Liberty'. Typhus swept through the slums. Ten thousand patients were treated in Cork Street Fever Hospital in 1826 and, when no more beds were left, tents were erected in the hospital grounds and in Phoenix Park, where, in the snows of winter, patients froze to death.

*

What happened to Dublin explains, if not everything, then many things about Mangan's youth: it explains why his father went bankrupt and why he was put to drudge work at a young age to support his family, and it goes some way to explaining the puzzling lack of sources and recollections – bankrupt people and ruined communities lose their stuff and repress their memories – and it offers a plausible suggestion for why neither Mangan nor any other writer or artist made Dublin their setting: it was bad enough living it, no one wanted to read about it.

The political and economic decline of Dublin is obviously central to the story of Mangan's youth, but he blanks it in his memoirs and it isn't foregrounded in either of the main biographies. I get why Mangan never mentions the catastrophic economic crises that coincided exactly with his removal from school in 1817/18, and his nervous breakdown in 1824/5.* Most nationalist writers would be keen to blame the Act of Union and the British government, but Mangan didn't have the kind of empirical, dispassionate mind that observes socio-economic conditions and understands their effect on individuals. He had a mind swirling with startling images – when people enter his memoirs, they arrive like characters in a fairy tale, without background or context. His father occupied an overweening place in his psyche; such a castrating, God-like figure might carry within him the seeds of his own destruction but shouldn't be brought down by external forces. And Mangan liked to see himself as a uniquely unfortunate being, marked out for a terrible fate; he wasn't about to generalise his misfortunes by sharing them with the rest of the Liberties.

I also get why the Smiths emphasise the father's extravagance. They were preternaturally shrewd and cautious, hanging on to their holdings through successive recessions, and to people like that any risk-taking is culpable. And anyway they were just responding to questions from journalists and would not have seen the need to point out the obvious: the collapse of the economy after Waterloo. But this isn't true of O'Donoghue, writing a biography in the 1890s, when readers' memories had faded. Why did he not recall the

---

*He refers to a few nervous breakdowns in his memoirs, without dating them. The case for dating a breakdown to 1824/5, the year when the final protections were removed from the textile industry, is that he contributed no poems to the almanacs that year, and James Tighe references a breakdown in his 1826 poem on Mangan.

significance of 1817 as a year of deep recession and hunger? And Shannon-Mangan was researching her biography a good decade after Chuto and Lloyd had reset the narrative, but her opening chapters return us to the private space of domestic abuse, with politics and the economy barely mentioned.

The only reason I can hazard is that both O'Donoghue and Shannon-Mangan were in thrall to Mangan's singular vision. I sympathise: when you are in his world, squeezed into his dark places – the mousehole, the father's intestines, the pestiferous offices, the mysterious semi-blindness of his 'fifth to thirteenth' year – it is nearly impossible to see out, and anyway you are not much interested in the outside because you are trying to find your way around the mind of this remarkable personage who seems to defy all expectations: a poor Catholic who leaves school at fifteen but translates from all languages; a revolutionary who never gets arrested, fined or censored but is instead published in an arch Unionist journal; the most celebrated Famine poet who never actually mentions the Famine …

Exceptionalism is what defines Mangan. Yeats, aged twenty-two, shrewdly ended an essay by observing: 'He never startles us by saying beautiful things we have long felt. He does not say look at yourself in the mirror; but rather, "Look at me – I am so strange, so exotic, so different."' I'm not sure that I would have realised the vital influence of the economy and the political situation on his character if it weren't for Lloyd who opens his book with the observation that Mangan's life is framed by two unsuccessful rebellions, Robert Emmet's in 1803 and Young Ireland's in 1848, and implicit in this framing are the two politico-economic catastrophes that shadow the rebellions: the Act of Union and the Famine. When you line up Mangan's personal dates with key dates in Irish history, everything falls into place in a way that seems almost too neat:

Reduced to these neat columns, Mangan appears as almost

1798	United Irish Rebellion	Parents' marriage
1800	Act of Union	
1803	Robert Emmet Rebellion	Birth
1817/18	post-Waterloo Recession	Father goes bankrupt & Mangan taken from school
1824	Collapse Liberties textiles	Nervous breakdown
1826	Almanacs cease publication	Start of Mangan's silent period
1829	Catholic emancipation	
1831	Renaissance in Irish publishing	Adopts 'Clarence', starts contributing to *The Comet*
1846	The Famine	Becomes major contributor to *The Nation*
1848	Young Ireland Rebellion	Hospitalised, writes (and loses) the long memoir
1849	Cholera epidemic	Dies of cholera and malnutrition

entirely reactive, his whole life and career determined by the fall and rise and fall again of Irish political hopes and economic growth.

*

A surviving few photos from the late nineteenth and early twentieth centuries suggest the world that Mangan knew. These early photographers must have had great feeling for the Liberties' shadows, poverty and hidden places. They sought out tiny weavers' cottages, glistening cobblestones with drains running through them, once-fine houses with huge windows divided into cracked panes of glass and rows of thick coats hanging outside pawnbrokers.

In March 1849 when he was ill, malnourished and soon to die,

Mangan was moved to write with unprecedented specificity about the Dublin of his youth in a passage that adopts just the noir and ghostly atmosphere of the photographs. This happens in the middle of an essay he was writing on the Gothic novelist Charles Maturin for the series 'Sketches and Reminiscences of Irish Writers':

> I saw Maturin but on three occasions, and on all three within two months of his death. I was then a mere boy;* and ... the reader ... will appreciate the force of the impulse which urged me one morning to follow the author of 'Melmoth' into the porch of St Peter's Church, in Aungier-street, and hear him read the burial service. Maturin, however, did not read – he simply repeated; but with a grandeur of emphasis, and an impressive power of manner, that chained me to the spot. His eyes, while he spoke, continually wandered from side to side and at length rested on me, who reddened up to the roots of the hair at being

---

*Maturin died in 1824 – a date which Mangan gives correctly in a later paragraph. In 1824 Mangan was twenty-one and not a 'mere boy' but he had a fixed pathology that he was six years younger than he was so he may have imagined he was fifteen in 1824. Alternatively he may have been 'a mere boy' when he followed Maturin, but the passage depends on Maturin being close to death.

even for a moment noticed by a man that ranked far higher in my estimation than Napoleon Bonaparte. I observed that, after having concluded the service, he whispered somewhat to the clerk at his side, and then again looked steadfastly at me. ...

The second time that I saw Maturin he had been just officiating, as on the former occasion, at a funeral. He stalked along York-street, with an abstracted, or rather distracted air; the white scarf and hat-band which he had received remaining still wreathed around his beautifully-shaped person, and exhibiting to the gaze of the amused and amazed pedestrians whom he almost literally *encountered* in his path, a boot upon one foot and a shoe on the other! ...

The third and last time that I beheld this marvellous man I remember well. It was somewhere about a fortnight before his death, on a balmy autumn evening in 1824. He slowly descended the steps of his own house, which perhaps some future Transatlantic biographer may thank me for informing him was at No. 42, in York-street,* and took his way in the direction of Whitefriar-street. Thence he passed into Bride-street, proceeded up through Werburgh-street, into Castle-street, and passed the Royal Exchange into Dame-street, every second person staring at him and the extraordinary double-belted and treble-caped rug of an old garment, neither coat nor cloak, which enveloped his person. ... Instead of passing along Dame-street, where he would have been 'the observed of all observers,' he wended his way along the dark and forlorn locality of Dame-lane, and having reached the end of this not very classical thoroughfare, crossed over to Anglesea-street, where I lost sight of him. Perhaps he went into one of those bibliopolitan establishments

---

*The impulse to record detail is highly unusual in Mangan but he may have it wrong – the *Dictionary of Irish Biography* puts Maturin's address as 37 York Street.

wherewith that Paternoster-row of Dublin abounds. I never saw him afterwards!

[...] Where the remains of my distinguished countryman repose, I confess I know not. Maturin was killed off in a mistake and buried in a hurry. He died of an apothecary's blunder.

In this astonishing passage the dying Mangan fuses with his dying subject. Since he was known as the 'Man in the Cloak', notorious around Dublin for his own 'trebled-caped' attire and for wending along 'dark and forlorn localities', no one could miss the self-portraiture in this account of Genius walking in the shadow of death, particularly since the final route taken is a Mangan Liberties route.

Maturin moves in this passage from praying a soul into the next world to becoming himself the dying soul and forgotten corpse, and by the same progression, Mangan moves from being 'steadfastly' invested by the older writer to merging with him in a 'double-belted and treble-caped' coat and following him into the unknown grave that he always insisted upon for himself. (He doesn't however mention another striking convergence: Maturin died of an overdose of laudanum, which Mangan would have known; perhaps laudanum was a step too far in his identification.)

The voyeuristic and solipsistic merging of self and subject recalls the ragman poem, which stands as this passage's hauntingly light-hearted companion piece – in both texts the narrator is observing a double-cloaked eccentric 'wending forth' while crowds 'stare' at him 'entranced', but where the early poem is witty, open to the

---

*Maturin was buried in St Peter's in Aungier Street, which wasn't a secret, but the church was demolished in the 1980s and Maturin's remains reinterred in a communal crypt in St Luke's in the Coombe, a Huguenot church closed in 1975, damaged by arson in 1986 and still awaiting renovation, so Mangan's words are true today: few Dubliners know where the remains of this 'distinguished countryman' repose.

possibilities of 're-creation' and takes place at daytime, the later passage is spectral. The uncharacteristic reference to the 'future biographer' suggests an anxiety to shore memory against ruin, to name streets and routes against oblivion. Buried in the final image of the unknown grave are Emmet, Maturin, Mangan and the rebellious, mercantile Liberties that fissured with the Act of Union and Emmet's rebellion, and went out with the cotton looms.*

Although he doesn't usually weave Dublin into the danse macabre, Mangan was always a poet of entropy. No matter how joyfully he might start out writing about knights and maidens, bells and parapets, roses and pearls, sooner or later all tends to decay, corrosion and dissolution, which is psychological and symbolic, but also physical and structural. His poetry is an endless spool of 'demolished towers' and 'forsaken walls' and remnants 'crumbling to sad decay' and 'spectral wrecks and withered blossoms' and 'beauties now mouldering low in the clay'. I made a list of his favourite words; shrivelled, dreary, wrecked, mould, pall, crumbling, ruins, droop are typical, and even when he is being positive, the words are transient and evanescent: waft, float, sway. Nothing is firm, stable, rooted. His inveterate deployment of the negative prefix and suffix amounts to a tragicomic compulsion to maim and reduce: unurned, unsouled, unsparkling, unreturning, unwarmed, unbeheld, lampless, hueless, urnless, chantless, mateless.

He turned away from the Liberties the way one looks away from tragedy, but the area, which he never left, couldn't help but get into his writing. Its crumbling buildings and closed-down mills, its boarded-up shops and sputtering gutters, the decay of fine townhouses into tenements, the degradation of textile workers into beggars, the 'dismally monotonous echo' of apathy and dejection, which infected the no-hope lives of those around him – all this comes through in images of decay and desolation but transmuted to other places and other times.

When you have read enough of him, you begin to understand that his opaque approach is so innate and compulsive that to rail against him for not being Isherwood with his shutter open, recording, or Joyce with his grocer's assistant's mind, taking inventory, is to miss the point, is to seek to turn him into someone else and to deny him his uncanny premonition. Though he witnessed its decay he didn't live to see the Georgian Liberties demolished but throughout his work you hear, faint but insistent, the pulse of the buried Liberties. In his brilliant late poem 'The Saw Mill', the narrator falls asleep to the sound of the saw mill sawing but awakes to the knowledge of death. Though this mill serves the timber, rather than the textile, industry, it gestures to the industrial mills that turned so busily in his childhood, and the final image, the greatest of all Mangan's images of coffins, sets the materiality of wood against the fade of oblivion:

I awoke, and heard four planks
Fall down with a saddening echo.
I heard four planks
Fall down with a hollow echo.

*

It was on one of my final melancholy tours of the Liberties that I wandered up John Dillon Street in the shadow of St Nicholas of Myra – one of the 'seven chapels' that went up after Emancipation – and found myself straggling into a long blank corner that turns into a dead end where four tiny red-brick houses are shoved up against a school or other institutional building, and was amazed and gratified to discover that this happenstance of a corner-into-cul-de-sac is called, brilliantly and quite inaccurately, Clarence

Mangan Square. I saluted the genius who named it. Here, finally, I could imagine Mangan's ghost pausing to make a mordant pun on the square that isn't, before fading back into the shadowy lanes and alleys.

That was in late April or early May 2015 and it can't have been more than a few weeks later that I was cycling with Frank through the Tenters towards my house in the long stretch of the evening, watching the folds of his trousers rising and falling to expose his purple socks, and his handlebars wobbling under the weight of his overloaded bags as he looked up and around at the low-rise pebble-dash semi-Ds, and said with gallant irony and saving self-mockery, 'I used to canvas in places like this!' and I heard, for the first time in six months, the delighted sound of my outraged laughter rise up, up on the balmy air to meet the mad chirrup of the birds flying home to roost in the trees in Oscar Square.

And it was three or four or five years after that – on our way back from Piglet on Cow's Lane, a restaurant raised on or near the site of Mangan's old school in Saul's Court – that we cycled up Dame Street and turned onto Lord Edward Street and spotted on the wall of The Bull and Castle a plaque to Mangan, which had not been there during my looping tours, and Frank, who never let a significant event go unrecorded, posed me in front of it. I look at the photo now and there I am, in plain joy, madly grinning because here we are, back in the picture, Mangan and me! Where we were not, here we are now!

The grin is mad because it thinks that now is forever. You would never see a grin like that on Mangan's face: the hollow echo doesn't let up and gives him tinnitus.

J.C.M. at the translator's

Mangan's is a life of two distinct parts. If you were to stage it, you could open with a prelude that takes the form of a monologue delivered by an actor silhouetted in shadow speaking in a ghostly tone as if from a distance. The monologue is the text of the long memoir, with a few almanac poems thrown in. At one point, the actor falls silent for a lengthy period, and maybe the lights go out. The most dramatic moment comes at the end, when the actor stops abruptly after saying 'Stop, what do you[—]'

It is then up to the director to manage the transition to Clarence Mangan and the play proper. You could get the actor to start spouting German or a cacophony of languages. Or bring on supporting actors, all talking at once, waving different newspapers and pamphlets. Or you could go all Pirandello, planting actors in the audience as biographers and critics, commenting on the action in a way that becomes increasingly annoying. The important thing is that there should be a complete change of mood and tone between the prelude and the play proper and everything should get louder, brighter, busier and more populous (for Act One, things narrow down in Act Two when he dons his cloak).

This isn't just conceit and me 'using the novelist's art of arrangement, suggestion, dramatic effect to expound the private life' as Virginia Woolf characterises the efforts of biographers who are novelists manqués. This is exactly how Mangan's life does separate according to the surviving biographical sources, with 1831 as the dividing line. Up until that year, he is plain James Mangan, and everything is absent and shadowed: his poetry a trickle of puzzle verse, e.g. acrostics, rebuses, riddles and enigmas, which have to be 'solved' via visual and aural clues. In 1826, this trickle dries up and the five silent years that follow are called by his biographer D.J. O'Donoghue his 'barren period' and by his friend and editor John Mitchel, 'a gap that painstaking biography will never fill up, a vacuum and obscure gulf which no eye hath fathomed or measured'. The bare silhouette he had done at 'the age of 19 years' seems to encapsulate his shadowy youth.

From the unfathomable 'gap, vacuum and obscure gulf' of being James Mangan, he rebirthed himself as Clarence Mangan, the National Poet, a process that gets underway in 1831, the year he met John Sheehan, who invited him to contribute to his radical new paper *The Comet*, and the year which ends with a cryptic comment in *The Comet* (4 December): 'J.C.M. is at the translator's: as soon as it can be deciphered, we will answer his letter.' The 'C' stands for Clarence: this is the first public mention of the name under which he will become famous. Mangan, otherwise negligent about dates, is precise about it being 1831 that 'I entered upon my career' and this is the exact moment that the memoir breaks off.

Two pivotal questions about Mangan's obscure youth have exercised biographers: why from ages fifteen to twenty-three was he publishing only puzzle poems, and only in the almanacs, which weren't literary magazines but info-journals with listings for markets, tides, weather and festivals? And why did he fall silent for five long years during which he published almost nothing?

The memoir has nothing to say about the first question and, in fact, makes no mention of the almanacs, perhaps because eight years writing brain-teasers for info-journals is a seriously unglamorous and unacceptably long apprenticeship for a Romantic poet. Romantics are supposed to follow the model of Byron, Shelley, Keats and Pushkin and sprint out of the starting blocks in their teens. In his biography, O'Donoghue connived with Mangan to bury his apprenticeship:

Between 1818 and 1826 Mangan wrote very frequently for the almanacs but there is no need to dwell upon these youthful whimsicalities. They may have helped to form his genius, but it is impossible to deny that they vitiated it to a considerable extent. His fondness for exercising his powers of rhyme, his delight in the mechanical difficulties of verse, and his inordinate display of his mastery over them, are traceable to his feats of literary agility in the almanacs. An enormous proportion of his subsequent literary work is characterised by visibly painful efforts to appear gay and festive when his mind and heart are overwhelmed by woe.

This remarkable paragraph comes in chapter two of O'Donoghue's biography and I'm not sure the book ever recovers from it. If Mangan's 'youthful whimsicalities' in the almanacs 'helped form his genius' and are responsible for the atmosphere of 'an enormous proportion of his subsequent literary work' then surely there is *every* 'need to dwell on them'? Already, page 19, we have hit a nerve which, as you read on, settles into a theme: O'Donoghue really dislikes Mangan's sense of humour. He was following the lead of Gavan Duffy and John Mitchel who objected to Mangan's 'abominable' joking and 'Fescennine buffoonery', but it is O'Donoghue's idea to link this tendency to the almanacs. His image of Mangan as a fundamentally earnest person permanently derailed into buffoonery by his youthful apprenticeship doesn't give you much confidence in his judgment as biographer.

In contrast to the conspiracy of silence around the almanacs, the 'barren period' 1826–31 gets a lot of attention and is always presented as a crucible for his future cloaking and despair. In his memoir, Mangan recalled 'a settled melancholy, a sort of torpor and weariness of life … this deplorable interior state, one which worlds and diadems should not bribe me into experiencing again'; Mitchel has him entering this period 'a bright-haired youth and emerg[ing] a withered and stricken man'. For a century and a half everyone thought he produced nothing during these years, but in the 1990s the editors of the *Collected Works* unearthed eight poems published across four journals between 1827 and 1830, which spoils the immaculate perfection of the total silence but is still vanishingly few.

Why should Mangan fall silent (or almost silent)? Because he was depressed. But why was he depressed? Because of the office job, he says in the memoir. Because of a failed love affair, says Mitchel. Melancholy is Romantic, but there is a disconnect between the enthusiastic boy submitting puzzle poems to the almanacs and the anguished youth so depressed he ceases publishing altogether. I think Mangan dropped the almanacs from his memoirs to remove the disconnect and superimpose a cohesive narrative of silence and despair lasting his entire youth.

The 'barren period' is another one of those seminal moments in Mangan's life, which people like to ascribe to his unique and hermetic character, but which is better understood through the socio-economics of Dublin. His first biographer, John McCall, grasped this very well. McCall was a Liberties publican like Mangan's father and as a young man he had worked in grocers in Wexford Street and Camden Street so would have seen Mangan out and about, and maybe spoken to him, though sadly he doesn't mention this in his short biographical articles. It is perhaps his immersion in the milieu that gives McCall his sober authority and allows him to resist the alluring myth. In his succinct way, he provides the explanation for the pivotal questions around Mangan's long ludic apprenticeship and barren period:

> In Mangan's juvenile days there were no magazines nor cheap periodicals of any kind published in this country through the medium of which young aspiring poets could give their varied inspirations to the world. In fact Jones' two almanacks were the

only publications in our metropolis which encouraged such light poetical flights of fancy.

With this casual aside, McCall laid bare the publishing wasteland that met Mangan and other Irish writers of the period. Dubbed, 'the greatest source of information on nineteenth-century literature and journalism in Dublin', McCall knew what he was talking about and only O'Donoghue's deep investment in Mangan as a melancholic depressive explains why he didn't follow up on this lead when he came to write his own biography a decade later.

Journalism, printing and publishing, which had flourished in Dublin through the eighteenth century thanks to undercutting British publishers, were virtually destroyed by the Act of Union – directly through legal acts, and indirectly through the poisoning of political and cultural life. In 1816 a Dublin bookseller, Charles Palmer Archer, wrote that he 'never in all my life knew business so bad' and five years later a wholesale agent in Dublin for a London publisher gave evidence to a Commission of Inquiry:

> Printing of books is comparatively nothing in Ireland except a description of Catholic books of a very cheap sort … and also a few school-books used exclusively in Ireland. Since the Act of Union the book trade is almost annihilated; it was on the same footing as America previous to that time, and every new book was reprinted here; but since the Copyright Act has been extended, that cannot now be done openly.

The situation was no better for newspapers or magazines. Taxes, including duty on newsprint, kept prices exorbitantly high, while revenue from advertising declined 'from £21,000 in 1813 to below £15,000 in 1829 – a reflection both of the country's declining commercial prosperity and of the advertisers' lack of confidence in the power of the press'. By 1830 the average number of advertisements per issue of a newspaper was eighty in England, fifty-seven in Scotland, and sixteen in Ireland.

If advertisers had little interest in the press, it's because it was partisan, polemical, dull and censored. There was little objective reporting since editors and printers were continually being prosecuted, fined and imprisoned for alleged attacks on the government and for covering the activities of Daniel O'Connell and the Catholic Committee. Printers and publishers like Hugh Fitzpatrick, John Magee and Michael Staunton went to jail for alleged libel, while others like James Magee avoided imprisonment by public apologies and moderating the paper's line, and still others like Philip Whitfield Harvey and F. W. Conway were in the pay of Dublin Castle. The pervasive atmosphere of fear and suspicion was disastrous for cultural as well as political journalism. The Tory press was propped up by government support, but other papers found it difficult to survive. Neither the liberal *New Irish Magazine and Monthly National Advocate*, established 1821, nor the Orange *Hibernian Magazine*, established 1820, lasted more than a year, and literary magazines like the *Dublin Magazine* (1820) and *Belfast Magazine and Literary Journal* (1825) had the shelf-life of vegetables. Barbara Hayley, historian of the nineteenth-century press in Ireland, puts it succinctly:

> The conflict of Catholic-Whig-Irish Nationalist versus Protestant-Tory-English Unionist was a fact of Irish life after the Union. Up to the passing of the Catholic Emancipation Act in 1829, the conflict was particularly bitter and magazines were exclusively polemical, disseminating violently Protestant or Catholic, Unionist or anti-Unionist propaganda and very little else … Most Irish magazines were like tracts in appearance and contents: dreary productions on coarse paper with rough type and crude

woodcuts, hammering home their religious and political causes in editorials, articles and slogans. The literary content of these magazines was slight and desperately partisan.

The contrast with Britain was painful: this was the era of the great literary magazines, *Blackwood's, Edinburgh Review* and the *Quarterly Review* and of the great publishing houses, John Murray, Constable's, and Longman's. There being no comparison between the two islands, most Irish writers did the obvious thing. In 1842 William Carleton used the preface to a new edition of his bestselling *Traits and Stories of the Irish Peasantry* to make a point about the brain drain:

> In truth, until within the last ten or twelve years, an Irish author never thought of publishing in his own country, and the consequence was that our literary men followed the example of our great landlords: they became absentees, and drained the country of its intellectual wealth precisely as the others exhausted it of its rents.

Of Mangan's near-contemporaries, the Cork virtuoso William Maginn started contributing to *Blackwood's* in 1819 and moved to London in 1824, where he became famous and started *Fraser's Magazine*; the Limerick writer Gerard Griffin moved to London in 1823 and worked as a journalist and drama critic for a few years and all his books, including his masterpiece, *The Collegians* (1829), had London publishers; Mangan's idol, the Rev. Charles Maturin, was kept in Dublin by parish duties but his plays were performed in London and his books published by John Murray. Even the Cork poet J.J. Callanan, who died young and shared with Mangan the sense of being an outcast, had six poems published in *Blackwood's Magazine* in 1823.

Mangan had no British career at all – not even one poem in a British journal. He had to support his family, but he could have done what other writers did: gone to London and sent money back or stayed home and sent work to British editors and publishers. John Mitchel congratulated Mangan for 'never deigning to attorn to English criticism' but such kamikaze economic nationalism wouldn't have occurred to Mangan who wrote for whoever would pay him – he was happy to contribute to the ultra-Unionist *Dublin University Magazine* in its sectarian years. It was his fragile, neurotic character that prevented him leaving the Liberties or establishing relations with British publishers, and I also wonder if, on an unconscious level, he knew that staying put was the right thing for his writing.

Writers (good ones) carry within them an unconscious sense of what they will have to do to release their voice. Trying to express something unique is so difficult and the odds on the world taking notice so slim, that there is no easy or predictable route to success and no prototype of the writer's life. For Mangan, as for Anna Akhmatova remaining in Soviet Russia, success involved staying put and enduring, rather than taking the seemingly more decisive and adventurous option of exile. His peculiar gift found its greatest expression in an oblique engagement with the buried Gaelic past, which he had to be on site to discover.

Anyway, having decided to stay – or more passively, feeling unable to leave – Mangan made the most of his limited opportunities. The almanacs were the only outlet for a fledgling poet in Ireland in the 1810s and 20s, so that is where he went, aged fifteen, and he managed to subvert them to his purposes, as he would every subsequent journal he ever wrote for. The formulaic requirements to plant clues and quizzes for wordplay poems were intended to produce clever wordplay rather than anything heartfelt or experimental but Mangan, while outwardly conforming, managed to smuggle in lines like these:

Oh! can we through life know an hour like the one
Whose airy-winged moments have found us
Employed musing deeply, unseen and alone,
On the trophies of death spread around us?

Here is his signature solitude and negative prefix, and his first
unforgettable image – only Mangan would gloat over tombstones
as 'trophies of death'. Instead of the almanacs shaping Mangan, as
O'Donoghue claimed, he shaped them into a platform for work that is
strange, melancholic and burlesque. He had no choice about this, there
being no other publishing outlet, and lack of choice also explains his
barren period: in 1826 both almanacs folded and there was nowhere
else to go since the publishing situation in Dublin was as bad as ever
and the economic situation worse following the removal of protective
tariffs from cotton. There could be no question of Mangan leaving his
job. His promise was being crushed so grindingly as to make a mockery
of Cyril Connolly's genteel complaints about the pram at the door.

He published just one poem in 1827, none for the next two years
and then, over the course of a few weeks, between 29 December
1829 and February 1830, he suddenly published five poems; four in
The Friend and one in *Dublin Monthly Magazine*. What caused this
dam-burst? The 'gap that painstaking biography will never fill up' still
yawns over Mangan's personal life, but we know what was happening
in Ireland: on 13 April 1829 the Roman Catholic Relief Act was passed
to enable Daniel O'Connell to take his elected seat for Co. Clare in the
House of Commons, which he did on 4 February 1830. Thirty years
after it was promised, Catholic Emancipation was finally delivered and
in the most dramatic circumstances, forced by O'Connell's victory
on a hardline Tory government and an unyielding king, who tried
to get the government dismissed and then threatened to abdicate. In
a tantrum, George IV broke and trod on the pen handed to him to
sign the legislation into law. He was handed another pen, and signed.

*

In the last passage of the long memoir, the narrator starts to tell the story of how he 'entered on his career' in 1831: he takes a desultory ramble one day in June and stops for a rest 'on a long knoll of grass by a stream-side beyond Rathfarnham, while the sun is setting' and starts reading his book, *Les Pensées de Pascal*, when he is 'suddenly approached and accosted by a fashionably dressed and intelligent looking young man' whom he has previously 'observed sauntering about this neighbourhood'. They embark on a conversation about life, death and the universe which ends mid-question – '"Stop," said I. "What do you[—]"'

This ending isn't as abrupt and haphazard as it seems at first reading. The structure of the memoir is almost classical, with the hero going through a series of trials, setbacks and humiliations before being rescued by a glorious stranger who arrives by the side of a stream like one of those disguised gods who help mortals in the Greek myths. Although the scene isn't resolved, all the auspices are positive and renewing: there's a stream, it's the first mention of the sun, the first time the narrator gets out to nature, the first time he is approached *and* accosted by someone, his first recorded conversation, and one of the few times he steps ironically outside himself to observe how he must appear and sound to a normal person. The friendly stranger is so upbeat and buoyant and the narrator so negative and gloomy that the conversation is comical, I think intentionally. The narrator's flat nihilistic contempt – 'I have pleasure in nothing, and I admire nothing. I hate scenery and suns' – is as amusingly postured as a punk lyric. Most movingly, the narrator, who has been met at every turn by 'coarse ribaldry, vile and vulgar oaths and brutal indifference' is, for the first time, addressed as 'friend'.

With this final scene, narrator and reader are rescued from the claustrophobic offices, pestilent hospitals, unkind workmates, cycles of depression and the office grind. Although the manuscript 'stops', we can construe its ending: the 'fashionably-dressed and intelligent-looking young man' has been identified as probably John Sheehan, editor of *The Comet*, the most exciting of the new journals to spring up after Emancipation, and the sure end of the unfinished conversation is that he will be intrigued enough to urge the narrator to write for him.

The passage is, I think, an allegory on the astonishing impact of Catholic Emancipation, both on Mangan's career and on the country at large: the memoir can be read as a long winter of discontent made glorious summer by O'Connell (with the dangling, irresolute ending signalling this as a brief sunny interlude rather than happy ever after).

Emancipation was transformative politically, culturally and socially. A notice in the liberal paper, the *Morning Register*, on New Year's Day 1831 shows its galvanising effect:

> There will be a Meeting of the Law Clerks of the City of Dublin on Monday, 3rd January next ... to take into consideration the propriety of petitioning both Houses of Parliament for a Repeal of the Legislative Union between Great Britain and Ireland.

This was signed by dozens of law clerks, including 'James Mangan' and the meeting duly took place with five thousand clerks in attendance, including presumably Mangan. This is very moving: five thousand clerks, many of them I'm guessing as miserable and suffocated in the 1820s as Mangan, converging to make what would have seemed two years earlier a lunatic demand. Mangan was never a natural political activist and within eighteen months of this petition he would be writing to a friend, mocking the repeal movement and claiming the whole idea of liberty was overrated, but he wasn't immune to the excitement. And he was much luckier than any other law clerk – he could take advantage of the literary renaissance catalysed by Emancipation.

With politics no longer bitterly polarised, space opened in the press for social issues, jokes, satire, stories, poems and feature articles. The decade started with a sheaf of comic, exuberant titles like *The Comet* and the *Dublin Satirist* and ripened into a crop of serious, long-lasting literary journals, notably the *Dublin University Magazine*, Ireland's answer to *Blackwood's*, which lasted forty years. It became possible for a writer to have a literary career while remaining in Ireland.

*

This moment in *The Comet* 4 December 1831 – 'J.C.M. is at the translator's' – is so seminal that I have to stop myself making grandstanding statements like 'modern Irish literature begins here'. The two nouns, J.C.M. and translator, are inextricably linked: he would not have found one without the other and he needed both to become famous.

In terms of his career – about which he was more opportunistic than he lets on – learning fluent German positioned him to exploit the huge vogue for German literature gripping Britain and Ireland. His first translation, Goethe's 'Song', was published in 1830, which means that the preceding years, far from being 'barren', were germinating (pun intended). But translation went deeper than meeting market demand. Something happened when Mangan discovered translation: he was freed up. He went from publishing ten poems a year to more than sixty and the poems get freer, easier, longer, wittier.

Mangan had a fear of the blank page beyond even most writers and to get around this, he always needed scaffolding. In the almanacs the requirement to plant clues and puzzles was a kind of scaffolding – in an acrostic, for instance, letters in each line form a word, which is the 'answer' to the poem – and devising and placing these clues distracted Mangan from the blankness of the page. But translation proved more effective because now the starting page was already filled with words waiting to be re-made. The original poem becomes the edifice on which Mangan erects a new poem. Crucially – or he wouldn't have found the experience liberating – he gives himself a free hand, relieving himself of any requirement to be authentic or faithful to the original conception. He needs the original words, which act like founding stones, beams and rafters, because he can't seem to provide his own, but he chooses how to re-assemble them: his version might gesture to the original edifice but have a different feel, or he might remake it into something unrecognisable, or amuse himself by erecting a grotesque parody, and occasionally he will recreate a deadly accurate simulacrum, just to show that he can. But at all times, he only ever consults his own wishes; the intentions of the original author don't concern him.

Translators, even those with a robust attitude to the original source material, are never as cavalier as this. In general, translators don't take on the task unless they like and admire the original. The process of absorbing a text seems to instil respect, or at least loyalty. Having travelled with an author line by line and felt something of the agony and ecstasy that went into the creation, it seems a betrayal to knock the text down, only to reassemble it in a way that might horrify the original creator. Mangan's contemporaries had a dim sense of his assaults, but it wasn't until the 1980s that Jacques Chuto and David Lloyd revealed the full bloody offensive (see chapter 'The Scholar and the Prodigy').

When he found translation, he found his name and his fame. I can't see him becoming famous as James Mangan: it's too pedestrian and it doesn't scan. James Clarence Mangan has an aristocratic air and is a lovely dactyl, linking him to his American twin, Edgar Allan Poe, and it sounds like someone who might be fluent in all world languages, which you would never believe of James Mangan. And more important than its glittering dactylic surface, the name released something very deep in him.

In Shakespeare's *Richard III*, the Duke of Clarence, who stands in the way of Richard and the throne, is incarcerated by his brother in the Tower and then murdered. Mangan liked to recite a particular speech of Clarence's: an account of a terrible premonitory dream, which he relates to the Keeper of the Tower, in which he is on a ship and shoved overboard by his brother and arrives in Hell, where he is cursed by ghosts, including the ghost of the prince he once killed in battle:

> Then came wandring by,
> A shadow like an angel, with bright hair
> Dabbled in blood; and he shrieked out aloud,
> 'Clarence is come; false, fleeting, perjur'd Clarence,
> That stabbed me in the field by Tewksbury:
> Seize on him, Furies, take him unto torment!'
> With that, methought, a legion of foul fiends
> Environed me, and howled in mine ears
> Such hideous cries, that with the very noise
> I trembling waked, and for a season after,
> Could not believe but that I was in hell,
> Such terrible impression made my dream.

The way this dream fits to Mangan and his life and preoccupations is pretty uncanny: there's the torment, the 'season in hell', which he had passed through twice in the 1820s, and would go through again in the 1840s …

There's the guilt and self-accusation in 'false, fleeting, perjur'd Clarence'. Free-floating guilt was part of Mangan's makeup, and he seems to have sensed that it had its roots in childhood. In the opening paragraphs of the long memoir he writes of being haunted in boyhood 'by an indescribable feeling of something terrible' which 'rose on my imagination like one of those dreadful ideas which are said by some German writers of romance to infest the soul of a man apparently foredoomed to the commission of murder'.

Identifying with a murdered murderer satisfied his haunted and double-edged sense of himself. Crucially, it's only in a dream that the Duke can admit both his guilt and his fear, and can receive the truth, refracted: whatever his guilt over killing a man in open battle, it's not he, Clarence, who is 'false and perjur'd', it's Richard. The ghost that Clarence meets in hell is the accusatory ghost of the man he killed, but it's also the ghost of himself, accusing his brother who will shortly kill him. This kind of vertiginous refraction – like being spun through a hall of mirrors or falling endlessly without ever reaching the bottom – recalls numerous passages in Mangan where the ground is cut from under you, 'beneath every deep, a lower deep' as his favourite line from 'Faust' has it ...

Also 'false and perjur'd' because, as translator, Mangan plays the authors whom he translates false. He has no intention of rendering them accurately and authentically. And of course, he is now literally 'false Clarence' since he has falsified his name ...

In the play, Clarence is murdered by hit-men sent by his brother who drown him in a vat of wine, an extraordinarily literal rendering of a 'drunkard's death' which resonated with Mangan's fears for himself and is obliquely referenced in his short story 'An Extraordinary Adventure in the Shades', in which the narrator imagines himself 'driven into a box, three feet square; there cooped up – a beggarly bottle of wine allotted pour toute compagnie'.

The name is so psychically resonant that I wonder if it came to Mangan in a dream (making it a dream within a dream) and I lost confidence in Shannon-Mangan as a biographer when she suggested that he took the name, not from 'Richard III', but from a character in a Maria Edgeworth novel. I understand that every biographer has to reshuffle the deck but not at the expense of insight into their subject. I can't work out if her insistence that she has found 'another, in fact better explanation' for what was already the perfect explanation, was excitement at being the one to discover that Mangan read a book with another Clarence in it, or because she can't handle the image of her saint of saints as *false, fleeting, perjur'd.*

Mangan in love

In March 1887 a young Yeats revealed in an article for *Irish Fireside* the identity ('now for the first time named') of the woman who 'loved and jilted' Mangan: 'she was a Miss Stackpoole of Mount Pleasant-square, one of three sisters'. When the article came out, Yeats received a letter 'from a well-known Mangan enthusiast denying the whole story point blank'. Yeats accepted that he had 'no proof except for the word of an eccentric Protestant clergyman' but he subsequently got 'corroboration' from Mangan's former editor at *The Nation*, Charles Gavan Duffy, and went on to publish a further article in 1891 entitled 'Clarence Mangan's Love Affair', which delineates Duffy's evidence – or rather his *missing* evidence (go figure): 'a dozen or more unpublished letters of Mangan's' which Duffy had lent 'to the Irish Exhibition at Earl's Court, but has never been able to recover, owing to the scandalous neglect of the committee' – and provides a physical description of Miss Stackpoole: 'a very handsome girl, with a tint of red in her hair, a very fashionable colour in our day, whatever it was then'.

The articles do not seem very Yeatsian, or at least are not like our idea of Yeats as 'high and solitary and most stern'; he sounds more like one of those literary sleuths on *The New Yorker*, forensically sifting through scant evidence and cautiously withholding the names of his sources. What the unlikely articles speak to is the nineteenth century's deep investment in Mangan's mysterious love affair and an already rich tradition of treating it as a detective story with clues, pointers and tip-offs to be followed up and deciphered. This tradition, which shows no sign of letting up – since Yeats's essay, multiple writers have got stuck in and now I'm adding my own two cents – seems determinedly unromantic but also quite Manganese, as if love was for him just another one of the acrostics and rebuses that he set in the almanacs as riddles for his readers to decode.

The first the wider public knew of any affair was from an obituary article which appeared in the *Evening Packet* in autumn 1849, a few months after Mangan's death, written by the journalist James Price, who had met Mangan in 1831 or 1832 when they were both writing for *The Comet*:

> [Mangan] once, with unusual bitterness of manner, alluded to the priceless argosy of a heart's first affections, tossed amid the quick-sands of a woman's caprice; to a love, fresh, pure, fervent, and beautiful as ever lighted passion's flame in human bosom, its jealous agony derided and its first rapturous declaration chilled by cruel and bitter scorn. He was not form'd to win the love of women.

Price backs up his charged account by quoting from Mangan's autobiographical letter to an editor, James McGlashan, 'a copy of which', Price claims, 'I have before me':

> I formed an attachment to a young lady who gave me every encouragement for some months and then appeared to take delight in exciting me to jealousy. One evening – I well

remember it – she openly slighted me, and shunned me. *******
I escaped marriage with this girl, but it was at the expense of
my health and peace of mind. [Price's asterisks, which denote
elisions he made.]

The next the public heard of the love affair came less than a
year later from Mangan himself when his impersonal memoir was
published posthumously in *The Irishman* in August 1850. Here he
writes up the affair languidly and ironically in the third person:

Mangan was at one period of his mysterious life drawn away,
and entirely, into the snare of love, and was even within an ace
of becoming a Benedict. But certain strange circumstances
– the occurrence of which he has described to me as having
been foreshadowed to him in a dream – interposed their
ungallant proportions between the lady and him; and so he
abode a Maledict …*

That is all he says about his affair, and it is as fleeting and
ambiguous as you would expect but he has introduced the idea of
a 'snare' so it's not surprising – since his fans always do his bidding
– that subsequent critics and biographers have proved ensnared and
ensnaring, unable to let the matter go and continually complicating
it. In his 1859 essay, John Mitchel set the narrative of the love affair
which prevailed for well over a century:

In one at least of the great branches of education [Mangan] had
run through his curriculum regularly; he was loved and was

---

*Maledict means 'accursed' and is the antonym to Benedict, which means 'blessed' and more
particularly: 'a newly married man, especially one who has been long a bachelor'. (Until I
looked up this definition, I thought Mangan was making one of his ironic puns on becoming
a Benedictine monk.)

deceived. The instructress in this department was a certain fair and false 'Frances'; at least such is the name under which he addressed her in one of his dreary songs of sorrow. … He was on terms of visiting in a house where there were three sisters; one of them beautiful, *spirituelle*, and a coquette. The old story was here once more re-enacted in due order. Paradise opened before him: the imaginative and passionate soul of a devoted boy bended in homage before an enchantress. She received it, was pleased with it, even encouraged and stimulated it, by various arts known to that class of persons, until she was fully and proudly conscious of her absolute power over one other noble and gifted nature … then with a cold surprise, as wondering that he could be so guilty of such a foolish presumption, she exercised her undoubted prerogative and whistled him down the wind. His air-paradise was suddenly a darkness and a chaos … He never loved, and hardly looked upon, any woman forever more.

It is hard to overstate the impact of this account: it was adopted wholesale by Mangan's first two biographers, McCall and O'Donoghue, and by Yeats and the phrase 'whistled him down the wind' followed Mangan well into the twentieth century, sealing him as the jilted lover of a heartless girl. The description of this coquettish 'enchantress' is recognisable as the generic femme fatale in art and literature: Circe, Delilah, Salome, La Belle Dame Sans Merci, Becky Sharp in *Vanity Fair*, Milady in *The Three Musketeers*. Wherever she goes the femme fatale injects excitement and Mitchel's readers must have got a transgressive thrill to find Mangan in her coils. Nobody seems to have asked the obvious question: why would she bother with a poor, awkward, penniless, alcoholic and (in the period referred to) unknown poet? Femme fatales only ever make a pitch for powerful men, and they gravitate naturally to centres of wealth and power, so what was she even doing in Dublin? (And this is before getting into the larger question of whether femme fatales even exist outside literature … I can't say I've ever met one.)

But nobody doubted Mitchel and the story continued to gather legs. Yeats got his scoop by naming and locating the enchantress, and in his 1897 biography, O'Donoghue corroborated her identity and gave his biographer's blessing to Mitchel's account. However, the following year, Yeats's informant Sir Charles Gavan Duffy – now retired and knighted after a successful political career in Australia – published his memoirs, *My Life in Two Hemispheres*, in which he gives an alternate account of the love affair. This must have failed to cut through because a decade later he wrote testily into the *Dublin Review* saying that it was he who had told the story of the love affair to Mitchel who 'must have forgotten the precise details', which he now sets out again:

> Shortly after our acquaintance commenced, [Mangan] brought me to visit a County Clare family, Mrs Stacpoole and her daughters, living, I think, in Mount Street. I found them agreeable and accomplished, and I repeated my visit several times, always with Mangan. One night, coming away, he suddenly stopped in the moonlit street, and, laying his hands on my shoulders and looking into my face, demanded: 'Isn't it true you are becoming attached to Margaret?' and, finally, he said: 'I will save you from my fate by telling you a tragic history; when I knew Margaret first, I was greatly attracted to her charming manners and vivid esprit. I talked to her of everything I did and thought and hoped, and she listened as willingly, it seemed, as Desdemona to the Moor. I am not a self-confident man – far from it; but when I besought her to be my wife I believed I was not asking her in vain. What think you that I heard? That she was already two years a wife and was living under her maiden name till her husband returned from an adventure which he had undertaken to improve their fortune.' – 'You cannot think,' I said 'that she deceived you intentionally, since

you have not broken with her?' 'Ah, he said, 'she has made my life
desolate, but I cannot help returning like the moth to the flame.'

This 'wonderful tale', as Mangan might have dubbed it, isn't queried
by Duffy but he seems uneasy about it – in a footnote he admits that
'the curious nature of the denouement I probably did not mention [to
Mitchel], as it was too profound and painful a secret while the parties
were all living'. The tale refines Mitchel's and Yeats's accounts: the
exciting Margaret Stacpoole (of Mount Street rather than the even
more suggestive Mountpleasant Square), who always appears in a tizzy
of French adjectives, entrances the poet but then announces carelessly
that she is already secretly married to a glamorous adventurer! This is
where things stood until the indefatigable Shannon-Mangan arrived
at the end of the twentieth century to review the evidence.

Her findings are sensational. With characteristic energy she
tracked down Margaret Stacpoole's birth certificate and discovered
that in 1834, when she first met Mangan, Margaret was fifteen
years old, so cannot possibly have been 'two years a wife'. This is
obviously a game-changer. Shannon-Mangan, declaring herself
'almost certain' that Margaret made up the story, calls it a 'generous
and efficient fib' which 'spared the feelings' of both parties and
'allowed them to continue as friends'. But this demoting of Margaret
from femme fatale to big-hearted teenager goes against the evidence
from Mangan's poems and story where the girl is definitely wily
so Shannon-Mangan produces another revelation: after stress-
testing the dates, she concludes that since Price was adamant that
the affair that occasioned the 'Frances' poems was over before he
met Mangan in 1831 then Margaret, aged twelve in that year, can't
have been the muse … so there must have been two love affairs and
two girls: Margaret in 1834 and a nameless girl in 1830 or earlier,
about whom Shannon-Mangan can find out nothing although she
suspects, as Yeats did, that she had auburn hair …

At this point, I felt as I did as a child reading Beatrix Potter's *The Tale of the Pie and the Patty-Pan*, a dizzying story of an invitation to tea involving two neighbours, two pies, two ovens, one patty-pan and as many sleight-of-hand exits and entrances as a Feydeau farce, rendered with all the camp social anxiety of Mapp and Lucia. (Only Beatrix Potter could get away with visiting something so elegantly angsty, with it gestures to dualism, Platonic Forms and the opaque variegations of English etiquette, on very small children.) Instead of bringing the clarity she intends to the affair(s) Shannon-Mangan only churns up the murky narrative and deepens our sense of having entered a looking-glass world where girls multiply and time recedes, and everything hinges on dates (which given Mangan's way with dates is not very reassuring). And the churn only gets worse when she adverts, as do all the biographers, to a third girl, Catherine Hayes, whom Mangan tutored in French and German and who died of cholera in late 1832, and for whom he wrote 'Elegiac Verses on the Early Death of a Beloved Friend'. Nobody seems to think this sweet, innocent dead girl was the spirituelle coquette who broke his heart, but Price and Meehan do their best to cast her as Mangan's true love, with whom he was in 'perfect communion' and from whose death he never recovered, hence his sad celibacy.

*

To cut out the clamour, I went back to the poems and the story, published 1832/33, in which Mangan is alleged to have told the tale of his affair, and which are produced as evidence by Mitchel, O'Donoghue and Shannon-Mangan.

The first poem, published in *The Comet* on 16 December 1832, is addressed 'To xxxxx xxxxx' but within the text the girl is named as 'Frances'. She is indeed 'cold and cruel' and 'lavishes all her wiles to win her lover o'er' before 'turning him over to despair'; he ends up in an 'unremembered grave'. Six weeks later, 17 February 1833, came two 'Very Interesting Sonnets', again in *The Comet*, and addressed this time 'To Caroline'. In the first sonnet he accuses her of failing to realise that he loved her. He starts off defending himself – 'Have I not called thee angel-like and fair?' – but then admits to being among the 'shrouded few, who share their locked up thoughts with none'. He depicts Caroline as all movement – 'dark bright eyes' with 'flashing rays' – while he is cold and inert and his heart, where 'the memory of unuttered loves lie, alas! too faithfully inurned', is a mortician's urn.

In the second sonnet, the dream is over, 'the spell broken' and 'the enchantment dissolved' and that is the end of his love poems in *The Comet*, but five months later, in July 1833, he published, in the *Dublin Satirist*, a short story 'My Transformation, a Wonderful Tale', which begins with the narrator recalling his love for 'the beautiful and fascinating' Eleanor Campion, who doesn't reject 'his passion' but when he introduces her to his best friend, Lionel Delamaine, 'a young man of handsome figure, insinuating address, and extensive accomplishments', Lionel proves 'a villain' and 'Eleanor a forsworn traitress!' This is all recounted in two paragraphs, after which Eleanor and Lionel disappear from the tale and the narrator gets down to describing his misery.

These are the poems and story cited as evidence for Mangan's affair with a cold enchantress. The name-changing seems to prefigure the later biographical confusion over Catherine/Margaret but the consistently treacherous behaviour suggests a single perpetrator. Shannon-Mangan provides more helpful information: Mangan took one of the names, Caroline, from a short story by James Price, published in *The Comet* in August 1832. (This is the same James Price who brought the love affair to public attention in his obituary of Mangan.) Price's Caroline also has dark eyes and also plays the narrator false – he comes in one evening to find her 'on the sofa where I used to recline with her, leaning on the breast of a stranger'. Nothing so risqué happens in Mangan but he certainly appropriated this story and quite openly: the two sonnets are addressed 'To Caroline' and according to Shannon-Mangan, his own story sends up Price's style, which 'had now become something of a joke'.

This new information made me incredibly suspicious so I went off to Pearse Street Library, where you can still look at newspapers in hard copy and got out all the issues of *The Comet* between Price's story and Mangan's 'very interesting sonnets'. This proved a very interesting exercise. Price's story seems to have unleashed a vexation of cruel temptresses and broken-hearted poets onto the poetry pages. I counted ten poems on this theme by five different poets, including Mangan.

On 30 September 1832 Price, using his poetic acronym 'J.P. – E.', bemoans in 'Song of an Unhappy Love' that:

I must live on in anguish and I must exist to see
The form I lov'd another's – This, oh! This is misery

In the same issue, 'W.M.B.' (*Comet* poets never used their full names) has a poem 'To Fanny', depicting her as a kind of weaving spider:

Still may you vow and swear with hidden guile –
And plight again to make thy prey more sure
Then be detected as thou art by me
In all thy secret tricks as blighted fallacy.

Three weeks later, 21 October, W.M.B. has another poem, 'Original', describing a feckless girl binding garlands around his head:

You told me as wildly you bound them
That love mid their blossoms would stay
In sunshine [love] sported around them
But left them at eve to decay.

On 4 November, M.F. has a poem, 'The Coquette':

The clustering locks – the coral lock – the eye so darkly bright
Tis true she seemed a thing of light, amid the flattering throng
But cold and calm, with heart untouch'd, the coquette moved
along.

On 25 November J.P. – E. is back with 'Song of a Deceived One'. The narrator beats himself up – 'I felt I was not form'd to win the love / Of woman. I was plain' – but the girl is 'false!' and has 'left me blighted – sear'd in heart, and all / My feelings turned to bitterness and gall.'

On 2 December, 'Brasspen' joins the throng with 'Song', which describes parting from his love and returning to find her behaviour changed:

What – no more? I fear a cheat
I see it in the wile
Now lurking in these roguish eyes
Now playing in that smile.

On 9 December, J.P. – E. is back addressing a 'Miss M – G – '. She hasn't played him false but seeing her beauty and innocence recalls for him that 'too soon falsehood and treachery come / To wrap the young heart in their withering gloom'. A week later, 16 December, he is back with a poem addressed to 'Miss Fanny K – D –, Williamstown' whose 'dark black eyes' and 'raven hair' he admires but doesn't feel free to love because 'falsehood and untruth' have 'blighted' the 'trustingness of youth'. In the same edition appears Mangan's poem 'To xxxxx xxxxx', also addressed to a 'Frances'.

Did any of these excitingly cruel girls exist? The dark bright eyes and clustering locks and roguish smile and 'Fanny/Frances' are a constant, but I don't think the poets intended readers to believe that they were drawing from life – it's exciting to think of a sultry temptress going through *Comet* poets like a knife through butter but it's beyond credibility that all five should have had the same experience with the same woman. They are kicking around a theme, and because they have the luxury of a large, readership they expect their attentive readers to be in on their game. They are the nineteenth century equivalent of tweeters, bloggers and podcasters.

By the new year, the *Comet* editors were growing tired of the theme. The section 'Letters to Correspondents' on 12 January 1833, has this jocular note for Mangan:

> No, Clarence dear, we will not, cannot, ought not admit your indescribable Ode, half in praise, half in censure of the beautiful 'starry-eyed Miss E – of Summerhill and her fascinating sister Anna' … You say 'you have wept in silence and in sorrow over the shattered wreck of all your hopes!' Devil a tear ever dropped from your eyes. We know you well. You are a mystifier, *Clarence* – a humbugger of the first water.

A month later, Mangan makes his valedictory farewell to 'Caroline' of the generic 'dark bright eyes', and the fascinating temptresses now disappear from *The Comet*'s pages. What makes the episode memorable isn't that Mangan was exploring a real-life event that happened to him – he wasn't – it's that he saw off the other poets to win the slam. He is the only one to make something arresting and original out of a generic trope. The other poets tell a straightforward tale of jilted love using routine rhyme and metre – nothing prepares you for the ambiguities, evasions and convolutions with which Mangan disrupts the account.

The doubts appear in the first few lines of his first poem in the series, 'To xxxxx xxxxx':

> The charm that gilded life is over
> I live to feel I live in vain
> And worlds were worthless to recover
> The dazzling dream of mine again.

This suggests something surface and superficial, rather than a profound heartfelt connection, but the girl soon makes her invariable appearance, wily, smiling and false, and we are back in femme fatale territory, but with a strange circumlocution:

> Oh, cold and cruel she, who while
> She lavishes all wiles to win
> Her lover o'er, can smile and smile,
> Yet be all dark and false within.
> Who, when his glances on another
> Too idly and too long have dwelt,
> Will sigh as if she sought to smother
> The grief her bosom never felt;

So: she pretends to sigh, to give the false impression that she is stifling an emotion she never felt, about something he wasn't guilty of anyway (his glance was 'idle'). After this vertiginous swoop, the girl continues on, witching, wanton and weaving, until the narrator makes a sudden confession: his love was 'untold' – worse, his words were actually cold!

Me, Frances! me thou never knewest,
Nor sawest, that if my speech was cold,
The love is deepest oft, and truest
That burns within the breast untold.

He blames her for not having the perception to see that his behaviour actually means the opposite – not cold but burning – but he's uneasy about demanding such superlative understanding. The reader of the poem now starts to wonder whether the girl's cold behaviour is a reaction to his seeming indifference. Maybe she was trying to excite him to jealousy? At the end, he is in his favourite resting place, 'mine unremembered grave', while she is in 'a bower or beauty' where winds and lightning bolts can't reach her. It is not clear whose fault their mutual isolation is.

None of the other poets come anywhere near this subtlety or ambiguity. They recount a potentially interesting relationship drama but without the personal experience to animate the event, their accounts fall flat. Mangan doesn't have the personal experience either, so instead he creates a kind of fan dance, where it becomes impossible to tell who is in love with whom, who is testing whom, and who is to blame for the failure of the relationship. This inconclusiveness draws attention to the artificiality of the whole exercise. None of the poets is actually the jilted lover they claim to be, and all are riffing off a trope, but only Mangan works in the ambiguities and evasions to imply that the tale has no firm foundations in genuine experience. This makes him, conversely, the most honest as well as the most artificial of the poets.

This reading of the poem isn't immediately obvious – Mangan is never obvious – but the editors of *The Comet* seem to have had a shrewd idea of what he was about when they mocked his claim to have 'wept in silence and in sorrow'. Given that his editors were on to his 'humbugging' at the time, and that Chuto and Lloyd got on to him in the 1980s, I'm a bit confused as to why these poems and short story are still being taken as personal experience. Nobody thinks, reading his later poems, that he was in love with Marianne or Moreen or any of the girls he borrowed from other poets. When he discovered translation, he found a legitimate means of ransacking the experience of others, but from the start he was looking to his reading for themes; his own life was peculiarly uneventful in terms of even ordinary pleasures like travelling, sex, romantic encounters, social engagements, sporting activities, etc. He didn't fake emotion, but he did borrow experience. I guess the reason these poems are taken as authentic experience is because he made four separate assertions – verbally to Price and Duffy, in writing to McGlashan, and in his impersonal memoir – that he suffered a love affair which sounds very like the situation in the poems and story.

But these assertions, on closer examination, are deeply problematic. Price's recall of their conversation is a paraphrase – if Mangan did confide in him, he definitely didn't confide in those hectic mixed metaphors – and even when we have Mangan's actual words, in his letter to McGlashun, what he is saying isn't obvious:

> I formed an attachment to a young lady who gave me every encouragement for some months and then appeared to take delight in exciting me to jealousy. One evening – I well remember it – she openly slighted me, and shunned me. *******
> I escaped marriage with this girl, but it was at the expense of my health and peace of mind.

Mangan is careful to emerge from this account as the victim, but his language gives him away: it is the girl who is the victim. She encourages him and then tries 'slighting' him to 'excite' a proposal of marriage which gives him the perfect excuse to 'escape'. Had the girl wept or pleaded, it would have been trickier since in every situation he has to cast himself the victim, but she shuns him and he is away, safely the victim, but too gleeful to resist the final gloat: 'I escaped marriage'.

Maybe this is what happened. Maybe Mangan was the shunner, not the shunned. But maybe not. I don't see that there is any onus on us to take Mangan at his word. Just because he was allegedly confiding in friends and readers, why should these versions be believed any more than the poems or stories? He was quite capable of working up a situation from a slender premise and then presenting it as having happened. Who really believes that Margaret was secretly married or that such a young girl made up the fantastic tale? Only Shannon-Mangan, who will insist on taking Mangan at his word, so that, like the great naturalist Philip Gosse refusing the evidence of evolution because it conflicted with his religious beliefs, she throws away the conclusions of her own brilliant research. Unearthing the game-changing proof of Margaret's age, she allows it to modify the account but not to challenge her faith-based view of Mangan as a sincere, truthful, suffering soul.

'Almost certainly' Mangan was making up the tale, not Margaret. A PhD student in Queen's Belfast, Nigel Oxley, found his likely literary model: Goethe's *The Sorrows of Young Werther*. In the most famous of all Romantic novels, which launched a wave of copycat suicides, Werther falls in love with the orphaned Lotte. She is engaged to another, but he keeps visiting her until, unable to bear it, he kills himself. Mangan's words to Duffy – 'she has made my life desolate, but I cannot help returning like the moth to the flame' – are pure Werther.

Mangan was trying it on with Duffy, just as he was trying it on in *The Comet*, and was probably also trying it on to McGlashan and in his impersonal memoir. He liked to trick, and his work is full of occluded jokes. But since his intention is to confuse and evade rather than to deceive outright, he leaves wistful clues – the gloating verb 'escape' and the riff on a famous novel – and finally, like a 1980s soap opera whose plot has got out of hand, he plays the hoary old get-out clause: 'it was all a dream'.

Looking back over the poems, story and memoir where he recounts his 'love affair(s)', I realise that they are all presented as dreams. 'To xxxxx xxxxx' opens with a 'dazzling dream' and the second 'interesting' sonnet deploys seven variations of dream/unreality in case we haven't got the message:

> Still I did adore the unreal image loftily enshrined
> In the recesses of mine own sick mind
> Enough: – the spell is broke – the dream is o'er –
> The enchantment is dissolved – the world appears
> The thing it is – a theatre, a mart

In 'My Transformation, a Wonderful Tale', the narrator is prey to a strange vision before he takes the ruinous step of introducing his love to his friend:

> I well remember that on the very evening of the introduction a presentiment of overshadowing evil hung like a cloud above my spirit. I saw, as on the glass of a magic mirror, the form and character of the change that was about to be wrought upon the spirit of my dream.

This is anxiously layering and refracting – not just a mirror, but a magic mirror, not just a dream but the spirit of a dream (something almost impossibly transient). Sixteen years later, the same strange 'presentiment' creeps into the account in the impersonal memoir of the love affair: 'Certain strange circumstances – the occurrence of which [Mangan] has described to me as having been foreshadowed to him in a dream – interposed their ungallant proportions between the lady and him.' The 'ungallantry' here is dislocated: it may attach to another suitor; it may attach to the girl; it may attach to Mangan himself. Either way, in this, his last word on the subject, he has transmuted the affair to a dream.

*

I arrived at my conclusions – that Mangan 'escaped' the girl and/or that the affair only happened in his fantasies – through minute sifting of the evidence. I was proud of my hard slog and deductive reasoning until I re-read *Dubliners* and realised that Joyce had said it all already.

In 'Araby', the third story in *Dubliners*, Joyce gives what are, for him, two overt clues to his sources: the story is set in an oriental bazaar and the love interest is referred to as 'Mangan's sister'. It took decades for critics to pick up on his hint, but once the connection was made (by a scholar, Harry Stone, in 1965), numerous other Mangan allusions in the story were seized on and decoded. More recently, in a brilliant essay entitled 'Joyce and the Mangan in the Mac', Peter van de Kamp suggests that another character in *Dubliners* also derives from Mangan: Mr Duffy in 'A Painful Case' who has a moustache, like Mangan, and lives 'at a little distance from his body, regarding his own acts with doubtful sideglances' and has 'an odd autobiographical habit which led him to compose in his mind from time to time a short sentence about himself containing a subject in the third person and a predicate in the past tense' – an exact description of what Mangan does in his impersonal memoir.

Both the nameless boy and Mr Duffy are cast adrift in love. The boy sets out on a grail quest to buy a keepsake for the girl next door but arrives too late and the bazaar is closing. Mr Duffy gets closer: he meets a married woman at a concert, 'finds courage to make an appointment' and begins to go 'often to her little cottage outside

Dublin' where 'little by little their thoughts entangle' although Mr Duffy still hears 'the strange impersonal voice, which he recognised as his own, insisting on the soul's incurable loneliness'. One night Mrs Sinico 'caught up his hand passionately and pressed it to her cheek'. Mr Duffy, 'very much surprised' and 'disillusioned', arranges to meet her a last time 'to break off their intercourse'. As they walk back towards the tram, 'she trembles so violently that fearing another collapse on her part, he bade her goodbye quickly and left her'. Four years later, he reads in the paper of her death, knocked down by a train, while drunk.

Remarkably, the two stories enact the exact scenarios which I so painstakingly assigned to Mangan's love affair(s): fantasy/dream and gloating escape. In 'Araby', the affair is an infatuation built on a few words and glances, with an unsuspecting girl cast as muse and without any hope, or even wish, of consummation (she is going on a retreat and the sister motif brings in the incest taboo). Mr Duffy, for his part, cruelly and prudishly 'breaks off the intercourse' when the woman manifests her need and escapes back into his 'incurable loneliness'. I think these two stories are, among other things, an oblique commentary on the great literary *whodunnit* of the age: Mangan's love affair. Although Joyce had access to most of the sources I've quoted, I am in awe of his radical insight. My own sceptical approach to the love affair was primed by Chuto and Lloyd's iconoclastic dismantling of the Mangan myth, whereas Joyce was writing at a time of deep belief in Mangan as jilted lover.

How Joyce had the insight to push back against the prevailing narrative is one of the mysteries of genius, but Peter Van de Kamp offers a sensational lead. The title of his essay, 'Joyce and the Mangan in the Mac' conjoins the Man in the Cloak and the mysterious Man in the Mackintosh in Ulysses with the street flasher, and the essay opens with a brilliantly salacious anecdote from the poet Austin Clarke of meeting Joyce in Paris:

Some weeks later as we were sitting in a cheap café in a side street under the shadow of Saint Sulpice, drinking Pernod Fils, Joyce after a long silence said 'La poesia de Mangan e de Yeats è quella di segatora di chi sela da fa [*sic*] solo.' ... He emphasized their obsession with hands, quoting Mangan and pointing to the frequency with which Yeats refers to pearl-pale hands ... I glanced at the drooping figure, I wondered if he had been addicted in youth to our national vice.

The Italian translates as: 'The poetry of Mangan and Yeats is the poetry of those who wank alone' which explains why Joyce said it in Italian and why Clarke didn't translate, although he may as well have, since it's pretty obvious what he means by 'our national vice'. Clarke, fourteen years younger than Joyce, seems to be casting himself as the fourth generation of literary Irish masturbators in a tradition handed down from Mangan. The image is irresistible – the two (lapsed) Irish Catholics fingering their great forebearers in the shadow of Saint Sulpice (where the Marquis de Sade was baptised) – and it is an astonishing moment in the narrative of Mangan in Love: sex has finally entered, veiled by Italian and euphemism, but bringing its usual frisson of danger.

Reading Clarke's anecdote is to realise just how absent sex is from Mangan's work. There is no flesh, smells, carnality, lubricity, nothing down and dirty. He is squeamish: 'My heart is a monk, and thy bosom his cloister / So sleeps the bright pearl in the shell of the oyster' goes one of his couplets (and what a weird transgendered image: a monk cloistered in a bosom!). But Joyce is right. There are lots and lots of hands. I dashed off a new list (this is not exhaustive):

- 'mute each eye, unnerved each hand'
- 'and with her hands the lattice raised'
- 'and quitted quick a nerveless hand'

- 'What happiness was mine, when first I pressed / Thy hand! And dared to raise it to a breast'
- 'Thy phrenetic hand hath destroyed / The fabric – it crashes!'
- 'A lily-white glove accidentally / Slipped from her lily-white hand / And by eddying swirls was carried / Or hurried / Down towards the sand'
- 'a palace plundered by every hand / Is the hundred-leafed rose'
- 'Your holy delicate white hands / Shall girdle me with steel'
- 'the work of impious hands'

These hands are not very sensual or sexy in themselves – except perhaps the hand releasing into the 'eddying swirls' – but cumulatively they amount to a manual obsession. Van de Kamp opens his essay with the Clarke anecdote because, as he goes on to demonstrate, Joyce gives this manual obsession to the boy in 'Araby' and to Mr Duffy, and he subtly characterises both as solitary masturbators. (Van de Kamp calls the boy 'a sly voyeur, who shares Duffy's manual fixation' so that I formed the rather tragic impression that the boy grows up to be Duffy.) The essay convinced me that Mangan 'who shared his locked up thoughts with none' was onanistic but I was amazed that Joyce was able to pick this up from the poems. I wondered was it a case, as Clarke seems to be suggesting, of 'you spot it, you got it' but *pace* the national vice, I imagine Joyce as less addicted to solitary masturbation than most young men (he had prostitutes and then he had Nora).

In *Brideshead Revisited*, Evelyn Waugh describes a significant moment (also involving hands) between the young Charles Ryder and Julia Flyte: 'As I took the cigarette from my lips and put it in hers, I caught a thin bat's squeak of sexuality, inaudible to any but me.' The first time I read this I was about fourteen and had never taken or received a cigarette from anyone's lips but I recognised immediately that inaudible squeak as something I had heard all my life – in the sandpit, in the playground, probably in the cradle if I could only remember because 'we are sexual from the moment we are born to the moment we die', I agree with John McGahern – and I still think a bat's squeak is the best metaphor for repressed sexuality/ desire. Eventually most of us get round, as Charles and Julia will, to speaking and enacting our desires, but this doesn't happen for the 'shrouded few, who share their locked up thoughts with none'. You need supersonic hearing to pick up the squeaks in Mangan, but Joyce is pretty batlike (terrible eyes, astonishing hearing).

By listening closely, I was able to pick up a few squeaks which are maybe what Joyce heard. There are two in the strange anecdote in Mangan's impersonal memoir which is one of the sources for the grail quest in 'Araby':

> A hair-brained [sic] girl, who lodged in his father's house, sent him out one day to buy a ballad: he had no covering on his head, and there was a tremendous shower of rain; but she told him that the rain would make him *grow*. He believed her – went out – strayed through many streets, and by-places, now abolished – found, at length, his way homeward – and for eight years afterwards – from his fifth year to his thirteenth – remained almost blind.

The italics on *'grow'* are Mangan's own. The myth that masturbation sends you blind goes back to the ancient Greeks who connected semen to tears and by Mangan's time it was a settled view. An early eighteenth-century monograph by a Dutch theologian, entitled *Onania, or the Heinous Sin of Self-Pollution, And All Its Frightful Consequences, In Both Sexes, Considered* lists the 'frightful consequences' including many – 'disturbances of the stomach and digestion, nausea, weakening of the organs of breathing, hoarseness, paralysis, disorders of the eye and ear, paleness, thinness, loss of memory, attacks of rage, madness, fever and finally suicide' – that

Mangan self-diagnoses with in the longer memoir. In contemporary descriptions of him he is always thin, pale, melancholic, near-sighted, and sometimes also maddened, enraged and suicidal, as if he were a walking illustration of 'the frightful consequences of the abominable practice'. Rousseau's *Confessions* – which Mangan mentions in the opening of the memoir – are frank about indulging in the 'vice' and hysterical about the implications. Not even the radical Rousseau thought masturbation a good thing and the idea that it saps the bodily powers persisted well into the twentieth century, hence Clarke's pointed adjective 'drooping' to describe (the pale, emaciated, near-blind) Joyce.

The onanistic squeak in the impersonal memoir chimes with another faint squeak in the longer memoir, describing another childhood scene:

> For me, I sought refuge in books and solitude. My brothers and sister indulged in habits of healthy exercise, and strengthened their constitutions morally and physically … But I shut myself up in a close room: I isolated myself in such a manner from my own nearest relatives that with one voice they all proclaimed me 'mad'. Perhaps I was: this much at least is certain, that it was precisely at this period – from my tenth to my fourteenth year – that the seeds of moral insanity were developed within me which afterwards grew into a tree of giant altitude.

Mangan shutting himself in a 'close room' to read as his 'seeds' grow 'in altitude' is adverting to the steamy passages in his books (particularly, I'm guessing, Byron and *The Arabian Nights*) but he is also making a more subtle suggestion: it is not just the reading matter that encourages masturbation; the very act of *being alone* in a room encourages a relationship with yourself, which, if carried to extremes, may prevent intimacy with others.

Another squeak comes in the account of a dream, which radically disrupts a critical essay on the German poet Justinus Kerner:

> oh! that was a glorious moment, when we beheld Stamboul arise before our mind's eye in all its multifarious gorgeousness, glittering with mosques, kiosks, minarets, temples, turrets, and the rest of them! We surveyed them with extacy. We knew that we were dreaming, and that we might perpetuate any devilment with impunity. 'Here, to all appearance, we are,' we exclaimed; 'the streets are redolent with life around us; the firm earth is resonant under our boots – the sun hath a saffron, but clear brightness in Heaven – and yet all this is the merest sham – for we are at this moment at home in our own bedchamber … What is to withhold us, if we please, from annihilating this proud city by the breath of our nostrils? First, however, let us signalise ourselves in some less startling way.' Our attention was by-and-by attracted by a colossal pillar, inscribed with sentences from the Dutch poets … A man then came by, bestriding a rhinoceros. This time we were not to be hoaxed; and we merely demanded of the rhinoceros whether he was going to hunt. 'Following the horn, at least,' answered the rhinoceros; and we laughed so intemperately at this piece of wit that death appeared for a time almost inevitable …

When I first read this, I recognised the nose that 'annihilates the city' as the same nose that threatens to 'extend itself from College Green through Dame-street' in Mangan's first short story, 'An Extraordinary Adventure in the Shades', and I figured this nose as a Manganese motif but couldn't think what it might signify until I woke up one morning with the absolute certainty that the tumescent nose, which segues into the rhinoceros' horn in the dream-recital and which 'blocks up the entrance to the tavern' in the short story, rendering 'all intercourse thus impracticable', must be the penis. I confidently googled 'meaning of a large/expanding nose in a dream' and was disappointed in the results – they seemed to rely on Pinocchio, a book published long after Mangan's dream – but this did not shake me from my dream intuition, particularly when, after more googling, I learnt that the nose is the only other body part to have erectile tissue, and that nose-size has been proven to correlate to penis-size and of course the nose, like the penis, ejaculates … Mangan is having a wet dream.

Mangan 'segato da solo' (wanked alone) which means that he did have a sexual relationship: with himself. It would be nice if he weren't consumed by shame over this and great if we could add a partner but, still, this is a bit better than the dusty, monkish celibacy that has encased him for so long. A final question remains: what/who was he masturbating to? what were his sexual fantasies? The critic Patrick Rafroidi picked up another bat's squeak from the long memoir, which helps answer this. Mangan describes one of his hospitalisations:

There was a poor child in the convalescent ward of the institution, who was afflicted from head to foot with an actual leprosy; and there being no vacant bed to be had, I was compelled to share that of this miserable being, which, such was my ignorance of the nature of contagion, I did without the slightest suspicion of the inevitable result. But in a few days after my dismissal from the hospital the result but too plainly shewed itself on my person in the form of a malady nearly as hideous and loathsome as that of the wretched boy himself; and though all external traces of it have long since disappeared, its moral efforts remain incorporated with my mental constitution to this hour, and will probably continue with me through life.

Rafroidi hears the bat's squeak in the hysterical horror at being placed in bed with a boy. This is the only moment in all Mangan where anyone gets into bed with anyone and where skin comes in visceral contact with skin. Leprosy is here a metaphor for homosexuality, which imparts no 'external traces' but has 'moral effects', which 'continue through life'. The passage is full of shame, guilt, repression and disgust but it is fleshier and more visceral than the love poems, and it casts an interesting light on Mangan's friendships with young men, to one of whom, Joseph Brenan, he wrote a poem 'Brother and yet more than brother', and to another, Gavan Duffy, he addressed a letter, 'My hAnDy young MAN' (suggesting that when he 'laid his hands' on Duffy's shoulders and 'looked into his face', it wasn't Margaret's marriage he was trying to prevent). And it sends me back to his nasal dream where sure enough there are 'turrets' and 'colossal pillars' and a man 'bestriding a rhinoceros' 'following the horn', and not a woman, or breast, or yonic symbol in sight. I am wary about outing historical figures, particularly on such slender evidence, but so much about Mangan is queer-coded – his sense of shame, fraught anxiety, opacity, self-invention and re-invention, costume – that it seems coy not to conclude from the bat squeaks that he was gay, and that this was one more reason for his obsessive secrecy.

Mangan at *The Nation*

On 15 October 1842 a new paper, *The Nation*, was launched in Dublin. By lunchtime, it had sold out and within a few weeks it was the most popular weekly newspaper ever to have been published in Ireland. With a circulation of 250,000, it was alleged to have a regular audience of a million people. Ireland's population was eight million, with just over half the men and two-fifths of women literate (1841 census). Henry MacManus's painting 'Reading The Nation' in the National Gallery shows how *The Nation* got its audience: a bespectacled elderly gentleman reads aloud to a group of yokels.

The 'most notable journalistic venture in Irish history' was the brainchild of three men: Thomas Davis, John Blake Dillon and Mangan's 'handy young man', Charles Gavan Duffy. Both Davis and Duffy left accounts of the genesis of the paper: the three men met in the Four Courts and walked up to Phoenix Park, planning the new journal. At the Park, they 'discussed it over again on a bench under a big elm, facing to Kilmainham'. This scene was captured in a sketch 'Birth of the Nation', showing Duffy in the centre writing energetically and Thomas Davis bareheaded, having set down his hat and cane as if divesting himself of privilege, all three animated under the shelter of the living Irish tree and turning away from the stony symbol of British power in the Park, the Wellington monument.

The three were members of the Repeal Association and their talents and interests were complementary: Davis, a Protestant Trinity graduate, had given considerable thought to pluralist nationalism and non-denominational education; Dillon, son of a Roscommon Catholic farmer and shopkeeper, pushed tenure and land reform; and Duffy, a Monaghan Catholic and former editor of the *Belfast Vindicator,* ensured an attractive layout and the right explosive mix of news, opinion, scandal, local doings, sport, poetry and obituaries.

In the first issue, a note 'To the Subscribers' indicates the preparation that went into the venture:

> There never was any such Newspaper in the country which commenced with such a circulation as ours, nor, we venture to affirm, with half of it. … Lest it should be supposed that we have not fulfilled our pledge respecting the size of the Paper, we must request our readers to measure the sheet of THE NATION, before it is cut with the largest Paper they can find, that they may convince themselves it is, as we promised it should be, THE LARGEST PAPER EVER PUBLISHED IN IRELAND.

The Largest Paper Ever Published in Ireland looks crowded and script-heavy to our eyes. However, in comparison with other papers of the era it was a model of spacious, clear layout. This boosted its circulation, as did the clever balance of news and politics against light entertainment and sensationalism. Each issue included shipping and agricultural news, foreign affairs, regional news often syndicated from local papers, transcripts of debates in the House of Commons, editorials, and reports from the law courts. It was with a sense of déjà vu of the ubiquity of the issue in Irish history that I read (29 October and 5 November 1842) of 'The Trial of John Bond, a man aged forty-five years, and whose appearance was anything but prepossessing, and Jane Read, an interesting girl about nineteen years of age, both indicted for having solicited to procure the abortion or miscarriage of the said Jane Read'.

A decisive factor in the paper's early success was O'Connell's support. Every issue carried news of the Repeal Association, and at O'Connell's demand, Repeal wardens ordered bundles of the paper for distribution at their meetings. This in turn helped ignite the movement, which had been stagnating. O'Connell would later fall out with *The Nation*, but in the early years the friendship was mutually beneficial. In its mission to repeal the Union, *The Nation* was keen on poetry, of a particular kind. Davis's friend and mentor Thomas Wallis recalled that 'all the founders of *The Nation* agreed in the resolve that, come whence it would, poetry – real living poetry, gushing warm from the heart, and not mechanically mimicking obsolete and ungenerous forms – was worth a trial, as a fosterer of national feeling, and an excitement of national hope.' In its third issue, 29 October, *The Nation* set out its stall:

Ireland, a rising, vigorous and virtuous nation (unlike England) is now, in fact, as of old, essentially a poetic or bardic nation, with a fresh imaginative population … Our POET'S CORNER shall be regularly supplied with numerous and varied effusions in this fascinating department of literature, from our ablest pens; so that the ramparts of the fortress of corruption, which we propose to level, may be cleared by the lighter but unceasing crackle of such sparkling musketry.

I think Duffy wrote this. It is a mess of mixed metaphors, but he is clearly trying to weaponise poetry for the national struggle, an idea imported from the Romantic movement in Europe. In 1806, in a Berlin occupied by Napoleon, the Romantic philosopher Johann Gottlieb Fichte had given a series of 'Addresses to the German Nation', praising German language, tradition and literature and tying cultural distinctiveness to political independence. The lectures inspired some bad rabble-rousing poems from minor German Romantics and the message spread to the rest of Europe. In Poland in 1830, Adam Mickiewicz's early revolutionary verse inspired insurgents who urged him to return from exile to fight, and in Brussels the same year, the audience at a performance of an opera by Daniel Auber rose up and rioted in the streets after the duet '*Amour sacré de la patrie*', triggering the Belgian revolution.

Duffy dreamed of turning *The Nation* into a platform for poetry that would send people out on the streets. In his search for 'the ablest pens', he had his sights set on Mangan, who was Ireland's most famous poet and, if enigmatic in his political approach, certainly a Catholic in favour of Repeal. Mangan contributed a piece of doggerel to the first issue, ending:

> Then arise! fling aside your dark mantle of slumber
> And welcome in chorus The Nation's First Number!

This is writing by numbers but at least it shows willing. Mangan had a few short comic pieces in the next two issues of *The Nation* but he then virtually disappears for the next three and a half years until suddenly re-emerging in February 1846. There is a story behind this.

*

By the launch of '*The Nation*'s First Number', Mangan was a well-known Dublin street character and was on his way to becoming his myth: The Man in the Cloak. The moment he adopted his signature look is nearly as important as 'J.C.M. at the translator's' but we don't have the date for when he first donned his cloak-and-coat. I put it somewhere between 1838 and 1840. Duffy, who first met him in 1836, recalled that 'when our acquaintance was still new, [Mangan] was as cheerful as it was ever his nature to be, and his appearance was less eccentric, his garments fresher'. In 1838 Mangan signed an essay 'The Man in the Cloak', which isn't proof since he may have adopted the pseudonym before literally inhabiting the role, but in March 1841 he published a weird essay, 'My Bugle and How I Blow it', which riffs on his identity as the Man in the Cloak and is so self-referential – he knows that readers know he's talking about himself – that we can take it that by this time he was literally under the cloak, or, as he insists in the essay, *in* the cloak.

Almost every description of Mangan starts and ends with his appearance as if no one ever got any closer to him. Fr Meehan left a detailed description:

> He was about five feet six or seven in height, slightly stooped, and attenuated as one of Memling's monks. His head was large, beautifully shaped, his eyes blue, his features exceedingly fine and 'sicklied o'er' … The dress of this spectral-looking man was singularly remarkable, taken down at haphazard from some peg in an old clothes shop – a baggy pantaloon that was never intended for him, a short coat closely buttoned, a blue cloth cloak still shorter and tucked so tightly to his person that no-one could see there even the faintest shadow of those lines called by painters and sculptors drapery. The hat was in keeping with this habiliment, broad-leafed and steeple-shaped, the model of which he must have found in some picture of Hudibras.

William Wakeman, who worked with Mangan on the Ordnance Survey, added some props to the costume:

He possessed very weak eyes and used a huge pair of green spectacles; he had narrow shoulders, and was flat-chested, so much so, that for appearance sake the breast of his coat was thickly padded … Out of doors he wore a tight little cloak, and his hat exactly resembled those which broomstick-riding witches are usually represented with. Sometimes, even in the most settled weather, he might be seen parading the streets with a voluminous umbrella under each arm.

The look was an extraordinary compound of dandy, romantic, tramp and paranoiac. It repelled contact – people do not easily approach a man in a cloak as Mangan recognised ironically in 'My Bugle and Why I Blow It' – and this helped fulfil his chilling teenage prophesy of 'scorning all, and shunned by all, by turns'. It was also functional: if you're sleeping rough (as he was in his final years), it is useful to have your bedding on your back. Certainly the look was peripathetic and turned him into one of those Dublin street characters known by their sobriquets, like his contemporary, Zozimus, or the ones I recall from my college days: the Diceman and the Poet of Grafton Street.

Mangan's look was studied and deliberative. Wakeman felt that 'he seemed to court the reputation of an oddity' and I think this is right and that he was motivated by his reading of the Romantics. Like their heirs, twentieth-century rock stars, the Romantics were performance artists who made their lives extensions of their art. Dublin's most famous Romantic, Charles Maturin, had a distinctive look, which the *Dublin University Magazine* called 'coxcomb'. Nobody would say that of Mangan's look and neither was he dashing like his idol, Byron, but then he didn't have to be since his poetry didn't boast of sexual conquest. Romanticism wasn't about slavishly following a specific look; it was about the life mirroring the work and back round again. Through his cloak, and carefully cultivated air of mystery, and shaded green spectacles (a distinctly Romantic prop*), Mangan successfully connected his melancholic, fleeting, lonely verse to his solitary, shadowy, mysterious life.

Because his look was as definite in its own way as Charlie Chaplin's, it has inspired artists. The sketch that Charles Mills provided for D.J. O'Donoghue's centenary edition of the poems (1903) has all the accessories, except the green spectacles, but the stance is too sprightly, and I find the image slightly twee (next page, top).

I prefer the Harry Kernoff woodcut that I bought at the stall at the Christmas Fair in the Point. It gets across the shadow and mystery, but I think Mangan looks a bit naked, stripped of his costume and props (next page, bottom left).

My favourite is this sketch done by my brother, which captures the shrouded look, and the shadows and phantoms, the lurch of drink and drugs, the Liberties streets (next page, bottom right).

This was the man whom Duffy was pinning his hopes on to provide the 'unceasing crackle of sparkling musketry' to 'excite national hopes'. Duffy knew he had his work cut out because a few years earlier he had asked Mangan for political articles for the *Belfast Vindicator* and Mangan had refused – 'I have had no experience in that *genre d'écrire* and I should inevitably blunder' – and sent instead some whimsical squibs he called 'facetiae', 'whim-whams', 'scraps and scrapings'. These might be described as political in the broad sense of being anarchic and satirical, but they weren't the chest-thumping nationalism that Duffy was hoping for.

It was beyond Duffy (and, to be fair, everyone else) to notice the subtle politics that Mangan was sneaking into the conservative *Dublin University Magazine*. In an 1837 article on Turkish and Persian poetry he had launched a remarkable attack on the European

---

*Wordsworth wore green spectacles, as did Beau Brummell and, in another one of the uncanny Poe–Mangan links, Edgar Allan Poe gave them to his fictional detective C. Auguste Dupin.

JAMES CLARENCE MANGAN

(From a Drawing by Charles Mills)

"JAMES CLARENCE MANGAN"

'Orientalists', accusing them of 'regarding the Asiatics as a subordinate and degraded caste of mortals' and of 'communicating few or no impressions of Asia that were not imperfect and unsatisfactory … Because the two continents differed – because the moral character of Europe was reckoned austerer than that of Asia – because Asia was not Europe, the literature of Asia was pronounced unworthy of a comparison with the literature of Europe'.

This is uncannily like Edward Said's *Orientalism*, the iconic text of my undergraduate degree, and I can imagine the excitement of my professors had they come across this passage which proves what they were telling us: that the Irish, having been 'othered' by England, had special insight into orientalism. Thanks to Said's fame, Mangan's argument now reads like a direct attack on Empire and, since it appeared in a unionist journal, an obvious provocation, but I guess it didn't read that way then, his ideas being in advance of his time. Had Mangan sent such a sophisticated argument into *The Nation*, I doubt they would have printed it.

Duffy, resigned to not getting bellicose political essays, focused on eliciting poems to 'foster national feeling'. This took him three and a half years and he only succeeded through a national catastrophe. The story of Mangan at *The Nation* is hilarious but obfuscated. I needed a magnifying glass to work it out.

*

The Nation had two poetry sections, 'Poet's Corner' and 'College Green Rhymes', where it featured three or four poems per issue. These were, for the most part, truly terrible: e.g.

> Be bold, united, firmly set / Nor flinch in word or tone / We'll be a glorious nation yet / Redeemed – erect – alone ('Songs of the Nation')

Oh! 'twere merry unto the grave to go / If one were sure to be buried so (by 'A True Celt')

Lo! Freedom again hath appear'd on our hills. / Already the isle her divinity fills (by 'Shamrock')

They don't just seem terrible to us now with all our learned postmodernist scorn towards rhyme and patriotism; no one rated them at the time either. Even O'Connell sneered publicly at 'the poor rhymed dullness' of *The Nation*'s ballads, and he wasn't known for his literary taste and his massive ego should have been stroked by a particularly nauseating eulogy in the paper (5 November 1842) ending 'And as his eyes were raised to heav'n – from whence his mission came / He stood amid the thousands there a monarch, save in name'.

Clearly there was a house style: solemn, uplifting, patriotic and earnest, which Mangan snubbed when he sent in 'The Blackwater – a Ditty Eulogistic of that Magnificent River' with its run of rhymes mimicking the flow of the river: crack-water, slack water, track water, lack water, arrack-water, tabac-water, snack water; brack water, attack water, etc. Duffy refused this poem for the poetry column but I spotted it – this is where the magnifying glass comes in – buried in the small print of the column 'Answers to Correspondents' on 22 March 1845 accompanied by a little homily definitely written by Duffy (he reproduces it in his memoirs): 'Horace Walpole holds that it is only a man of genius can trifle agreeably, and here we have the truest poet this country has produced in our days … writing versicles very much akin to the nonsense verse with which Swift and his friends made war against spleen and blue devils.'

'Answers to Correspondents' was the slush pile – where stuff that wasn't judged good enough to for the main poetry pages, ended up. It's not where you'd expect to find the country's 'truest poet' but it's where most of Mangan's poems for *The Nation* appeared until 1846. Almost all the rejected poems are comic pieces like 'The Blackwater' and were consigned to the slush pile with Duffy's little headmasterly notes urging a more serious approach, e.g. 'Last, and by no means least comes one whose name will some day be illustrious in literature. It must not be written here with a mere bagatelle thrown off in a moment of relaxation; but it will write itself in marble' (*The Nation*, 18 March 1843).

It wasn't that Duffy disliked comic verse; when he first met Mangan in 1836, he confessed to him that he preferred his comic verse in *The Comet* to his serious translations, and he occasionally let humour into the main poetry section of *The Nation*, as long as it was political, e.g. 'This is the house that Paddy Built' (10 December 1842), a tedious satire on the parliament at Westminster. What he seems to have objected to in Mangan's verse was its lack of politics and atmosphere of exuberant silliness. Perhaps he felt obscurely that he was being mocked and perhaps he was right. Duffy took to the review pages to try and get Mangan to come onside – 'How we wish the author of "The Barmecides" would lend his help to an Irish ballad history! His power of making his verses racy of the soil cannot be doubted (*The Nation*, 16 November 1844).

The Nation was Ireland's most popular paper and Mangan was hyper-competitive and badly needed the money and yet he kept sending in 'whim-whams' and 'facetiae' that he knew would be rejected. I find his provocative obstinacy magnificent, particularly when I worked out what lay behind it (beyond innate contrariness). Mangan wasn't fundamentally opposed to revolutionary uprising – he would go on to write incendiary stuff for John Mitchel – but he was phobic about Duffy's chest-thumping nationalism. Duffy didn't have much taste in poetry, but he had enough to know that he was printing terrible stuff and excluding clever stuff like, for instance, 'The Queen of Spain', Mangan's translation of an anonymous

German children's song about the real-life Isabel II of Spain, who was three years old when she succeeded her father to the throne in 1833. Mangan's version keeps the nursery rhyme feel:

The baby Queen of Spain,
How happy she must be!
Her crowns are two, her years are three;
She governs Leon and Castile;
She has the world to lose or gain.
O, dear! what rapture must she feel,
The may-as-yet or may-not be,
The baby may-be Queen of Spain!

In its chillingly jolly way – I love the refrain that gets its knickers in a twist – the poem is anti-monarchical, riffing on the absurdity of placing a crown on a toddler. That should have pleased the revolutionary Duffy, but he was nervous of Mangan's 'nonsense' and so this too went into the small print of 'Answers to Correspondents'. Refusing witty poems that don't meet your political agenda and accepting bad poetry that does is propaganda. Irony, rather than truth, is the antonym to propaganda and Mangan was the consummate ironist. A line from his memoir seems like his answer to Duffy: 'I cannot do so if I would, and I know that I would not if I could.'

And maybe he was also getting a fetishistic kick out of denying his 'handy young man' (who had gone and got married). I dislike Duffy for his propaganda (and for his failure to visit the dying Mangan in hospital or attend his funeral because he was dancing attendance on the famous British essayist, Thomas Carlyle) so I took 'diseased gratification' in tracking their hilariously dysfunctional relationship through the small print and was sorry to see Mangan suddenly give in and submit two rabble-rousing poems in late 1844.

These made it straight into the main poetry section, signed with his initials, J.C.M., in case anyone should miss that they are the work of the 'truest poet in Ireland', which they could well have because the two German translations 'A Lane for Freedom' (23 November) and 'Our Fatherland' (28 December) are very tired. 'A Lane for Freedom' calls for armed uprising:

> Why waste your burning energy
> In void and vain defiance,
> And phrases fierce but fugitive?
> Tis deeds, not words, that I weigh –
> Your swords and guns alone can give
> To Freedom's course a highway!

Poets weigh words, not deeds, and Mangan always identified with what was 'fugitive' and 'wasted': the poem is somewhere between apathetic and subversive of its own bellicose messaging. A letter Mangan wrote to Duffy at this time reinforces this sense of apathy and continual underminings:

> My poor mother lies dangerously ill – and I cannot leave her … Before the end of the week … I will call at *The Nation* office … to arrange the plan, or system, upon which my poor contributions to *The Nation* shall be – I will not say *received*, but – *proffered*. I will write for you, from the beginning of next year, either in prose or verse, as you please.
>
> I would express to you, my dear friend, my sincere regret, that you are compelled to devote such a large proportion of your journal to 'frothy speeches' (I quote the words of your own paper). Believe me, that until you remedy this defect, the great mass of earnest readers will peruse even *The Nation* with some degree of apathy and indifference.

This explains why Mangan is finally giving in to the demand for propaganda – to get money for his mother – and his words follow the contortions of his restlessly divided mind: his promise to 'arrange a plan' is undermined by the sarcasm of the italicised verbs, which gesture to all the *proffered* poems consigned to the slush pile, which is then undone by his submissive pledge to give Duffy what he pleases, which is in turn undercut by his demurely ferocious attack on the 'frothy' speeches, for which read also frothy poems, and the admission, like a knife in Duffy's heart, that the paper leaves him apathetic and indifferent …

Fortunately, his mother recovered, and he went back to his Bartleby-like refusals. In the whole of 1845, he had just one poem in the main poetry section, the rousing 'Baghdad is Taken!' (30 August) about the conquest of that city in 1638. On 7 February 1846 he sent in an immensely clever and witty poem, which didn't make it out of the slush pile. 'The Iron Man' is a translation from an obscure German poet describing a real-life statue in Strasbourg of a soldier 'looking down on the market below'. The German poem juxtaposes the age and immovability of the statue with the constantly changing life around it. From this rather trite trope, Mangan scripted an ironic anti-war poem:

> In Strasbourg town, be it known, there stands
> An Iron Man on a pillar.
> He bears a lance and a shield in his hands,
> And he wears a heavy old helmet:
> He is covered with rust and dust, and hath
> A drearyish obsolete look from the path.
> The crowd pass him by, but there still are
> A few quaint folk of the middle age sect,
> Who bow to him often with a deal of respect,
> And cry: 'Hail friend! We are well met.'

II

For me, I confess when I eye this wight
I fancy I gaze on an emblem
Of the spirit of war in our age of light!
He too, seems armed as whilome;
But the rust of opinion is on his lance,
And there he stands and he can't advance,
For the People, when chiefs assemble 'em,
Fight now-a-days – shy! Even Germany cowers,
And France has forgotten her ginger-bread towers,
And Albion skulks in her isle home!

What a brilliant poem! On any reading it stands out for its startlingly unrhythmic 'drearyish obsolete look' but when you spot it in the sin bin of 'Answers to Correspondents', it gives the finger to the patriotic rhyming of 'Poet's Corner'. The rusting Iron Man recalls Ozymandias but where Shelley aims his mockery at the statue (or its subject), here the mockery is refracted – on the pompous statue certainly, but also on the town of Strasbourg and on all Europe, which glorifies war through its emblems but 'fights shy', and in a final sleight-of-hand the attack extends to the whole idea of war: the 'gingerbread towers' reduce French fortifications to something out of Hansel and Gretel.

Mangan embeds one of his hermetic jokes in his poem: he knows that Duffy will demote it to 'Answers to Correspondents' where readers will 'pass it by'. This remains the fate of both the poem – which is constantly passed by for anthologies – and the statue itself, which is still in situ in Strasbourg in the square named for it but is so submerged within a whirling traffic artery that commuters continually pass it by.

Three and a half years into *The Nation*, Duffy and Mangan remained at a stand-off: propagandist and refusenik. And then, two weeks after 'The Iron Man', an original Mangan poem, not a translation, 'The Warning Voice' featured in the main section of the paper and excited Duffy to slavering praise – a few issues later he called it 'the most impressive poem, perhaps, we have ever published'.

I don't agree, and neither I'm guessing do others because 'The Warning Voice' isn't included in any recent Mangan anthology. It opens: 'Ye faithful! – ye Noble! / A day is at hand / Of trial and trouble / And woe to the land' and goes on to warn of Terror, Shame, expiring Hope, phrenetic Sorrow, darkness, suffering, sore tribulation, stormy commotion, Dearth, Sadness, etc. It is all very portentous and non-specific – the reader never learns why all this horror is coming – but it is no surprise that Duffy loved this poem since it has an explicit call to arms: 'To this generation … The struggle of class against class / The Sword and the War-vest'.

'The Warning Voice' marks the beginning of a new phase for Mangan at *The Nation*. In the remaining ten months of 1846, he had twenty-eight poems published in the main section, averaging more than one a fortnight, and these included a few rabble-rousers and many Irish ballads that were 'racy of the soil'. How did Duffy get what he wanted? The clue is in the paragraph that preceded the 'The Warning Voice':

THE FAMINE – O'CONNELL'S MOTION. Once more the grim phantom of Irish misery has been held up before the averted eyes of our Legislators. They will not look at their own hideous work. They seem, in words, to admit the coming death, disease, and death – speak with conventional phrase of sympathy about it – hint obscurely at some beggarly relief they have been providing – and then wave their hands and bid the spectre vanish.

O'Connell has, however, drawn from them the acknowledgement on the part of Government to do something.

> We shall see, in course of time, what they have in store for us besides an Insurrection Act. But we warn our countrymen not to trust them.

This explains the poem's desperate urgency and its unusual absence of irony: after a lifetime of fearing 'impending doom', Mangan has something calamitous to warn about. Our knowledge of the horror that the poem was responding to, and the far worse horrors to come, preserves for 'The Warning Voice' something of the outsized acclaim that Duffy and other nineteenth-century commentators heaped on it. And it marks the breaking of the impasse between editor and poet. It was nothing Duffy said or did, but he got lucky, if that is not too grotesque a word to use for a national calamity: within a few months, Mangan's famine masterpieces including 'Siberia', 'Dark Rosaleen' and 'A Vision of Connaught' would reach *The Nation*'s million listeners.

Mangan's requiem

Mangan's autobiography belongs to his childhood and youth in theme and content, but in conception and delivery it belongs to the last months of his life. In obvious and not so obvious ways, it is his requiem.

For all of the twentieth century, the idea of the memoir's missing half remained as a tantalising possibility for Manganistas. The idea feeds into a wider narrative of his absent archive, those missing letters, papers and manuscripts perhaps still stashed around Dublin and the world (maybe taken by Duffy and John Mitchel to Australia or America). In the John McCall Papers in the National Library of Ireland, there is a reference to some Mangan papers held in 'McNally's house in Brookefield', which set my pulse going the way I guess it has raced scholars' pulses for well over a century. The idea that material might still emerge was given a boost in 1920 when an unusually long and buoyant letter did turn up, and turned out to be authentic, but as the decades went by, hopes faded, until in 2001 the legend of the lost remnant of memoir had a final unlikely surge.

On 28 September 2001 the *Times Literary Supplement* included, in its back-page column of miscellanies, the following paragraph:

The Irish poet James Clarence Mangan (1803–1849) was the subject of Brian Moore's brilliant novel, *The Mangan Inheritance*. His real life is somewhat obscure and scholars have long wondered about the fate of his 'lost Autobiography' described by one as 'the last great unpublished work of Irish literature'. A section of it was published in the nineteenth century by a Catholic priest, Fr Meehan, who however claimed that Mangan was an heretic, and that no more of his dreadful writing existed. Now, though, the remainder of the autobiography has turned up, thanks to the researches of the Dublin poet, James McCabe. It amounts to about ten pages and appears in the Irish literary magazine, *Metre*.

Five months later, the same column came back to the subject with a shamefaced update:

The other day we received a letter from Jacques Chuto, co-editor of the ongoing *Complete Works* of J.C. Mangan, on the subject of the discovery [of the 'lost Autobiography']: 'Your readers will perhaps be interested to hear that this text will not be included in the volumes of Mangan's prose soon to be published. McCabe's "find" is in fact a fake.' So *Metre* has been hoaxed? No – they are the hoaxers. Professor Chuto continues: 'It was concocted, as McCabe has gleefully informed me, "to tomfool a few English".'

Our resident expert on Clarence Mangan is his twentieth century namesake, Gerald Mangan, who wrote about his poetry in the *TLS* of September nineteenth, 1997. He was naturally intrigued to hear of the discovery, brought to light by *Metre*, and like us he was taken in. 'Mangan himself was famous for pseudonymous impostures of the kind,' he told us. 'But even an expert has to read McCabe's spoof very closely to detect the tell-tale flaws. It's an abuse of the reader's confidence.'

The *TLS's* 'resident expert on Clarence Mangan' – the coincidence of whose name seems to have created such a misleading sense of security – seems to be spinning in all directions: he says the imposture is in the spirit of Mangan but also that it's an abuse of the reader's confidence (true, those statements aren't mutually exclusive). But when you turn to *Metre* to read the 'lost autobiography' you wonder how anyone, expert or not, was ever taken in. Here is how it is introduced by its supposed finder, James McCabe:

> Late last summer, I followed a trail from Pearse Street via SS Michael and St John's to a damp and draughty loft in Copper Alley where, right enough, fifteen music notebooks and countless loose leaves found in an old tea-chest held the last great unpublished work of Irish literature. My only guess as to why this treasure trove has remained undisturbed until now despite the frenetic activity of the Manganites remains the simple fact that none of them have been Dubliners, and none of them have thought of doing what any Dubliner would have done – follow his nose …

This is a piece of obvious pastiche and burlesque. Even if you don't pick up on the sly Manganese allusions – e.g. the music notebooks; Copper Alley where his cousins lived; 'following the nose' from his dream and his first short story – and even if you don't know that Copper Alley was bulldozed decades ago and now only survives in the name of a pub, and that there are no houses left in the Liberties dating from Mangan's period, and that there hasn't been a tea chest spotted in Ireland since the 1980s, and that numerous Manganistas, including John McCall, James Joyce, David Lloyd and David Wheatley have been Dubliners … even if you're not Irish and have never been in Dublin and have never heard of Mangan, you would spot this as pastiche because: a *tea chest in an attic containing a long lost treasure trove!* This is Tintin.

The text itself does a better job at verisimilitude with lots of convincingly Manganese lines – 'I am in this respect quite a phenomenon: I am literally all nerves and no muscles' – but some of it reads suspiciously like exposition with its overt references to bars and people that Mangan is known to have frequented, and it doesn't manage the vertiginous swoop, Mangan's 'disappear here', when the text is suddenly whisked from under you, and there are none, or few, of the stray unattributed quotes from other authors which Mangan liked to embed in his prose, and which gave Chuto and the other editors so much work tracking them down.

What the *TLS*'s willingness to be 'taken in' speaks to is their complete ignorance of Mangan, unsurprising since he never had a UK reputation, and to a romantic view of Ireland that is strangely persistent in Britain. Though Ireland more and more resembles just another prosperous western European democracy, it can still appear to British readers like a land of leprechauns and poteen. I think the *TLS* was taken in because its editors wanted Ireland to be a country where the long-lost manuscripts of alcoholic geniuses turn up in attics down ghostly alleys, undisturbed after a century and a half.

The hoax hugely annoyed Chuto who complained to *Metre*'s editor, David Wheatley, that at a time when he and the other editors were trying to establish a comprehensive, authoritative Collected Works, the fake would create 'a new confusion'. I'm generally on Chuto's side in the Mangan wars but for once I think that his sense of humour deserted him, probably because he picked up on the dig at the 'frenetic activity of Manganites … none of them Dubliners' as a surly reference to him (a Breton) and the other editors of the collected works (Dutch and American). I don't think the pastiche was ever going to create any real confusion. It seems a clever way of reviving attention for Mangan and highlighting his exciting impostures, as well as a tribute to the memoir's enduring mystery, its refusal to be explained away.

It was a summer's evening when I met the author of the hoax, James McCabe, in the snug of the Stag's Head, off Dame Street. He seemed to arrive out of the gloom, suddenly standing before me, slim and restless, saying conspiratorially that this was where he and David Wheatley had 'plotted the hoax' and that 'it was a tavern in Mangan's time, and he probably drank here'. This was excellent scene-setting, but our conversation proved to be at frustratingly cross-purposes: he wanted to tell me everything he knew about Mangan, whereas I wanted to cut to the chase and talk about the hoax, a subject in which he seemed curiously uninterested. When pressed, he said off-handedly that he had written the second part of the autobiography 'ages before it was published in *Metre*' and added carelessly ,'I might go back and finish it one day' before getting back to telling me that Hermann Melville based his character Bartleby the Scrivener on Mangan – a theory I'd come across but which seems to me incredibly unlikely since Melville wrote his short story in 1853, six years before John Mitchel introduced Mangan to America. (I agree that in his obstinate reticence and passive aggression, Bartleby is a very Mangan-like figure, but I think that says more about what the job of scrivening does to you.)

As McCabe discoursed on 'the artist figure without a patron, a trope in Gaelic writing', the word that came irresistibly to mind was man[gan]splaining and I began to feel like I was trapped in one of those biographies so stuffed with information that it shields, rather than reveals, its subject, so that in desperation I cut him off rudely mid-sentence to ask: 'But what do you think Mangan was *like*?' He paused briefly and then pronounced, 'I think he was a very playful, slightly wizardy type of character,' which put me so forcibly in mind of Ireland's current president, that I began to despair – there is nothing Mangan-like about our president – but then, with a sudden abrupt turn, McCabe said: 'In his poems, he always uses the past and future tense, never the present, which is fascinating to me, it's almost like he doesn't exist' and that was fascinating to *me* – Mangan's 'disappear here' – so I tried to get him to expand on it, but he had moved on. And so it went: in and around discoursing on Manganalia that I already knew, he would say something arresting that I would leap on – e.g. 'the poem that hooked me was "A Vision of Connaught", that's the gateway poem';* or 'that essay "The Sixty-Drop Dose of Laudanum" is like Coleridge's table-talk';† or 'I did my MA on Mangan; it was called "The Apparitional Moment" and I wrote it in gobbledy-gook, proto-*Finnegans Wake* language.'

It seems characteristic that, after we parted, McCabe began sending me academic essays on Mangan which I hadn't asked for but didn't send me his thesis which I did ask for repeatedly since I felt it would provide the clue as to how he produced the parody of Mangan's memoir. Eventually I came to see his obstinacy in telling me only what he wanted to impart, and not what I wanted to hear, as peculiarly Manganese. And I was indebted to him for an insight which brought me closer to solving the mystery of the memoir.

At the end of our conversation, he took from his bag a deck of tarot cards and fanned them out in front of me, instructing me to 'pick one'. I plucked from the clustered centre and got an absolute shiver of fear and gratification when I saw that I had picked the Devil. McCabe was as off-hand and unsurprised at this as at everything else: 'not *necessarily bad*,' he said, taking the card out of my hand to return it to the pack. 'It denotes obsession.' Later, when I looked up tarot meanings, I found that the Devil also means addiction, the shadow side and unhealthy co-dependency, which, being an

---

*A brilliant aperçu – among Manganistas I've spoken to, including Shane MacGowan, David Lloyd and a former Provost of Trinity, 'A Vision of Connaught' is the poem that drew us all in.

†A Max Beerbohm cartoon entitled 'The Table Talk of Samuel Taylor Coleridge' depicting the poet at the head of a table talking into his glass, flanked by two rows of identically bald men, yawning in unison like walruses, reminds me of Duffy's description of Mangan's 'delightful monologues on poetry and metaphysics', which seems to suppress a shudder of horror at the memory of being submitted to those monologues …

uncannily accurate description of Mangan and my relationship to him, I took as a Sign, though I was unnerved to discover that the card can also mean entrapment and restriction, a Sign perhaps that I was lost in the labyrinth of research … This was hardly flattering but I was always envious of those other Manganistas like Shane MacGowan, Brian Moore, David Lloyd and David Wheatley, to whom the Master appeared as a ghost in their dreams and visions. I was constantly inviting him into *my* dreams but he never came and I couldn't help taking this as a snub – on my gender perhaps since Mangan's sensibility, though not at all macho, is somehow very masculine, or on my prosaicness, my not being a poet, novelist or rockstar – and for this reason I was ready to accept meekly every unflattering implication of the card, since any contact was better than none, though I regretted not registering whether I had drawn the card upright or reversed (it makes all the difference, apparently).

It seemed very Mangan to contact me through the occult, but when I looked up images of the Rider Waite tarot Devil with his faun's legs and heron's feet, his blazing eyes and cuckold's horns and, most sinister of all somehow, his hairy paunch, he seemed to me in his aggressive aura and insignia so exactly Mangan's opposite, that I began to grow doubtful whether the card was in fact a Sign from Mangan, and wondered if perhaps it denoted someone else entirely, some sinister figure from my past perhaps. And then one afternoon, a few weeks after I had met McCabe, it came to me, in the sudden random unconnected way that you recall a dream from the night before, just who the Devil it was.

*

The long memoir is one of the few creative works of Mangan's that survives in manuscript – the other surviving manuscripts are mostly letters – and it is also the text of Mangan's about which we have the most information: we know when it was written, and where, and how Mangan reacted to criticism of it. We have one man to thank for both its preservation and its contextualising: Fr C.P.M. Meehan, who asked Mangan to write the memoir and kept it safe (until he lost it) and, when it was finally published, annotated and explained it.

I was always aware of Fr Meehan's role in the memoir, and I always included him in the telling, but the way you might include a minor character in a play, who appears on stage at a critical moment to advance the plot but is too inconsequential to be given a personality or a backstory. I'm not sure at what point it was that I realised that Meehan's fingerprints are all over the narrative, and not just on the inside cover of the music book where he signed off.

My main interest initially was in *why* Meehan had got Mangan to write the memoir. He was a historian as well as a priest, so maybe he wanted Mangan's recollections for the record? And he was, like Mangan, a Young Irelander, committed to the repeal of the Union – maybe he hoped Mangan's life story would inspire young people to take up the nationalist cause? And he was a follower of Fr Mathew, 'the apostle of temperance', and had tried to persuade Mangan to take the pledge not to drink, but without success, so maybe he hoped that going back over past events would give Mangan insight into his addictions?

All, or any, of these reasons would explain why Meehan took against the memoir on reading it since it didn't fulfil any of these expectations, but at the periphery of my mind I was also registering just how present Meehan is throughout. He is always *there* – not just at the memoir's conception, but at its first reading, its critical reception. Every time you have a query about the memoir, up he pops telling you how it came about and what you should think, and this began to make me suspicious, the way the police grow suspicious when someone keeps returning to the scene of the crime. It suddenly struck me as astonishing that he has emerged as the hero of the tale, the man who commissioned the memoir and with 'characteristic generosity' allowed it to be published, when in fact he denounced it, mislaid it, publicly denigrated it, and may be responsible for fragmenting it (his words in the inside cover – 'the remnant [sequel] of the biography never came into my possession; and I fear the author either lost or destroyed it' – are precise and suggest that he *did* see this remnant but didn't try to ensure that the two parts remained together).

And then I came across two pieces of information, the effect of which I can only describe in the lurid terms of Gothic literature: the hairs stood up on the back of my neck.

The first came via the critic David Lloyd, who noticed something highly significant in two passages of Mangan's, written within months of each other. The first, the description of his father in the long memoir, is well known (it even gets into *Finnegans Wake*):

> [My father's] temper was not merely quick and irascible, but it also embodied much of that calm concentrated spirit of Milesian* fierceness … His nature was truly noble … If anyone can imagine such an idea as a human boa-constrictor *without his alimentative propensities*, he will be able to form some notion of the character of my father. … His grand worldly fault was – improvidence. To any one who applied to him for money he uniformly gave double or treble the sum requested of him.

The second is from Mangan's profile of Fr Meehan for his series 'Sketches and Reminiscences of Irish Writers' and presumably written shortly after the memoir since it was published in *The Irishman* (12 May 1849):

---

* The Milesians, alleged to be Iberian warriors who conquered Ireland around 1000 BC, were a medieval invention but were taken as historical fact until the late nineteenth century.

The disposition and temper of Mr Meehan are lively, quick and bordering on choleric. His Milesian blood courses rather too hotly through his veins. He is carried away by impulse … But he is a man of a lofty and generous nature. Anything like hypocrisy is as alien from his heart and soul as the snake is from his native land.

Freud says that we go through life casually assigning to the people we meet the roles of our parents or primary carers and acting out our relations to them, but you don't have to be an analyst to spot Mangan's assignation of the biological father to the spiritual father – he bestows on both men quick, Milesian tempers, impulsive lofty souls and boundless generosity, and he seals the link through the snake.

Meehan was nine years younger than Mangan but as a curate of a prominent parish and a noted preacher, he was an authority figure and he tended to infantilise Mangan, describing him as 'wayward, irresolute', in need of 'words of encouragement and gentle attentions', which makes Mangan sound about nine years old (the world is full of wayward children; I never heard of a wayward adult). And of course, as a priest he was addressed by everyone as 'Father', a word which Mangan can never encounter without alarm bells going off.

Mangan wasn't exaggerating Meehan's temper: according to the entry on Meehan in the *Dictionary of Irish Biography*, written by Patrick Maume, 'he suffered badly from indigestion for most of his life, and this aggravated a testy personality and a waspish tongue. He regularly fell out with friends, and few parishioners were foolhardy enough to brave his confessional.' The image of the furious priest turning on his poor parishioners as they confess their pathetic sins is irresistible, but it was another piece of information in the entry that caught my attention and sealed my view of Meehan. Maume reveals that he wrote for *The Nation* under the pen-name of 'Clericus'. I checked 'Clericus' out and he was quite as bad as other *Nation* poets ('Then, lovely Erin, weep no more – / the night of thy bondage shall soon be o'er'). Now the relationship between Mangan and Meehan was revealed to me as that of true artist to failed artist: Mozart to Salieri.

The envy and malignancy of the mediocre composer Antonio Salieri towards the genius Wolfgang Amadeus Mozart is imprinted on me because both my younger sister and Frank were obsessed with Miloš Forman's film *Amadeus*, which dramatises their relationship. In my mind the hitherto faceless Fr Meehan began to take on the features of F. Murray Abrahamson who plays Salieri in the film – the lowered eyes, soft voice and tight mouth in public, the unmasked rage and fury in private. I imagined Meehan railing like Salieri against God for bestowing Genius on this unworthy specimen, this useless addict and spendthrift, who shocked all Dublin by his drinking 'in the lowest and obscurest taverns, and in company with the offal of the human species'. Mangan must have known who 'Clericus' was – they wrote for the same paper – but in his profile of Meehan for 'Sketches of Irish Writers' he doesn't mention his poetry but praises him as a historian and critic, specifying his 'peculiar power of appreciating poetry at a glance'. The blanking of Meehan's creativity is possibly worse than Mozart farting as he plays a parody of Salieri's compositions.

Fr Meehan is Mangan's father, and he is Salieri, with the memoir as Mangan's requiem. These images played through my mind and were drawn together by the tarot card because both Mangan senior and Salieri are explicitly depicted as satanic. In *Amadeus*, the previously devout Salieri denounces God, breaks the crucifix, and vows to destroy the genius whom He has created and in the memoir Mangan uses three diabolic metaphors – snake, cat and huntsman – to depict the father as a Lucifer figure (a 'princely soul but no prudence') who addresses his son in cloven-hoofed terms – 'could he not behoof himself' – and wrests him from the paradise of reading to cast him into hell of the office, with its 'pestiferous atmosphere, the chimney of which smoked continually, and emitted a sulphurous exhalation'.

If Meehan is a failed poet jealous of Mangan and an irascible man with a waspish tongue whose parishioners are too scared to confess to him and whom Mangan equates with his satanic father, then this puts the commissioning and writing of Mangan's 'confessions' into a whole new light.

Meehan asks Mangan to write his life story for reasons that are both disinterested and malign. Probably he does want to get Mangan's testimony for posterity and to help him manage his addictions but, whether he admits it to himself or not, he is also jealous and proprietorial. His intention isn't, like Salieri's, to claim authorship of the 'requiem', which would be impossible, but he would like to position himself as its 'onlie begetter', the man who brought it into being. He excitedly envisages the memoir of a nationalist and/or a penitent sinner, which will end the way all such confessions should: with a stirring cry for Irish freedom and/or a mea culpa and pledge to never drink again. What he doesn't realise is that by making this demand of Mangan, he is setting himself up for failure and not just because Mangan is identifying him with his terrifying father, but because Mangan's overt meekness is deceptive, and he never gives editors what they want.

To fulfil the commission to write about his younger years, Mangan goes back to live on Fishamble Street, site of his childhood home, where he is provoked into writing an insulting account of his biological father, which has the effect, as must be his subconscious intent, of antagonising his spiritual father. When Meehan reacts with predictable rage and dismissiveness, Mangan performs one of his disappearing acts: he admits to dreaming the tale up and offers to destroy it. Meehan won't give up the music book (and by this refusal establishes his ownership of it) but he does enable, or ignore, the destruction or disappearance of the second half, the mysterious 'remnant', and at some point over the next three decades he does let the music book 'escape his keeping' (a studiedly impersonal phrase, which serves to release him from blame for losing it). Once the memoir is in the public domain, he inserts himself back into the narrative, re-publishing it himself, together with annotations and an introduction calculated to devalue it.

Shannon-Mangan is more alert than previous biographers to Meehan's sinister role in the narrative of the memoir; she is sure that 'Mangan must have been very hurt by Meehan's response'. My immediate riposte was that Mangan can't have been 'very hurt' because he provoked the response, but then I realised that she is on to something: provocation doesn't exclude hurt and is consistent with the pattern, familiar to therapists, of abused people seeking out relationships that re-enact the abuse they suffered as a child.

For the longest time I was puzzled by Yeats's handwringing over the memoir being 'full of terrible untrue things that [Mangan] believed' because why wouldn't a poet get that another poet might be writing figuratively and metaphorically? But what Yeats was responding to is the memoir's inchoate, repetitive quality, which is not that of a misery memoir but of a dream, or the closest thing we get to a dream in waking life, the free association of psychoanalysis. The memoir reads like one of Freud's case studies and like them it brings you back to the original hurt of childhood 'where tiny is tiny and massive is massive' and this is not a place where adult readers are ever comfortable because we are supposed to grow out of childish things and the spectacle of a grown man behaving like a child is always embarrassing, unnerving, *wrong*. Even the usually adoring Shannon-Mangan rebukes Mangan for being so upset with his father for removing him from school, pointing out that 'there was nothing unusual in a fifteen-year-old being put to work' and commending his parents for selecting an occupation 'congenial to his temperament'. She is in effect telling him to 'grow up' but Mangan, back near his childhood home, has regressed to childhood and is projecting his hurt onto Meehan, the 'father' forcing him to revisit his past. And because Meehan is not a trained therapist, the session doesn't go well – instead of keeping quiet and letting Mangan free-associate, Meehan is projecting his own unresolved issues, his anger and sense of artistic failure, onto Mangan, who gets stuck in what analysts call the repetition compulsion, going around and around the same images of sickness and serpents. And yet something is shifting all the same (perhaps the mere act of free-associating is having an effect) because in the final scene of the memoir, with its encouraging images of sun, nature and human interaction, the narrator seems to be on his way to escaping the cycle.

Unfortunately, it is at exactly this point that Meehan breaks off the session. By questioning Mangan's recall and truthfulness, and by overseeing the severing of the narrative, he suspends Mangan mid-session, deprives him of ownership of his own story, and prevents closure. Meehan knows nothing about analysis obviously, but he is also breaking the code of the confessional – a priest, like an analyst, should listen to his parishioners with tolerance, not cut them off mid-sentence with accusations of lying and blasphemy ('that is not a *faithful* picture').

What is remarkable is Mangan's intuition about what is taking place, in contrast to Meehan's impregnable obtuseness still intact three decades later when he smugly recorded their exchanges. Mangan's 'I dreamed it' signals subliminal awareness and establishes his paradoxical control of the narrative. Meehan is the memoir's father, midwife, archivist, annotator, critic and vandaliser and, in fulfilling these roles, he emerges as the villain of the piece. The villain is conventionally seen as master of any situation he is in, but just as in S&M, where paradoxically the masochist is ultimately dominant, Meehan is ultimately Mangan's instrument:

the person chosen and manipulated to deliver the story in the way that Mangan wants it told. Meehan's comments are intended to denigrate the memoir but instead they accentuate our sense of it as a piece of perfect Manganese: a relict whose survival is a kind of miracle, a fragment whose sequel may still be out there, and a nightmare spilling unfiltered from the psyche. When Meehan triumphantly claims for himself the last word, calling the memoir a '*rêve d'une vie*', apparently unaware that he is parroting Mangan's 'I dreamt it', you feel towards him a tender, if patronising, sympathy; he has no idea that he is being played.

The death and burial of James Clarence Mangan

When Mangan died, everyone in attendance at his sickbed, morgue or funeral – and everyone listening in through the rumour mill in Dublin – had their say. There are many more sources for his death and burial than for his first three decades of life, and enough supporting characters and atmospheric touches that it can be recounted with all the ghoulish specificity of a Gothic horror story:

On Wednesday 13 June 1849 the celebrated eye doctor William Wilde takes a walk from his surgery in Westland Row up to the Liberties. It is warm and sunny, like previous days, and this is causing panic: 'Our fears proportionately increase with the growing heat of the weather,' writes the *Belfast News Letter* grimly. The country is in the grip of a cholera epidemic and, as everyone knows, cholera flares in the heat, though no one knows why exactly. The Liberties is one of the worst-hit areas in the country, no surprises there – within a fortnight, the *Waterford News and Star* will announce with veiled triumph that 'Cholera is now principally confined to the filthy parts of Dublin'.

The Liberties *is* filthy and horribly overcrowded – in 1840 the journalist and philanthropist Mrs Hall had found 108 people living in one house and that was before the potato blight and the influx of hundreds of thousands of rural migrants fleeing starvation, disease and eviction. By 1849 migrants are coming from both directions: up from the southwestern seaboard and returned from British ports that are refusing to take any more disease-ridden Irish peasants. Dublin doesn't want to take them either – a city councillor observes that 'two thirds of Dublin's cholera cases are among vagrants, from distant parts of the country, who came to Dublin in a state of great destitution, in fact almost dead from starvation'.

Over a hundred people this week will be admitted to the cholera sheds in Kilmainham, where infectious patients are isolated, and half of them will die. The Board of Health has begged people to seek help as soon they have the 'premonitory symptoms' of cholera, which are minutely described as 'laxity of the bowels and vomiting, the matter discharged resembling whey, or thin gruel, or barley water'. But too many sit it out until they get the cramps and 'the skin on the hands and feet becomes wrinkled – the surface of the body cold, damp and clammy – the tongue moist, often white and loaded, always flabby and chilled, like a piece of dead fish'. These are the symptoms of extreme dehydration and when they manifest, patients have no more than twelve hours to live.

As Dr Wilde makes his way up Dame Street and into the Liberties, the smell becomes unbearable: it is the stench of overflowing gutters and open sewers (just one privy to each yard) mixed in with the rotting animal hides curing in the tanners, and bones boiled down to make glue, and the sweat and scuzz of unwashed clothes and bodies festering in the heat, and hanging over it all the unmistakeable fishy odour of cholera. This smell doesn't just disgust people, it terrifies them because they believe cholera is airborne. In London, Dr John Snow is putting the finishing touches to his seminal paper 'On the Mode of Communication of Cholera', which will prove that the disease is waterborne, but which will be ignored until the next cholera outbreak in 1855. For now, the medical profession concurs with the doctor who writes into the *Westmeath Independent*: 'That the sable poison ferments tissues through the medium of the atmosphere can hardly be controverted.'

Dr Wilde knows all about infectious disease – he has recently commissioned and edited a series on Famine fevers for a medical journal. It seems amazing, incredible really, that he should choose this moment to go to the Liberties 'on one of his antiquarian researches', but this is what the record states. Finding his way to 'a wretched hovel in Bride Street', he upturns a rare relic: the poet James Clarence Mangan 'in a state of indescribable misery and squalor', having dragged himself out of the cholera sheds and 'retired here to die'.

Six weeks earlier, when the first cases of cholera were reported in Ireland, Mangan had informed friends of his 'presentiment that he was doomed to fall victim to it' but he did nothing to save himself, 'maintaining that there was no such thing *in rerum natura* as contagion, and consequently that precautions of all sorts were unnecessary and delusive'. Remarkably for a pandemic-denier, he survived the cholera sheds, suggesting that he presented in time before he got the cramps and the flabby, chilled tongue, but when Dr Wilde discovers him in the hovel, he is in 'a pitiable condition': 'a shrunken and attenuated form, a wan, worn, ghastly face … fearful emaciation and pallor'. The whole country has this look, but in Mangan's case it's not just famine and cholera; it's the booze, laudanum and sleeping rough; he hasn't had a proper meal or a home since the death of his mother, three years ago.

Dr Wilde recognises the pitiable specimen – all of Dublin recognises Mangan and Wilde is betrothed to Jane Elgee, who as 'Speranza' is a fellow poet on *The Nation* – and now he sets about getting him to Meath Street Hospital, just ten minutes away by foot – but how does he get him there? Does he call for hospital porters? Does he carry him himself? Can he bear to lay hands on the wretched specimen who has become a kind of cockroach, 'crawling through our streets, grotesque in figure, mean in attire'? But Dr Wilde isn't squeamish. He is the 'dirtiest man in Dublin' – Shaw will call him 'beyond soap and water just as his Nietzschean son was beyond good and evil' – so perhaps picking up the diseased poet is nothing to him. Perhaps after admitting him to hospital, he returns to the Liberties to reprise his antiquarian hunt, *without washing his hands ...*

In Meath Street Mangan regains his status as not just another Liberties cholera victim but as the national poet. The head physician of the hospital is Dr William Stokes, Regius Professor of Medicine in Trinity College, 'a man whose worth is proverbial, whose fame is European'. He 'watches over Mangan personally for three days' for which he earns this pathetic encomium: 'You are the first man who has spoken a kind word to me for years,' a remark Dr Stokes treasures and repeats to his daughter, not recognising the classic junkie sense of victimhood and rank ingratitude (Mangan is a sponge who soaks up people's near-constant goodwill). The famous patient is also entrusted to Dr Gilbert, 'who knew him well and intimately and who did all in his power to alleviate the poor poet's bodily afflictions'.

The kind attention and the 'cleanliness and restoratives bring Mangan back for a very brief space to look upon dear life again with natural longing' – a wistful statement since the poet's 'natural longing' has only ever been for death but he does revive enough to 'pore over' the 'well-worn volume of German poetry' that he has brought with him from the hovel, and to start scribbling away 'on whatever strange scraps of paper happened to be within reach'. Noticing this, Dr Gilbert arranges 'without having the sufferer's suspicions aroused' to have 'a quantity of paper transmitted to him from time to time, ostensibly as wrappers around medicine bottles, powders etc, likewise giving peremptory orders to the nurse to on no account disturb her patient, but leave him as much as possible to himself'. (Why the elaborate subterfuge? Why not just present him upfront with paper for writing? But the 'medicine wrappers' fit with a pattern of Mangan writing on whatever is at hand, as in the music book, and seem the perfect medium for his last words.)

He is 'assiduously waited on by a few friends' but the records don't specify which few. His famous friends are scattered or imprisoned: John Mitchel is a convict in Van Diemen's Land; Gavan Duffy is out of prison but apparently too busy preparing his tour of the west with Thomas Carlyle to visit. Anyway, Mangan doesn't have friends. He has colleagues and fans and well-wishers and benefactors, but if, as Yeats says, it takes 'heart-revealing intimacy' to 'find a friend' then this is beyond him, as he admits to himself with his usual mixture of pride and self-loathing: 'What cared I if those who attempted to break down, with their feeble fingers, the adamantine barrier that levered me from a communion with mankind, perceiving the futility of their enterprise, retired from my presence with disgust and despair?'

One who does come, but only because Mangan has asked for him, is his confessor, Fr Meehan, who so recently commissioned and took possession of his memoir. With his sinister talent for always being on hand as Mangan's recording angel, Fr Meehan now takes note of the poet's astonishing last words: 'I feel that I am going. I know that I must go unhousel'd and unanneal'd but you must not let me go unshriven and unanointed.' Fr Meehan recognises this as the terrifying plaint of the ghost in Hamlet who, having died without the Eucharist (unhousel'd) or extreme unction (unanneal'd), is denied heaven, but he doesn't know why Mangan would be quoting this when there is a priest on the ward, ready to administer at any hour. He decides nervously that the words must be 'playful', and a century and a half later Ellen Shannon-Mangan will concur, pointing out insightfully that the quote is a pun on 'un-housed' and 'un-annalled', which is to say homeless, without biography or archive, exactly Mangan's condition on his deathbed. Mordant playfulness is what we expect of the dying Mangan, but something more sinister is going on: he is signalling his intention to become a ghost. He knows this will discomfort Fr Meehan because the Church's position on ghosts is that you can pray them into heaven but if they start making excessive demands, then they must be exorcised. In the unconscious power struggle played out between poet and priest over the memoir, Mangan was the son provoking the father, but on his deathbed, he subverts this: by evoking the ghost, he becomes the father laying it on the son to do the necessary to free his soul from torment. What this might be is suggested by his words: Meehan must play his part in 'enshrining' and 'anointing' Mangan's poetic legacy.

Moving quickly on from the blasphemy of willed ghosthood, Fr Meehan gives us Mangan's final moments, which are edifyingly Catholic: 'The priest in attendance being called, heard his confession, and administered the Last Unction; Mangan with hands crossed on his breast and eyes uplifted, manifesting sentiments of most edifying piety, and with a smile on his lips faintly ejaculating "O, Mary, Queen of Mercy!" That was on Wednesday, twentieth June, and about ten o'clock that night, his soul was summoned to the Judgment Seat of God.'

When Dr Gilbert enters the ward and finds his patient dead, 'his first inquiry naturally was to ascertain if all of the old papers under the patient's pillow, and which he had amused himself scribbling on in his lucid intervals, were preserved intact?' (I love that 'first inquiry naturally', even his doctor is more interested in his poems than his health.) The papers aren't preserved – the 'fussy attendant', in an excess of hygiene, 'has just consigned the whole collection to the fire-grate', and the last written words of James Clarence Mangan have gone up in smoke.

His body is removed to the hospital morgue, where it remains for three days 'because of the difficulty of procuring either coffin or hearse, owing to the awful mortality then desolating the city'. But death has wrought a miracle: it has changed the poet from cockroach to angel:

Those who remember Clarence Mangan of late, crawling through our streets, grotesque in figure, mean in attire; bread, a comb, pens, and MS. sticking from his pockets, his hair long and unkempt, and with the dreamy enthusiasm of the opium-eater flickering at times across his sallow features, could have no idea how beautiful, yes, absolutely beautiful he looked in death. Nor physical pain nor mental anguish left a trace on his intellectual features. Unwrinkled was his domelike forehead, fit temple for the soul that had dwelt therein.

(This is Price writing; you would recognise those mixed metaphors anywhere.)

Dr Stokes makes a plaster cast for a death mask (which goes missing and is spotted, a century later in a bookshop, by Joyce's friend C.P. Curran) and on the morning of Thursday twenty-first, another 'sultry day', he calls into his young friend, the artist Frederic Burton, to ask him to come to the morgue – 'you never saw anything so beautiful in your entire life'. Burton finds 'the sight of poor Mangan … intensely interesting and pathetic' and makes an astonishing sketch, which he will present to the National Gallery of Ireland in 1872. Most reproductions crop the image, and you have to see the original to get the full effect of the long serpentine tendrils of hair, which give Mangan the drowned pre-Raphaelite look of Millais' Ophelia, but also suggest the Medusa, a ghastly association but not supererogatory

– Mangan has a thing about snakes and a petrifying glance; in his poems he turns living things to stone.

On Friday 22 June an obituary notice appears in *Saunders's News-Letter*, beginning 'Clarence Mangan is no more.' The next day he is buried in Glasnevin Cemetery. Five people attend his funeral. Three are named as his cousin Michael Smith, his confessor Fr Meehan and the journalist Joseph Brenan, whom Mangan addressed in a poem as 'brother and yet more than brother'; a fourth is referenced opaquely as 'one who had been for many years connected with *The Nation*' (Shannon-Mangan thinks this is Bernard Fulham, editor of *The Irishman*); the fifth is a blank. In his obituary in *The Irishman*, Joseph Brenan whips himself into an italicised frenzy:

> *Five* friends who knew the man and appreciated him – who were not lip-friends but heart-friends – attended him to his grave. *Five* humble individuals formed the burial cortege of one who, in another country, would have been attended by a royal following; *five* out of all to whose pleasure and instruction his genius ministered for years – a small number, passing small!

Fr Meehan says it was three.

News of the poet's death goes around the country. The tone of the newspapers is sombre but unsurprised. Just five months earlier 'an humble mechanic', signing himself 'Honestus', had written into *The Pilot* to describe Mangan's 'suffering and destitution' and 'venture an appeal on his behalf', which led to the 'State Prisoners in Kilmainham Gaol' (e.g. the political activists arrested after the Young Ireland uprising) contributing £3 10s to a 'Fund for the Relief of James Clarence Mangan'. The papers have been waiting for this death for a while and now they all rush out with virtually identical wording on 'poor Mangan'. In the *Waterford News and Star*, the death entry appears on 29 June, at the bottom of page 2, preceded by an astonishingly grisly sentence:

> A human being was devoured by dogs in the townland of Knock, County Tipperary, this week.
> DEATH OF CLARENCE MANGAN. –It is with deep regret we announce the death of Clarence Mangan, the poet. Poor Mangan's lot was a sad one. He lived a life of misery –unknown except through his writings, which will live after him.

(Note 'a human being', not 'a corpse'. These macabre inserts are a feature of the rural press during the Famine.)

The Anglo-Celt (10 August) strikes the note of rage and shame that will define how Mangan is remembered for the next century and a half:

> The Parnassian genius that wove an unfading chaplet for his country, culled from 'many lands,' perished of penury, untended and unwept. Shame upon us as a people! Double shame upon the wealthy Dublin men, who thus allowed one of their nation's brightest gems to sink dishonoured (so far as they could dishonour him) into a pauper's grave!

The grave *is* left 'untended' for years and when his Plunkett cousins do finally put up a headstone – he is in their family plot – it is only his name, no mention of his poetry or fame, and the death date is wrong. And anyway, the rumour is that he isn't even in that plot but is in with 11,000 other victims in the mass cholera pit, which, as Glasnevin tour guides will still tell you, is under the grave of Parnell.

Wherever it is his body is laid, Mangan doesn't stay in his tomb. Within a short time, his friends and acquaintances begin recalling him in ghostly terms. Joseph Brenan recalls seeing him 'moving with noiseless step' as 'the shadows grew blacker on the walls'; for Thomas D'Arcy McGee he is 'the man without a shadow … like an anatomy new risen from the dead'; John Savage remembers him 'gliding, even as a shadow on the wall … with silver-white locks, like a tender halo'; and John Mitchel sealed the spectral imagery in his famous description of his first sight of Mangan, perched on a ladder in the gloom of Trinity's Long Room, 'an unearthly and ghostly creature' with 'corpse-like features still as marble'. And once the men who knew him pass on themselves, the accounts of actual hauntings start up, beginning with Yeats whose poem 'To Ireland in the Coming

Times' places Mangan among 'the elemental things that go / about my table to and for'. By the twentieth century the hauntings have become a trope, with Manganistas from Joyce to Shane MacGowan leaving hair-raising descriptions of their visitations.

*

'The Death and Burial of James Clarence Mangan' took nearly fifty years to tell in full – three key witnesses, the doctor, the priest and the artist, sat on their accounts for decades – but even before their testimonies completed the tale, it was playing out like a great set piece of Irish Gothic, prefiguring the vampirism of *Carmilla* and *Dracula* and gesturing back to the blasphemy of *Melmoth* and forward to the burlesque misery of *An Béal Bocht*, with a chorus, or motif, from Amadeus. ('Like Mozart!' says Frank ecstatically when I tell him the sorry tale of the pauper's burial and I know he is seeing the end of Forman's film, the long-angled lens tracking the lone mourners walking behind the plywood coffin to the plangent sound of the most magnificent requiem ever written.)

All those involved in, or merely observers of, Mangan's final illness, death and burial felt compelled to record the details with an assiduousness that no one seems to have felt about recording any other episode in his life – the ten days from 13 June, when he was admitted to the Meath Hospital, to the 23rd, when he was buried, is the best sourced period of his biography by a considerable distance. But despite the throng of witnesses and commentators, the accounts converge to a remarkable extent. There are some discrepancies, particularly around Mangan's entry to the Meath Hospital, but, like the detail of whether five mourners or three followed his coffin, these are not very substantive, which makes me wary because the memories of different witnesses, especially when filtered through journalists, should always contradict each other, as anyone who has attended a law court and then read the media reports knows. The accounts certainly shouldn't converge to read like a piece of thematically cohesive fiction, as Mangan's Death and Burial does.

Like the plot of a war film, the tale takes its rationale from the need to crystallise mass horror, which is unimaginable, into a single compelling personal narrative. Mangan is one more Famine victim among the millions, just another homeless man succumbing too young to disease and malnutrition, but he is also the National Poet, who has earned himself that title because of his response to the Famine and this makes him the perfect emblematic victim. The tale of his death and burial seeks the balance between nonentity (his identification with the million nameless victims) and celebrity (his status as the national poet). It begins in dark obscurity, the pauper dying alone in a Liberties hovel, and then moves into the light: through the offices of three wise men, who will all end up with monarchical honours – Wilde and Burton knighted, Stokes named Queen's Physician in Ireland – he is taken to a pristine hospital ward, attended by at least four staff (*four*, during the Famine!), his every wish anticipated, his every word noted down, last rites given, his beauty restored, his image preserved for posterity. In this way, the 'crawling' vermin is humanised and even beatified but, with death, darkness descends back down: his last writings go up in smoke; his funeral is grotesquely ill-attended; his grave is unmarked and has a perpetual question mark over it since his bones may be in a mass grave, and finally he reconciles the two conditions, dissolving, like all ghosts, into nonentity and celebrity.

The tale achieves dramatic resolution. A happier ending – surviving the Famine and overcoming his addictions to find peace, prosperity and companionship into old age – would be as unsatisfactory as Hamlet becoming the next king of Denmark, or Medea enjoying a contented marriage, or Mozart growing rich and old; while a less attested ending – death among the masses in the Kilmainham sheds or alone in the hovel – would feel random and meaningless. Behind the outrage which so many of the contemporary sources proclaim on Mangan's behalf – *miserable, unknown, untended, unwept, dishonoured, poor Mangan!* – you sense a satisfaction, which is less ghoulish and voyeuristic than artistic and cathartic.

His Death and Burial is instrumental to Mangan's nineteenth-century status as the National Poet and, for this reason perhaps, has proved compelling to creative artists. Of the three contemporary images taken of him, two – the death sketch and death mask – were done in the morgue, and playwrights wanting to say something about his life always start with his death. Louis D'Alton's successful debut, *The Man in the Cloak*, which launched a young Cyril Cusack in the title role in 1937 and was revived frequently, is set at the deathbed, and when I met James McCabe, he spoke of how he would like to make a film of Mangan's life which would open with the deathbed. And in April 2013 I went to see a new play in Bewley's Café Theatre, written by Gerard Lee, with the suggestive title of *Mangan's Last Gasp*.

Onto the rumpled set – a tenement room with a bed of crumpled sheets – came Dr Wilde, brandishing a death certificate and proclaiming in a nicely Manganese turn of phrase, that the lump in the bed is 'a corpse, unburied', at which the lump sat bolt upright and started talking. … For the rest of the play, poet and doctor went back and forth on Irish history and literature, the Famine, the tenements, social/medical care, and Mangan's life and work. The conceit, kept up throughout, is that the doctor is trying to complete the death notice for the poet who refuses to die; this casts Dr Wilde as the pragmatic straight man, the foil to Mangan's crazed visionary outpourings.

The place was full and I was gratified at Mangan's continuing pulling power, which encouraged me to spot a pun in the title – the 'last gasp' of his fame, or rather the fame of his death (the last gasp of his last gasp) – but when I realised the pair weren't going to get out of the hovel or let up on the expository dialogue, I began to fidget. I couldn't seem to get beyond the unlikelihood of dying patient and doctor lingering in the cholera miasma to argue the toss, and such pedantic literalness isn't a great sign – when you go to the theatre you tacitly agree to suspend disbelief.

I recognised the play as belonging to what you might term the 'extraordinary encounter' genre, which takes its inspiration from particular historical moments when famous people happen to converge in the same place, and was pioneered by Tom Stoppard with *Travesties* (Joyce, Lenin and Tristan Tzara in Zurich in 1917) and Michael Frayn with *Copenhagen* (Heisenberg and Bohr in 1941). I thought it perceptive of the playwright to draw on this genre because the enduring glamour of Mangan's death and burial, that which makes it resemble a piece of fiction rather than a random demise, has a lot to do with the renown, or future renown of Stokes, Wilde and Burton, and the enormous fame of Oscar, glimmering away behind his father, something adverted to in the play in a moment of high camp when Dr Wilde says 'I can resist anything except temptation'.

The Mangan actor (who was also the playwright, Gerard Lee) injected energy into his delivery, which wasn't wrong exactly since Mangan's poems pulsate with energy, what Joyce calls his 'line of firm, marching iambs', but this onward march, his lifeforce, is always coming up against its opposite, his death wish, which manifests as elusiveness and indirection, and the more you read him, the more you become convinced that the energetic flow, the marching metre and the monologues, are a desperate reaction against the downward pull, the ellipses and silences and double negatives, which are the real creative force. I felt that the production was too definite and concrete and that it should rather ebb and dissolve, though I couldn't think how that might be staged.

The Irish Times characterised the play as 'default melodrama'. Mangan's death does have elements of melodrama, but it really belongs to a different genre, what you might call the Chronicle of a Death Foretold. What makes it transfixing beyond the cameos for famous men and the lurid horror of the Famine, is that it all happened in exactly the way Mangan had always said that it would. The insistent wail from the obituarists and memoirists over 'poor Mangan!' sounds like one of his *own* poems or stories, right down to the faint note of burlesque and the overt fatalism. A few months after his death, *The Nation* commented that 'it is a curious fact that in turning over our memories of Clarence we find a number of poems having for their theme his grave!' but it isn't 'a number', it's an avalanche, and it's not just his grave that is his constant theme, it's his last illness, his death, his commemoration.

In poem after poem he is distinct and explicit about what his death will look like: he envisages that he will waste away – 'so meagre am I, too, no lath is like me; / Death for my shadowy thinness cannot see me' (what a brilliant line!) – and that he will be a victim of mass calamity and subject to a mass burial – 'Want-houselessness-famine, and lastly / Death in a thousand-corpsed grave, that momently waxeth wider' – and that there will be only 'lone mourners o'er the burial' and that his body will be carelessly disposed of, his ashes 'inurned', his grave 'unremembered' and his life 'unchronicled, unchanted'. He looks forward to oblivion – 'unfelt, untold, unknown must go the story to that tomb' – and to ghosthood/vampirism – 'incarcerated under the figure of a bat I should be doomed to flap my leathern wings dolefully through the sunless day'.

Maybe we all carry within a sense of our own deaths, or at least of our lifespans. When my father died suddenly, aged forty-nine, his cousin told me that he had always struck her, since he was a child, as being in a tremendous hurry, impatient to seize at life, and she felt that he had sensed within himself that he didn't have long. Her words conjured up his astounding energy, which was so bound up for me in his short, barrel-chested physicality that it brought to mind his exact physical opposites, Beckett and Shaw, and their long, lean Protestant bones, which seem to correlate to the long slow launch of their careers (neither famous till his forties) as if they had known that they had all the time in the world ... And I think of how Frank liked to quote affectionately and ruefully the words of his dear friend's son at the friend's funeral – 'Dad was never going to make old bones' – and how, each time he quoted this, it put the heart across me ...

So I don't find it particularly far-fetched that Mangan should have had a sense of his ending and that, being a romantic poet 'half in love with easeful death', his instinct wasn't to squash this sense down but to explore it and find the words to bring it into focus. I do think that is what happened, but I also think the opposite: that his death and burial didn't happen in exactly the way the sources claim but that he manipulated his survivors into presenting it in the way that he wanted them to. I suspected this from the convergence of people's memories and from the eerie way their language replicates the language of the poetry, and eventually I got proof.

*

O'Donoghue ends his biography, published 1897, with the thundering denunciation that 'the miserable headstone over Mangan's grave (placed there many years after his death by his uncle), is an eyesore to lovers of Irish literature, and his birth place is still unmarked by tablet or other memorial'. A few months later, the MP and journalist T.D. Sullivan visited the grave in Glasnevin and wrote up the experience in the *Dublin Weekly Nation* (16 April 1898) fulminating that 'the inscription on Mangan's tombstone records merely his name, his age and the date of his death. The poorest thing about the place of sepulchre is not the condition of the grave-plot … nor is it the size and pattern of the tombstone; it is the miserable baldness and coldness of the record placed over the mortal remains of one of the most gifted children of Ireland.'

This elicited a defensive response from one Denis Plunkett, who wrote into the *Dublin Weekly Nation* (30 April 1898) to identify himself as the son of Mangan's first cousin (sister of Michael Smith of Copper Alley) and her husband, John Plunkett. Denis clarified that 'it was always expected that Fr Meehan would write the epitaph for the grave. I myself mentioned the matter to Fr Meehan a few years before his death; the answer he gave was that the name Clarence Mangan was quite enough for an ungrateful country.'

No one seems to have taken any notice of this and a decade later, when a bust of Mangan was to be unveiled in Stephen's Green and the papers were again full of tales of his ill-attended funeral and bare headstone, Denis wrote into the *Evening Telegraph* (1 May 1909) to try again to set the record straight: 'My father, mother, brother and myself were some of the people who attended his funeral. My father buried him' – i.e. paid for the funeral and headstone. Denis was then interviewed by the paper and repeated his story about Fr Meehan and the epitaph and clarified that he was sixteen at the time of Mangan's death.

Here, finally, are the contradictory memories that bring awkward veracity to the suspiciously smooth tale. Denis' game-changing revelations do away with the lone mourners, the pauper's grave and the uninscripted tombstone to replace the shocking tale of neglect with a more mundane story of a sparse, but not grotesquely ill-attended funeral, and a family trying to do right by their gifted relative but constrained by the priest's orders. If he was sixteen at the time, Denis would know whether or not he was at the funeral. So who is telling the truth? Is he another one of the defensive Smiths, trying to rebut the accusation of mistreating the genius? Probably, but he comes across as too orthodox to be putting incendiary words into a priest's mouth, and anyway the words 'the name Clarence Mangan is quite enough for an ungrateful country' are exactly what we expect from the shrewd, irascible, myth-making Meehan, manifesting yet again his Zelig-like talent for appearing at key moments of Mangan's life and after-life.

And even if Denis was retrofitting himself, brother and parents into the funeral cortege, it doesn't explain why his recollections have never made it into the record. Why is there no mention of him or his memories in any of the biographies or critical treatments of Mangan? How come McCall and O'Donoghue, so assiduous about interviewing surviving relatives, didn't speak to Denis who lived in and around the Liberties? And how come the indefatigable Shannon-Mangan didn't turn up his revelations, which Denis had, after all, delivered on two separate occasions to two different newspapers? Admittedly they weren't 'papers of record' but biographical information on Mangan is so scarce that I find it difficult to believe that such a pivotal memory was allowed to fall casually by the wayside. And, Denis aside, how come nobody, except for O'Donoghue *in passim*, mentions what has to be part of the explanation for the poorly attended funeral, an explanation which will have occurred to anyone who lived through the Covid lockdowns, although I admit it only hit me when I opened the *Irish Times* on 1 May 2020 to a photo of Eavan Boland's coffin outside an empty church in Dundrum, and a few months later, 7 October, to a photo of Derek Mahon's coffin being wheeled by *five* mourners through a tunnel of rock to the Island Crematorium at Ringaskiddy in Cork. In 1849 there was no government prohibition to avoid wakes and funerals but everyone knew the risks: during a previous cholera outbreak, the *Tralee Mercury* (1 September 1832) noted that 'in almost every case where the sick person died in his own house, three or four of the same family have been attacked' and as far back as 1773, Eibhlín Dubh Ní Chonaill wrote in her great lament for her murdered husband that 'Were it not for the smallpox / And the black death / and the spotted fever / those rough horse-riders / would be rattling their reins / and making a tumult / on the way to your funeral.'

I suspect a kind of collective unconscious consensus to bury poor Denis' recollections and ignore the implications of death in the time of the cholera, for the reason that inconvenient truths are always buried: they destroy the stories we love. Apparently Mozart *wasn't* buried in a pauper's grave: an online article explains that the 'common belief stems from a misinterpretation of funerary practices in eighteenth-century Vienna, which doesn't sound terribly interesting but does explain the myth'. This wry acknowledgement that if the truth isn't 'terribly interesting' it has no hope of supplanting the myth is why I never bothered correcting the end of *Amadeus* to Frank, anticipating his eye-roll of boredom. If a rumour is artistically and aesthetically coherent then time will turn it into truth, something that Mangan, with his sophisticated grasp of form and representation, understood very well.

Denis's memories are the codicil to the Death and Burial of James Clarence Mangan, but they have been deemed unwitnessed and inadmissible. A final postscript: in 1981 Ellen Shannon-Mangan and her husband, Richard Mangan (the alleged descendant) persuaded the Cemeteries Committee to add this inscription to Mangan's 'bald' tombstone in Glasnevin:

Ireland's National Poet
O My Dark Rosaleen, Do not sigh, do not weep

Oh dear. Meehan is Mangan's instrument: whatever he does and says serves to burnish the myth and to progress the story

in the way that Mangan wants it told. When Meehan told Denis Plunkett to leave the gravestone unmarked because 'the name Clarence Mangan is quite enough for an ungrateful country', he was helping to deliver Mangan's self-fulfilling prophesy of his 'unremembered grave' and was subtly channelling the nationalist trope of the unmarked grave captured by Robert Emmet's 'let no man write my epitaph and let my tomb remain uninscribed and my memory in oblivion until other times and other men can do justice to my character'. I sympathise with Shannon-Mangan's wish to memorialise but how much cleverer and wittier if she had inscribed 'The Nameless One' rather than 'The National Poet'. The death date, at least, is still false.

Part Two: The afterlives

The type and shadow of his race

When my father died suddenly when I was twenty, I had to take the plane from Brussels, where I was, to Kerry, where he was. On the plane I read Auden's 'In memory of WB Yeats' for embarrassingly obvious reasons: of all the poets my father loved, he loved Yeats and Auden best, and this is Auden's poem on the death of Yeats and if the lines didn't precisely fit – my father disappeared in the heat of summer not 'the dead of winter' – they fitted well enough: when Auden says 'the day of his death was a dark cold day', that has nothing to do with the season or the temperature. But I regret reading this on the plane since it brought no comfort, and the poem is now spoiled for me. To approach it is to be returned to that sense of such numbness that I don't recall it as a feeling but a disassociated image of a figure, me, hunched in a plane seat. Only two lines from the poem have survived the experience: 'The brokers are roaring like beasts on the floor of the Bourse' because this predates the plane and belongs to my father reciting it every time he passed the Bourse in Brussels, and 'The current of his feeling failed; he became his admirers' because this came with me off the plane and into the wake and funeral, which are suffused in my memory with the golden light of the Kerry sun that shone all that week, and the warmth of my father's friends who descended from all over to be with us, and whom I witnessed, before my eyes, manifesting the truth of the line. His friends wanted to tell their tales of him, which was lovely, but since every tale carries the atmosphere of the teller, my father started to become his friends. Though it was a reciprocal process – they also became him – I was conscious of a kind of panic that the reality of him, subtle and mysterious like all reality, was being coarsened into a punchline. It was then perhaps that I began to develop my suspicion of biography as the process by which the subject becomes his admirers and – another line of the poem has just come back to me – 'the words of the dead man [get] modified in the guts of the living'.

Like Yeats, and like Auden (who is of course writing about himself), Mangan became his admirers. The words of writers are taken up and transformed by readers and for various reasons, not always to do with their lyricism, certain writers are particularly co-opted. Mangan's strangely persistent afterlife is because of some quality in him which earns him admirers or – just as useful for longevity – detractors. He 'becomes his admirers' in that every interpreter of his work, be that critic, biographer, singer or novelist, brings themselves to the interpretation, just as my father's friends brought themselves to their anecdotes, so that we have Mangan as saint (via Shannon-Mangan) and as postmodernist (David Lloyd) and punk rebel (Shane MacGowan). And he 'becomes his admirers' in the sense that they pass him down, like DNA, to the next generation. I would never have got to Mangan except through Shane and Joyce (via Frank).

It matters for a writer who their admirers are, and particularly their early admirers. I doubt that Joyce studies would be in such rude health if Ellmann hadn't brought out his stunning biography within two decades of Joyce's death. Mangan didn't get an Ellmann, but he did get, a decade after his death, the greatest Irish polemicist of the nineteenth century, who set the narrative for well over a century.

In May 1848, when Mangan was being admitted to St Vincent's charity hospital, one of his editors, John Mitchel, founder of the incendiary *United Irishman*, was arrested for sedition, tried, sentenced to fourteen years' transportation, and shipped out of Dublin. On the journey, he began keeping the journal that would make him famous, but he barely survived the trip: the first stop, Bermuda, was so humid and so worsened his asthma that he was moved onto the Cape of Good Hope, where the authorities were refusing to accept any more convicts, so he had to remain on sea in the ship's hull, only arriving in Van Diemen's Land in April 1850, at death's door. Good climate, exercise, and the arrival of his family helped his recuperation; in June 1853 he withdrew his parole, and the following month escaped the island, arriving, via Sydney, Tahiti and San Francisco, in New York on 29 November 1853, to be greeted by an enormous crowd of supporters.

He immediately capitalised on the romance of his escape by serially publishing, in *The Citizen*, his classic prison memoir and denunciation of British imperialism, *Jail Journal*. His 'blistering, anglophobic rhetoric' made him famous in America, but he was volatile, ornery and always happier with dissention, and he alienated his New York readers by his support of slavery – he claimed that plantation slaves had better lives than the exploited factory hands of Manchester or the starving cottiers of Mayo – and by his savage attacks on the Catholic archbishop of New York who had criticised the Young Irelanders.

In 1859, on the tenth anniversary of Mangan's death and in the febrile atmosphere that would lead to the secession of the Southern states the following year, Mitchel brought out the first American edition of Mangan's poems, with an introductory essay entitled

'James Clarence Mangan, his Life, Poetry, and Death'. This elegant, passionate and cunning essay is probably still the most influential thing about Mangan ever written. It was a break from American politics, which relieved Mitchel's admirers, and a break also from the visceral polemics of *Jail Journal*. It opens rousingly, overt in its aim to conscript Mangan as a scourge of British imperialism: 'For this Mangan was not only an Irishman; – not only an Irish papist; – not only an Irish papist rebel – but throughout his whole literary life of twenty years, he never deigned to attorn to English criticism, never published a line in any English periodical, or through any English bookseller.' But as the essay proceeds, Mitchel becomes uncharacteristically restrained, subtle and elegiac, ending on a gentle 'benison'. There is a sense that Mangan has put manners on him, that writing about someone so elusive, evasive and spectral has forced Mitchel to lower his tone and lay off the polemics. He indulges his genius for invective just once, in his famous attack on the 'fair and false' enchantress who 'whistled Mangan down the wind', but he ends by pardoning even her:

> As a beautiful dream, she entered into his existence once for all: as a tone of celestial music she pitched the key-note of his song; and, sweeping over all the choirs of his melodious desolation you may see that white hand. Let us bid her farewell then, not altogether in unkindness; for she was more than half the Mangan.

This uses Manganese motifs – the dream, hands, and 'more than half' (gesturing to Mangan's pun, repeated later in the essay, that the poems of the Persian poet Hafiz were *half his*) – to bring ambiguity and irony to the love affair, subverting the previous misogynistic attack on the 'false enchantress'. This acute sensitivity to Mangan's language and themes is apparent throughout.

The essay is subtitled 'Life, Poetry, and Death' and death makes an early and continuing appearance, long before the subject actually dies (which he does about halfway through, his death introduced by 'at last'). Mangan's first appearance is as an 'almost unknown', who has found 'no place' among the 'immortal names' and has 'lain so long in oblivion'. To be so overlooked is, as a poet, to be dead, and by the fourth paragraph (before even his birth has been announced), we are at his 'low grave in Glasnevin' and Mitchel is commanding his 'poor ghost' to 'keep still'.

After this introduction as an unread poet and restless ghost, Mangan is never allowed take flesh and breathe. In youth he is described in angelic terms: 'He was shy and sensitive, with exquisite sensibility and fine impulses; eye, ear, and soul open to all the beauty, music, and glory of heaven and earth; humble, generous and unexacting; modestly craving nothing in the world but celestial glorified life, seraphic love, and a throne among the immortal gods (that's all).' The humorous parenthesis hints at the opposite of modesty, the poet's pride – more fallen angel than seraph. Mitchel's Mangan is a creature of contrasts whose 'existence is twofold'. Overtly saintly, he has a dark twin: 'There were two Mangans: one well-known to the Muses, the other to the police; one soared through the empyrean and sought the stars – the other lay too often in the gutters of Peter street and Bride street.' Mitchel keeps the darkness under wraps; whole pages are devoted to the 'humble, affectionate, almost prayerful' Mangan, while his bad self is only hinted at:

> Sometimes he could not be found for weeks; and then he would reappear, like a ghost, or a ghoul, with a wildness in his blue, glittering eye, as of one who has seen spectres; and nothing gives so ghastly an idea of his condition of mind as the fact that the insane orgies of this rarely-gifted creature were transacted in the lowest and obscurest taverns, and in company with the

offal of the human species. From this thought one turns away with a shudder.

Mitchel is horrified (and titillated) by the company that this ghoulish Mangan keeps, but the censure doesn't extend to his drug and alcohol abuse which feeds into the essay's overt Christian motifs: 'Baffled, beaten, mocked and all alone amidst the wrecks of his world – is it wonderful that he sought at times to escape from consciousness by taking for bread, opium, and for water, brandy?' Unsurprisingly, since his 'character and will [are] essentially feeble', Mangan succumbs to his addictions and becomes 'a solitary, half-conscious dreamer and opium-eater', and it is as a ghost that Mitchel casts him in the celebrated passage where he describes his own first sighting of him in Trinity College Library:

> an acquaintance pointed out to me a man perched on the top of the ladder, with the whispered information that the man was Clarence Mangan. It was an unearthly and ghostly figure, in a brown garment; the same garment (to all appearance) which lasted till the day of his death. The blanched hair was totally unkempt; the corpse-like features still as marble; a large book was in his arms, and all his soul was in the book. I had never heard of Clarence Mangan before and knew not for what he was celebrated; whether as a magician, a poet, or a murderer; yet took a volume and spread it on a table, not to read, but with pretence of reading to gaze on the spectral creature upon the ladder.

This ghostly Mangan is multiply sealed off from the life around him: suspended above the ground, trapped amid ancient books, within a university walled off from the city, and he is still an unknown (although Mangan was only appointed to work in Trinity

Library in 1842, by which date he was a famous contributor to literary journals and Mitchel would have heard of him).*

After a few more descriptions of this 'ghastly death-in-life', Mitchel 'at last' lets the poet actually die and deposes him in Glasnevin cemetery, with the unsurprising aside that 'there is not, so far as I have learned, a stone to mark his last abode'. He now turns from the man who leaves the earth without having really lived, to the work 'his inner and more living life [which] affords a more pleasing spectacle'. The poems bear the stamp of the misery which produced them – they are 'the very soul of woe and terrible desolation' and bear the burden of 'dreary retrospection or a longing for peace in the grave' – but if the themes are mournful, the tone raises, energises and enlivens: 'ballads of wonderful power and passion', 'rolling and resounding stanzas', 'deliciously musical', 'marvellously impassioned'. The contrast is obvious without being overworked – his life was death-like but the work is alive, or at least waiting to be resurrected by the attention of the new readers whom Mitchel's essay will win.

Mitchel, who started out so defiantly claiming Mangan as a rebel poet snubbing English publishers, has now abandoned this crudely nationalistic line, and gives a more convincing reason for Mangan 'never sending a line of his verses to any London periodical': it was 'perhaps through diffidence; not feeling confident'. He admits that 'in the continual movements of political associations, whether under O'Connell or under … the Young Ireland Party, [Mangan] never took any ostensible part'. Quoting from a public letter that Mangan sent into the *United Irishman* in 1848, which commits to going 'to all lengths for the achievement of our national independence', he admits that 'this is the only expression (in prose) of [Mangan's]

---

*Jacques Chuto points out that Mitchel includes a poem 'Broken-hearted Lays' in the *Selected Verse* which wasn't reprinted anywhere after its publication in *The Comet* in 1833, which suggests that already, as a Trinity student in the early 1830s, Mitchel was reading Mangan.

political sentiments that I have ever seen or heard of' and notes with exquisite irony that 'the truth of history compels me to declare that it did not intimidate the British government much'.

By this stage of the essay, Mitchel is quite happy to release Mangan from active rebellion because he has found a more subtle and convincing use for him, as the symbol of the nation:

> His history and fate were indeed a type and shadow of the land he loved so well. The very soul of his melody is that plaintive and passionate yearning which breathes and throbs through all the music of Ireland. Like Ireland's, his gaze was ever backward, with vain and feeble complaint for vanished years. Like Ireland's, his light flickered upwards for a moment, and went out in the blackness of darkness.

The 'vain and feeble complaint for vanished years' refers to Mangan's fondness for recalling a lost (and non-existent) golden youth, which Mitchel implicitly links to Ireland's legendary past, while 'blackness of darkness' is the Famine, which claimed Mangan among its victims. Mitchel doesn't labour this point and doesn't have to: by the time he makes it, he has already established that Mangan was born walking into the shadow of death. Addressing Irish-American readers, he reminds them of Ireland's suffering and 'passionate yearning' to be free, and subtly suggests that by reading Mangan, they will be brought closer to the land they love so well. By remembering/resurrecting Mangan, they remember/resurrect Ireland.

*

The essay is stunning and is single-handedly responsible for Mangan's reputation in America (modestly significant by the start of the twentieth century though now bottomed out). American readers were thrilled to be introduced to this exotic being, with shades of Poe and Bartleby but transplanted to the fabulously squalid Irish setting. Remarkably, the essay succeeded in Ireland, where it went into numerous editions, for precisely the opposite reason: not its exoticism, but its familiarity. It sounded to Irish readers like a voice from the grave echoing long-buried memories … the twilight, shadows, spectres, pallor, melancholy, gliding, aloofness, all this comes back to them, seeded by Mangan's own poems and stories and by the obituaries and recollections of his friends. Mitchel's achievement was to subtly weave into one cohesive narrative all the elements of the myth wisping around Dublin. You can trace many of his images back to source: the striking phrase 'death-in-life' is Mangan's own; the 'creature, transacting in low taverns' comes out of Price's obituary ('crawling through our streets, grotesque in figure, mean in attire') and the seminal argument, 'his history and fate are indeed a type and shadow of the land he loved so well', was suggested by the Young Irelander John Savage who, in an 1851 article quoted by Mitchel, had called Mangan 'not the least powerful talisman by which a nation is moved'.

For the rest of the nineteenth century and well into the twentieth, you won't find a divergent view to Mitchel's and his stand-out phrases became common currency. I think Wilde's famous juxtaposition 'We are all in the gutter but some of us are looking at the stars' owes something to Mitchel's 'two Mangans', one who 'sought the stars' and the other who 'lay too often in the gutters'. And Mitchel's insistence on Mangan's obscurity and neglect explains Meehan's remark about the 'ungrateful country', which otherwise makes no sense since Mangan was published in all the major journals and distinguished establishment figures were always coming to his aid – Thomas Larcom employed him on the Ordnance Survey and Trinity College in its library although he arrived to work late and drunk.

It is not surprising to find Meehan – Young Irelander and instinctive mythologiser – channelling these nationalist tropes but only Mitchel's vast influence can explain why the rigorous, pedantic O'Donoghue went for the myth over the facts, and chose to introduce his biography with the generic justification:

> One of the strongest reasons for writing his life is to show that Mangan's work is not half so familiar to his countrymen as it should be … But for the exertions of Father Meehan and Mr. John McCall nothing but a few newspaper articles would have been devoted to Mangan's genius.

This was total rubbish as O'Donoghue must have known: Mitchel's *Selected Poems* had been reprinted at least seven times; John O'Daly's *Poets and Poetry of Munster* was on its third edition; Gill's *Selected Poems* was on its second edition; Fr Meehan had edited another selection and Yeats had featured Mangan strongly in his *Book of Irish Verse* (1895). O'Donoghue sternly termed all these 'grossly inadequate', but they were no more inadequate than other poets' selected editions, and Thomas Moore was the only Irish poet in the nineteenth century to receive a collected works. In the three decades between Mitchel's essay and O'Donoghue's biography, there were 295 mentions of Mangan in *The Nation* and 359 in *The Freeman's Journal*, according to an online search engine. To compare this with his best-known literary contemporaries: the respective figures for Samuel Ferguson are 122 mentions in *The Nation* and 342 in *The Freeman's Journal*, and for William Carleton 36 and 193. And Carleton and Ferguson were both alive for some of this period; in the decades after their deaths (in 1869 and 1886) newspaper mention of them slowed to a trickle, yet they were not, and are not, routinely introduced as neglected and overlooked.

O'Donoghue tries to shake off Mitchel's influence with some prim admonishing shots, scolding him for 'not knowing a great deal concerning Mangan's literary labours' and 'putting the facts very crudely', but he can't help parroting him, down to his errors. For instance, Mitchel writes of Mangan having 'a character and will essentially feeble' which, under O'Donoghue, becomes a 'weak and wavering character and enfeebled body', though as a historian he should have noted the exceptional willpower it took for a part-schooled Catholic to get into the country's most learned periodicals. He grudgingly praises what he calls Mitchel's 'adroit likening [of] the poet's history to that of Ireland', but when rephrasing the argument, shows that he hasn't grasped what Mitchel meant:

> From the opening of the year 1846, when the fearful shadow of an impending famine was cast over the country, Mangan, though he did not change his own habits or mode of life, almost entirely forgot his mannerism, and assumed the character of an almost inspired prophet ... Hitherto he had been contented with the name of 'poet', he now appeared as the great national poet of Ireland – the most splendidly endowed with imagination and keenness of vision of any Irishman of his time.

Mitchel's point is not 'though Mangan did not change his own habits or mode of life' but *because* he did not change them, that he is identified with the suffering land and assumes the status of inspired prophet and national poet. O'Donoghue is too puritanical about Mangan's 'habits' to absorb this, but five years later another Mitchel acolyte emerged who understood the point so completely that he reinterpreted it and changed Irish literature.

*

On 1 February 1902 James Joyce gave a lecture on Mangan to his college debating society, the L&H. It was the day before his twentieth birthday, always a significant date for him. His youngest brother, George, had recently taken ill with the typhoid fever that would lead to his death from peritonitis five weeks later.

Joyce was already famous in the L&H for his paper 'Drama and Life', delivered two years earlier, in which he had used a famous living foreign writer, Henrik Ibsen, to make provocative claims for the superiority of contemporary drama over classical. Now, in his first L&H paper since his earlier triumph, he chose an 'unknown' dead Irish writer to launch a subversive, if veiled, attack on nationalism.

Joyce's Mangan is wholly obscure and remote – he is 'sometimes spoken of in literary societies … a stranger in his country', his writings 'never collected and unknown, except for two American editions of selected poems and some pages of prose'. This is pure Mitchel, and the statement was even less true than when O'Donoghue had parroted it five years earlier because the Mangan publishing bonanza had continued and now even included UK reviews. When the chief secretary for Ireland, George Wyndham, quoted Mangan in the House of Commons, *The Freeman's Journal* (1 May 1903) had 'no doubt' that his 'declamation of the 'Lament for Kinkora' found recognising ears even on the English benches' since 'Mangan is one of the best edited poets of the century'.

Richard Ellmann, a bit confused by Joyce's pose, called his 'air of discovering Mangan, a little pretentious' but once you realise the debt to Mitchel, the pose can be seen as an early instance of what would become Joyce's signature technique of palimpsest or composting. This involves grabbing allusions from multiple sources – novels, poems, song lyrics, newspaper articles, myths, legends, history, jokes, advertising slogans, etc. – and layering them through his work to add depth, like a gardener adding compost to thin soil. Other writers do this – the creators of *The Simpsons*, for instance, layer in multiple allusions to American history and culture that go right over the heads of the children watching – but no one does it as subtly as Joyce, who snatches the faintest of refrains and then twists them out of recognition so that scholars are still trying to track his allusions, and the job will, as he noted gleefully, 'keep them busy for centuries'.

Mitchel isn't mentioned in the lecture but it is certainly his spectral Mangan being evoked and Joyce's delivery was well suited to summoning up the ghost – according to his brother, Stanislaus, and to his own estimation in *Stephen Hero*, 'he read quietly and distinctly, involving every hardihood of thought or expression in an envelope of low, innocuous melody'. According to his friend Con Curran, who was present at the lecture: 'Joyce's delivery remains in my memory – his voice metallic in its clearness and very deliberate as if coming from some old and distant oracle.' His audience, if rapt, was mystified. Felix Hackett, then an editorial assistant on the college magazine, *St Stephen's*, later characterised the paper as having 'the structure of a symphony' but recalled that 'the paper tried its audience hard. A symphony can scarcely be appreciated at a first hearing.' Unlike Joyce's Ibsen lecture, which was 'aggressive and declaratory', this was soft, winding, obfuscated and lyrical. The verbs and adjectives that he uses to describe Mangan and his writing – 'vague', 'contorted', 'interweaving like soft, luminous scarves', 'embroidering as in a web' – sound like a description of his own style in the lecture. Like Mitchel, he was suiting style to subject. Mangan has a way of infecting his critics.

Joyce's Mangan, like Mitchel's, is 'feeble-bodied', has been 'in love with death all his life' and has a nature 'so sensitive [that] he cannot forget his dreams in a secure, strenuous life'. He too is angelic – his 'vague face seems to live only because of those light shining eyes and of the fair silken hair above it, of which he is a little vain' – this, like Mitchel's sly parenthesis ('that's all'), topples the angelic Mangan with his own vanity and Joyce goes further with the Lucifer motif – 'his manner is such that none can say if it be pride or humility that looks out of that vague face'.

Joyce pushes Mitchel's acknowledgement that Mangan took 'no ostensible part' in the political associations of his day one step further to render Mangan 'little of a patriot' and for most of the essay he is concerned to free Mangan from Ireland and place him within the European Romantic tradition. In an extended homage, written in extravagantly purple prose, he accords Mangan's most famous image, 'Dark Rosaleen', full status as a romantic ideal. By comparing 'she whose white and holy hands have the virtue of enchanted hands, his virgin flower, and flower of flowers' to the great muses of European art, the Mona Lisa, Petrarch's Laura and Dante's Beatrice, Joyce lets Dark Rosaleen be emblematic, like them, of mystery, glory and beauty. This is placing Mangan and his iconic image of Ireland within the 'chivalrous' European tradition, but in the last movement of his symphonic lecture, Joyce abruptly changes gear to engage with Mitchel's seminal point that Mangan's 'history and fate were indeed a type and shadow of the land he loved so well' and the tone changes:

> Mangan is the type of his race. History encloses him so straitly that even his fiery moments do not set him free from it. … An eager spirit would cast down with violence the high traditions of Mangan's race – love of sorrow for the sake of sorrow and despair and fearful menaces – but where their voice is a supreme entreaty to be borne with, forbearance seems only a little grace; and what is so courteous and so patient as a great faith?
>
> … The life of the poet is intense – the life of Blake or of Dante – taking into its centre the life that surrounds it and flinging it abroad again amid planetary music. With Mangan a narrow and hysterical nationality receives a last justification, for when this feeble-bodied figure departs, dusk begins to veil the train of the gods, and he who listens may hear their footsteps leaving the world.

Beneath the flourishes, Joyce is absorbing Mitchel to come to a radically different conclusion. For Mitchel, there is something solemn and beautiful in the mournful history of Ireland and Mangan is aggrandised and beatified by his identification with it. Joyce, though not quite immune to the 'supreme entreaty' of the sorrowful Irish voice, is impatient and wrestling with the pieties. He finds nothing ennobling in being 'the type of his race' when the race is in straits. Literary genius reflects and validates the 'life that surrounds it' but what surrounds Mangan isn't the beauty of medieval Florence or the energy of eighteenth-century London; his poetry gives Ireland's 'narrow and hysterical' nationalism its justification.

In the essay's sharpest about-turn, Joyce turns viciously on Dark Rosaleen:

In the final view the figure which he worships is seen to be an abject queen upon whom because of the bloody crimes that she has done and of those as bloody that were done to her, madness is come and death is coming, but who will not believe that she is near to die and remembers only the rumours of voices challenging her sacred gardens and her fair, tall flowers that have become pabulum aprorum, the food of boars.

Dark Rosaleen has become an abject queen, and Kathleen Ny-Houlihan [Mangan's spelling] is the old sow that eats her farrow, and the 'flower of flowers' is pigswill! Implicit in the attack is the suggestion that if Mangan had been able to free himself from his history and traditions – if he'd had 'an eager' and 'strong' [e.g. a Joycean] spirit, which could turn 'with violence on the traditions of his race', his achievement would have been greater, and he would have gained a new perspective on Ireland and nationalism and helped to change the discourse. As it is, he leaves nothing in his wake but dusk and echoes of greatness.

This was an all-out attack on sacred cows, but with enough flourishes and subclauses to disguise the attack until the overt insult of 'narrow and hysterical nationality'. As soon as Joyce had finished speaking, a Derry student and ardent Gaelic Leaguer, Louis J. Walsh, was on his feet denouncing him for not making more of Mangan's Young Ireland connections and translations from the Irish, and the audience 'rallied with "timid courage" to the side of the new-found champion'. Reading this, I get an image of Joyce's thin ironic smile as he surveys his peers turning on him for neglecting Young Ireland, unable to locate his much more deadly attack on nationalism. The session ended memorably: the chair, William Magennis, after summing up the proceedings, declaimed from memory 'in magnificent and sympathetic style "The Nameless One", – thus proving how very well-known Mangan was. (Frank always insisted that the whole room joined in the declamation but I can't find this in any of the accounts of the session and I eventually concluded that Frank was conflating the audience's 'rallying' with the chair's 'magnificent declamation' but I also think he was right and that they did all join in: it was a famous poem in an era of learning poetry by heart so Magennis can't have been the only one to know it, and anyone who knew it would have joined in. I think the sound of the room chanting the famous lines – 'And tell how trampled, derided, hated / And worn by weakness, disease and wrong' – came down the years to Frank since he was auditor of the L&H when in college and had an intimate sense of its braying crowd.)

Reading the lecture now it seems full of ghosts: Mangan's obviously, and Mitchel's, and the obituarists and memoirists whose memories informed Mitchel, and the impending ghost of poor little George, lying in bed as the lecture rolled, waiting for his brother to come home and sing to him. Not quite fifteen, George was the same age Mangan was when taken from school and cast into the hell of the scrivener's office. George is present in 'the feeble-bodied figure departing the earth' and he reproaches the 'abject queen' [Ireland] for the 'bloody crimes' that she 'has done' and 'were done to her'. High among these crimes is the poverty, ignorance and superstition that are responsible for George's early death and 'inexpressively mean' burial: 'The entire apparatus of the State seemed to him at fault from its first to its last operation' is how Joyce characterises the death and burial in *Stephen Hero*, where the description of the child laid out on the deathbed seems to come straight out of Mitchel's essay: 'The wasted body that lay before him had existed by sufferance; the spirit that dwelt therein had literally never dared to live and had not learned anything by an abstention that it had not willed for itself.'

*

The 'feeble', 'shy', 'defensive' Mangan, evoked in the lecture feeds into the boy in 'Araby'. The last line of the story – 'Gazing up into the darkness I saw myself as a creature driven and derided by vanity; and my eyes burned with anguish and anger' – riffs on Mitchel's notable description: 'Like Ireland's, his gaze was ever backward, with vain and feeble complaint for vanished years. Like Ireland's, his light flickered upwards for a moment, and went out in the blackness of darkness.' I think that as Joyce ended his story, he heard the crowd in the Physics Theatre declaiming 'The Nameless One' after his lecture: 'Tell how trampled, derided, hated / And worn by weakness, disease and wrong'.

In *Portrait of the Artist as a Young Man*, Joyce fused a stand-out line from the lecture, 'History encloses him so straitly that even his fiery moments do not set him free of it', with a line from a Mangan poem, 'Horrible dream! Through which as in chains I struggle to waken', to synthesise Stephen Dedalus' famous pronouncement: 'History is a nightmare from which I am trying to wake up.' Mangan isn't mentioned by name in *Portrait of the Artist* but the national passivity and entrapment he is made to embody in the lecture is positioned as the nightmare against which Stephen must contend. The old man at the end of *Portrait* who acts as one of the spurs to drive Stephen into exile may owe something to Mangan:

> John Alphonsus Mulrennan has just returned from the west of Ireland. European and Asiatic papers please copy. He told us he met an old man there in a mountain cabin. Old man had red eyes and short pipe. Old man spoke Irish. Mulrennan spoke Irish. Then old man and Mulrennan spoke English. Mulrennan spoke to him about universe and stars. Old man sat, listened, smoked, spat. Then said:
> – Ah, there must be terrible queer creatures at the latter end of the world.

There are palimpsest suggestions of Mangan here: the tripartite name, the elderliness ('old and hoary at thirty-nine'), the Asiatic papers, the pipe (implying opium), the transitions from Irish to English, a sense of settling for imagining rather than experiencing the world, the stars (from Mitchel's essay), and a hint of the closing scene of the long memoir where the optimistic young man talks stirringly of God and love, only to be shut down. To combat the old man's vague imaginings of 'the latter end of the world', Stephen will 'go forth' to encounter the 'reality of experience'.

But there was another Mangan, immensely witty and anarchic, very far from the feeble dreamer. This irreverent Mangan, 'the mystifier and humbugger' who baited *The Comet* editors and tormented Duffy appears glancingly in Mitchel's essay but only to be dismissed for his 'grotesque, bitter, Fescennine buffoonery'. O'Donoghue played his part in the burying when he brought out a *Selected Poems* in 1903 in which he cuts facetious stanzas from poems, calling them 'the absurd and perverse tag', an act of literary vandalism so at odds with his otherwise scholarly and pedantic personality that it seems pathological.

In his lecture, Joyce went along with the sidelining but for complex reasons. I think he was entranced by the 'abominable joker' but already, aged twenty, had a sense that he would need him for his fiction. He took his time about it: there is no trace of the ludic, anarchic Mangan in *Dubliners* or *Portrait* but he emerges in *Ulysses* and erupts in *Finnegans Wake*. Jacques Chuto's excavations of the 'manganese' elements (Joyce deploys this exact word) in the *Wake* prove how often Joyce puns on Mangan's phrases and neologisms – 'ullahbluh!', 'hierarchitec-titiptitoploftical', 'barmicidal days', 'boysforus … bothforus', 'durck rosalon', 'ichabod', etc. – and suggest that the whole, anarchic, mystifying, punning, dreaming spirit of the *Wake* owes something to the 'Fescinnine buffoon' who 'owed no ode'.

But Joyce never let on what he was up to, and *Finnegans Wake* was (and remains) unread and under-studied so for the longest time nobody noticed that Mangan was lurking there. For more than a century after Mitchel's essay, the only Mangan visible to the public was the mournful lyricist. Mangan remained sheathed in 'the outward mask and semblance' of his myth until, in the last decades of the century, two critics emerged to lift the cloak and 'disperse by their wizard art the mists which envelop the shapes of actual life, and marshal those shapes before us apparelled, perhaps, in a more gorgeous vesture'.

The scholar and the prodigy

In 1949, on the centenary of his death, Mangan received the ultimate accolade from the newly declared Republic: he was put on a stamp.

He is in profile, as in all images of him, and the face is modelled on the death sketch by Frederic Burton, and coloured green, with Celtic lettering, flanked by a kind of Easter lily-meets-laurel wreath. After independence, he was put on the school curriculum and the stamp's iconography gives an idea of how he was being taught – as a suffering nationalist saint, one of those 'who sang to sweeten Ireland's wrongs' and prepared the way for freedom.

No stamp was produced in 1999 for the 150th centenary of his death. By then, he had been off the school curriculum for twenty-five years and was consequentially fading from the national memory. He had also received a complete identity makeover and, to reflect this, the image would have had to show a kind of fiendish imp rendered in expressionist / cubist / Dadaist style (which it's hard to imagine being commissioned).

The remaking of James Clarence Mangan in the last two decades of the twentieth century is the work of two men, Jacques Chuto and David Lloyd, and I became fixated on them not only because they are the two poles around whom contemporary Mangan studies orbits, but because they are perfect foils to each other. Each epitomises a particular archetype and there is a novelistic perfection to their contrasting skills: Chuto is meticulous, rigorous and exhaustive, the Scholar; Lloyd is swift, dazzling and provocative, the Prodigy, or Enfant Terrible. Each found the perfect outlet for their respective skills: Chuto edited and annotated the *Collected Works* and Lloyd wrote a terrifyingly avant-garde book of criticism, greeted on publication with shock and awe.

When I set out to make contact with Chuto, I couldn't find anything online – he had long retired from the University of Lille – but my googling did throw up that, as well as being a critic and a poet, he was Derek Mahon's French translator.

Derek was another poet I'd got drunk with. During the Celtic Tiger years, when we were both working on *The Dubliner* magazine, my sister and I would do the rounds of the innumerable launches which characterised that era: gallery openings, book launches, poetry readings, cocktail or wine tastings, gadget and cosmetics launches, fashion shows … they all took place at the same time, between 6 p.m. and 8 p.m., and drew more or less the same crowd, and served cheap wine (unless the product launch was booze) and you could take in two or three of an evening and call it work.

At an exhibition opening in the National Gallery, in its then new Millennium Wing, we met Derek. The exhibition was called, I think, 'American Beauty'. In my memory it is a summer evening and the room is overflowing with people who are there to be seen and Derek is wearing a linen suit and looks like a superbly relaxed and prosperous American businessman or diplomat, unless you look in his eyes, which you don't if you have any sense of self-preservation. His eyes are like those of the character Sharpsight in the Grimms' tale 'who keeps his eyes bandaged because without it his gaze would set things afire or break them into pieces'. Derek sweeps his shattering gaze around the exhibition and then gestures contemptuously to the nearest paintings: 'These are the Ashcan School, New York artists, very influenced by John B. Yeats when he moved over there. The Gallery has a roomful of John Yeats upstairs *and they haven't even made the connection.*'

I'm a sucker for erudite contempt. We abandoned the opening and its terrible wine and lousy curating and went I think to the side bar in the Shelbourne (before its Tiger makeover) and drank till last orders. That was all a long time ago and I hadn't seen Derek since, but now I wrote him a carefully flirtatious and effusive letter, recalling our meeting and asking for Chuto's contact details. Really, I wanted to go for another drink and talk about Mangan, but ten days after I'd posted my letter to West Cork, where Derek lived, a tiny envelope arrived through the door, the smallest envelope you've ever seen, which, when opened, contained Chuto's address in Paris and *nothing* else. I felt as snubbed as the National Gallery curators. I wish I'd saved that envelope, reminder in his own handwriting of the great Mahon putdown, but unlike Frank I don't have the collector's instinct.

I wrote Chuto another one of my carefully effusive letters and posted it to the Paris address that Derek had furnished. This had a better result. He replied by email with the beguiling heady intemperance I would come to know as characteristic:

I'd be interested to hear how you intend to produce something 'incisive, entertaining and intriguing' on the poor poet. And when I say 'poor' I don't refer to his life but to the way he has been handled by posterity. I thought the edition I co-edited would enable everyone to read the whole of Mangan and so stop them from writing any more nonsense about him. I was sadly mistaken. The sanctimonious Victorian approach has been replaced by the postmodern jargon-mongers. Ellen Shannon-Mangan's biography is good, but she tends to love Mangan so much that she can't bring herself to believe he ever lied. Clearly she hadn't met many drunkards in her life …

And we were off, plunged straight into gossip – contemporary gossip about other Manganistas, and 170-year-old gossip about the poet, e.g. was he or wasn't he a junkie? (Me: yes; Jacques, no) and did he have rotten teeth? (Jacques: 'I think the answer is yes'; Me: 'Oh God, it's actually terrifying to think how bad!') In his seventh email Jacques added a sharp P.S., 'You haven't asked me any real questions yet!' So I ventured a real, i.e. a scholarly, question, which like most academic questions, was really a theory posing as an inquiry, which he saw through, and snuffed out.

Jacques' poor eyesight was a leitmotif running through our correspondence – 'we do indeed see eye to eye, though I'm not sure that bodes well for you given the poor condition of *my* eyes' – which, he said, made travel too difficult so there was no luring him to Dublin. Instead, I went to Paris, and we met for lunch in the Brasserie Lipp on the Boulevard Saint-Germain, a Paris institution. He wore thick shaded spectacles, like Mangan, though his weren't tinted green, and his eyesight was indeed so bad that I felt guilty that he had had to navigate the metro alone. He had delicate hands and, despite being a Breton, which suggests to me a craggy, wind-hewn sailor's complexion, his skin was unlined and parchment pale. His general aura of decisiveness and impatience didn't remind me of Mangan, but he had what is indispensable for the Mangan scholar (and the lack of which condemns Shannon-Mangan's biography), an alert sense of humour.* Frank, also at the lunch, was much taken with his sarcastic laugh, which first aired when I asked how he had come to Mangan. He'd been looking for a subject for his thesis in Irish literature, he said, and was pointed towards the mystic poet Æ (aka George Russell) – 'Even if I were doing a three-year Anglo-Saxon PhD, I couldn't have done Æ …' The laugh dismissed both Æ and the unseemly haste of Irish and British PhDs (the magisterial French doctorate takes at least one and in Chuto's case two decades). By dessert I was suggesting that I might be brave enough to send him a chapter to look over; out came the sarcastic, self-mocking laugh – 'be careful, I am not easy …'

This 'not easy' became apparent in an email spat we got into on my return to Dublin. I'd given him Paul Muldoon's *To Ireland, I* as a present, knowing that it was a provocation, but that he would enjoy being provoked. A stunning if sporadically infuriating work, it picks up on refrains running through Irish literature and features Mangan's contemporary, Samuel Ferguson, very heavily, and Mangan not at all (he seems like the hole at the centre of the lectures). I think most readers follow the same trajectory: dazzled excitement and then a howl of 'no way' (mine came at the suggestion that 'the empty room from which Lucy sets out' to go through the wardrobe into Narnia 'is a version of the room in the Gresham Hotel from which Gabriel Conroy must set out on his journey westward' in 'The Dead').

Chuto's moment came earlier. After emailing equivocal approval of Muldoon's brilliance, he soon pounced: 'Muldoon has failed to pass (as I knew he would eventually) by misquoting Yeats's so well-known line on Davis, Mangan, Ferguson.'

---

*It was not at this lunch but later that I discovered his other Manganese trait: an addiction to gambling which sounds to have been compulsive before he knocked it on the head. As a result, he is particularly alert to the insignia of gambling in descriptions of Mangan (e.g. 'Mangan who likes a little loo') and to Mangan's extensive language of indebtedness (e.g. 'I owed you no ode' (only Mangan would see 'owed' in 'ode')).

I'd failed to notice that Muldoon had misquoted the Yeats line 'Nor may I less be counted one / With Davis, Mangan, Ferguson' as 'Would that I were counted one ...' but I didn't find this very serious and said so: it was a lecture so Muldoon was quoting from memory and it's part of oral literature that lines are remembered just a bit wrong, and I quite liked that in the published version he let his false memory stand (although maybe he just didn't notice). Chuto was having none of this: 'Muldoon smiles at Yeats's (or Ferguson's) "defective ear" perceptible in the "rhyme" *one / Ferguson*, without realizing that his misquotation of the first line makes it one syllable short, and that his own ear might therefore be slightly defective too.'

I made a final desperate plea that it was 'more interesting and revealing and honest of Muldoon to have left in this error that exposes him' but there was clearly no bridging the distance between Chuto's stickling accuracy and my sub-Freudian tenuousness. (When I told Frank of this exchange, he gave me one of his cold, ironic looks and said that it was appalling to have made such an argument to a great scholar.)

The meticulousness, obstinacy and semantic rigour illustrated by this exchange is clearly what is needed in an editor. Chuto was born to this task – there was a bad moment in 1994 when he had to hurry to Dublin in what he calls 'true *Oh the French are on the Sea* fashion' in order to rout a rival project, but he secured the prize, and assembled a team and between 1996 and 2004 the Irish Academic Press brought out *Mangan's Collected Works* in six volumes, together with a bibliography, under his general editorship.

This was a Herculean task requiring gargantuan energy, investigative flair, fluent German, fluent Manganese and the connoisseur's instinct. Only about 20 per cent of Mangan's poems had ever previously been anthologised and the rest were spread, often anonymously or pseudonymously, across a mishmash of journals, newspapers and periodicals. Chuto and his team had to track down the journals and then work out which among the unsigned/pseudonymous poems about twilight, roses, lost love and death were Mangan's. Once assigned, they had to work out whether the poem was an original or a translation and if a translation, track down the original (frequently, with Mangan misdirecting them) and compare the two versions to see where Mangan had digressed/customised/corrupted the meaning.

To give an idea of the difficulty involved, take the 'translations' of Eastern poets in the extended article 'Literae Orientales', which appeared in the *Dublin University Magazine* in March 1838. Their authorship isn't in doubt – they're signed Clarence Mangan – but everything else is. Did Mangan actually know Persian, Turkish, Arabic? Readers had their doubts, but it was Chuto who tracked down the source of the poems – a huge tome of translations of Eastern poets into German by Baron von Hammer-Purgstall. Almost all of Mangan's 'Oriental' poems are here, proving that he didn't know any Eastern languages; he just knew German.

It doesn't stop there: of the twenty-nine poems in 'Literae Orientales', thirteen aren't by the poet whom Mangan ascribes them to – some are by different poets, others may be his own compositions, and he amalgamates verses from different poems to make an ersatz poem. He gives himself a free hand in translation – in one poem he translates the line 'ihre sect ist Gott' as the exact opposite: 'their sect is mankind', and in another the phrase 'sick in mind and body' becomes 'farewell, thou troubled world' as if, growing impatient with mere sickness, he has decided to hasten things to their inevitable end.

None of Mangan's contemporaries had a clue what he was about (and short of having fluent German, a copy of the baron's book and the time and inclination to compare poem by poem, how could they?). Reading the *Collected Works* is like being handed a satnav in a terrain where you were relying on ancient, sporadic, handwritten directions. I think the supreme difficulty involved in tracking and pinning Mangan down is part of what attracted Chuto in the first place, whatever about being on the rebound from Æ.

Confronted with an anonymous or pseudonymous poem in a journal, how do you tell whether it's a Mangan, especially when his entire generation of poets are writing about the *same* things? They're all hung up on death, melancholy, roses and nationalism (I blame Byron). Reading through the poems in *The Nation*, I began playing a guessing game: if I hid the names and didn't consult the *Collected Works*, could I tell which was by Mangan? I aced a few rounds – obviously Mangan didn't write 'Haunted with gloomy thoughts for evermore / Like sheeted ghosts, peopling my solitude / I sigh for hopes that time may not restore' – and then I came upon 'The Peal of Another Trumpet' which begins:

> Youths of Ireland, patriots, friends!
> Know ye what shall be your course
> When the storm that now impends
> Shall come down in all its force

Shall come down in all its leaden *force*. I was confident that Mangan would never rely on such heavy obvious rhymes and forced rhythm – and the rest of the poem isn't much better, but buried in the middle I found these lines

> The swart slave of Kaffirland
> The frore denizen of the North
> The dusk Indian Mingo chief
> In his lone savannahs green
> The wild, wandering bedawheween
> Mid his wastes of sand and flame

The 'wastes', even more than the new-minted words and the

quick marching tempo, alerted me in this case – I'm preoccupied by Mangan's wastes – but I'm not sure that I'd pass a blind tasting of his poems. Shannon-Mangan was very excited when she discovered five potential Mangan poems in the *Morning Register* of the late 1820s. Chuto was having none of them for the *Collected Works*, but she included them defiantly in an appendix to her biography. I thought that two anyway sounded quite like Mangan on an off-day, of which he had many (he was a hack poet, paid by the line), plus the poems are early, from before he got into his stride. I asked Jacques why they hadn't made it into the *Collected Works*. His sarcastic laugh rang through the email: 'Poor Ellen, she wanted so much to have discovered unknown work by Mangan. But these poems are tame, packed with clichés and sometimes irregular. See the rhymes sun/on and boon/tone in "Poetical Portrait" and in the same poem the lengthening of the penultimate line to 10 instead of 8 syllables.'

Chuto is like one of those art connoisseurs called in to verify a potential Old Master, magnificently rubbishing the clumsy brushwork and garish palette of the rejected canvas. But since art connoisseurs can, and do, get it wrong all the time, I thought Ellen was right to fight for her discoveries and appendix them, although she had little hope of prevailing since her sense of the saintly wronged Mangan was so dated by the time she published her biography, that she burnt the credentials that her painstaking research should have earned her. In an amazing instance of the scholar as ostrich, she chose to ignore the ongoing revolution in Mangan studies and stubbornly reverted to the centenary postage-stamp view of him.

Her approach to David Lloyd and his dazzling discoveries is characteristic: she blanks him. He isn't cited once although his book was published twelve years before hers. True, he and Ellen could never see eye to eye, as Chuto might say, but refusing to confront the most incendiary Mangan critic of the age is like a toddler playing hide-and-seek, thinking that if she closes her eyes no one can see her. It seems of a piece with Ellen's childlike and touching attitude to her subject and it cemented for me the image of Lloyd as something terrifying and explosive, that burned you on touch.

*

Lloyd's book has a forbidding academic title, *Nationalism and Minor Literature: James Clarence Mangan and the Emergence of Irish Cultural Nationalism*, only saved from turgid scholarity by its pleasingly Manganese circularity. When this book was published in 1987 – reworked from a thesis submitted to Cambridge in 1982 – it was an event, not only in Mangan studies but in literary criticism. Malcolm Brown, professor of literature in the University of Washington, expressed the hope that this book might rejuvenate Irish Studies in America and five years after its publication the magisterial Denis Donoghue claimed that the book 'presented Irish criticism with a challenge that has not yet been taken up.'

Donoghue's words reminded me of the sly tailors in Andersen's tale of 'The Emperor's New Clothes', who spread it about that anyone who can't see the clothes isn't fit for their station, and when I did finally sit down to take up the challenge of Lloyd's book, the analogy came back to me. Not that I found Lloyd's book empty or void of meaning, but it did induce those feelings of insecurity and inadequacy that the tailors threatened on viewers. Like a difficult exercise targeting unused muscles, it actually hurts your brain to read this book. Written in the abstruse, convoluted, rarefied language of the structuralists and post-structuralists, it is so far from ordinary speech that you can't apply normal reasoning and compartmentalising to break down and manage the arguments. It made me feel like a juggler trying to keep five balls in the air – it required that kind of concentration, plus the threat that if you allowed any part of the argument to slip your mind, even momentarily, you'd be unable to hold up the rest.

If I felt this, reading the book nearly thirty years after its publication when its language and arguments have become somewhat mainstreamed, I can only imagine the shock for its first readers. Lloyd has taken over from Mitchel as the shaper of the discourse on Mangan – just as Mitchel's ideas and phrases turned up in lectures and papers for generations after his essay, so I started to trace 'Lloydisms' in the academic books and articles of the 1990s and 2000s.

In our correspondence Chuto would refer sarcastically to the 'mighty LLOYD', riffing on Mangan's inveterate capitalising of GOD (and the LORD above). Of course, I was desperate to meet the mighty LLOYD, but I avoided writing to him. I had it in my mind that I needed to run into him, though this was complicated because he lived in the States. When I heard that he would be at the IASIL [International Association for Study of Irish Literature] summer school in Lille, giving a paper (on Beckett rather than Mangan), I booked myself in.

I took a train to Lille from the Gare du Nord in Paris, which I nearly missed thanks to the horror of the connection at Châtelet-Les Halles. Works on the lines had pushed this already labyrinthine junction into chaos and I couldn't find the right metro line and ran up and down the underground tunnels, pleadingly approaching the kiosks selling coffee and newspapers who shook their heads indifferently and waved me away before I could get my question out. Somehow, I blurred my way onto an RER, which did get me to Gare du Nord, with minutes to spare, but since I'd left the metro system, I didn't have the right ticket, and had to jump the RER stile and run from imaginary yells onto the train as it pulled out, my heart thudding because I hadn't had time to double-check the platform number … And I wonder if this experience is not the source of the recurrent dreams I began to have some time later of being lost in train stations or ferry terminals in unknown cities, where people refuse to help or else direct me wrong, and when I take out my mobile to call Frank, I find all the numbers and letters have been rubbed off the keys and looking down I find that I've lost my shoes and it's snowing and my bare feet are turning blue … These dreams never end in triumph – I never find my way through, but in the most vivid of them, the only one whose details I ever recorded, I experience a brief moment of elation in the midst of all the frightening-yet-boring panic when I embark from a city-ferry to yet another unknown urban wasteland to find that the dark night is greying to dawn and a train passing by is carrying zoo animals, and I look in wonder at the lions and tigers pacing up and down wildly behind the bars of their cages, and am transfixed … And these dreams now strike me as replicating the experience of research in all its repetition, frustration, dead ends and sudden wildness – or at least of the open-ended, directionless research I'd got myself into with Mangan, very different to the smooth, well-signposted research of my MLitt – but this isn't how the dreams struck me at the time and maybe I'm being meretricious in framing them this way, too afraid to face up to what they are in fact trying to tell me, and too keen to claim for my unconscious the marvellous image of Mangan as a tiger pacing behind bars – 'chains, bolts and bars' he wrote in a very early poem, and chained, bolted and barred he remained.

Anyway, I made it to Lille on time, only to find that Lloyd hadn't made it. I sulked over the expenditure of so much time, money and stress for a no-show but contra Pascal, I've always found it's worthwhile making the effort to leave your room, and at the Mangan panel the next morning, the chair, Sinead Sturgeon, introduced us excitedly and endearingly to what she called 'a wonderful little poem that you want to wrap up and put in your pocket to take out to turn over', which made me think of a netsuke, which is a good moniker for the pithy poems that Mangan does so well, but not often enough. This poem, entitled 'Lamii's Apology for his Nonsense' is an original work posing as a translation and packs in a lot in just thirty-eight words:

I was a parrot, mute and happy, till,
Once on a time,
The fowlers pierced my woods and caught me;
Then blame me not; for I but echo still
In wayward rhyme
The melancholy wit they taught me.

The parrot is the poet-translator who mimics other writers waywardly and it is the ancient Gael living undisturbed in his woods before the 'fowlers' (a very Anglo-Saxon word) arrived to cart off his timber and teach him to 'echo' English. Colonial plunder made me think of Lloyd and I was gratified to find that if he wasn't physically present, he had fully occupied our minds: I don't recall any of the panellists referencing him in their papers, but it was open season at question time when someone referred mordantly to 'the Year Zero of Lloyd', a phrase which I considered worth my whole journey.

The idea behind the phrase Year Zero is that (to quote Wikipedia) 'all culture and traditions within a society must be completely destroyed or discarded and a new revolutionary culture must replace it, starting from scratch'. This gets across the scorched earth effect that Lloyd had on Mangan studies and the way in which his Mangan presents as something entirely new. Cloaked in the terrifyingly opaque and dense language that we associate with Lacan and Derrida, Lloyd's Mangan seems unrecognisable as any of the Mangans – the merry prankster, *poète maudit*, suffering saint, mournful lyricist, despairing ironist, etc. – that we have encountered before.

It was only when I forced myself to read the contorted essays that accompany Mangan's translations in the *Dublin University Magazine* that I began to hear in Lloyd an older note than Derrida's. Here is Mangan:

> Whether from an absence of sympathy with the unmitigated elements of the Ideal, or from a nervous dread of coming into hostile collision with that rather understood than expressed popular sentiment which overhastily supposes that wherever the Ideal is found unassociated with the Actual, it is necessarily excluded from the territory of the Possible, or else from what phrenologists would call a deficiency in constructiveness – a deficiency which, even where every other intellectual faculty is in full vigour, brings with it a consciousness of irremediable incapacity – [Schiller] shrank from drawing as largely and liberally on the resources of his own mind as an acquaintance with his works would lead us to believe he might have been justified in doing.

And here is Lloyd:

> The veils that his perverted translations cast around their object are lifted only to reveal counterfeit images that induce in the interested few an irreversible disposition to suspicion of rather than trust in appearances. The consequent multiplication of ungrounded appearances becomes the stimulus to an assiduous cultivation of suspicion with regard to the formative power of originality and authenticity.

Irremediable and *irreversible*: nobody can teach Mangan anything about density or opacity and Lloyd, ostensibly a poster-boy for post-structuralism, turns out to be a classic Mangan critic, infected, like the rest, by the master's style, with the difference that, alone among Mangan critics and biographers, he is infected by the language of the essays, not the poems or stories. Paradoxically the thing that most suggests Ground Zero in Lloyd's work – the opaque style – turns out to be the thing for which Lloyd is most indebted to Mangan.

Once I spotted the irremediable and unmitigated Manganese influence on Lloyd's prose, I could start to bring into focus his portrait of Mangan, although this wasn't easy since it's a jagged and cubist portrait, depicted from multiple perspectives. The face that is foregrounded and leaps out at you is of a coldly detached critic who uses translation 'as a mode of criticism', accentuating and parodying the mannerisms of the source poem so that the translation becomes a critique of the original: according to Lloyd, when Mangan distorts Schiller's poem 'Die Ideale' by layering in dreams, irony and stagecraft, this isn't, as Mitchel and everyone else has thought, in order to render his version more personal but because he wants to expose Schiller's philosophical stance as dreamy, stagey and unreal.

While I loved the sly savagery of making the translation critique the poem, I couldn't get with the detachment and methodical rigour of this translator-as-critic who seems more intent on 'providing a survey of German romanticism' than exploring the self. I just didn't recognise him. But when I glanced again at Lloyd's cubist portrait, I got an angle on someone more arresting and familiar.

*

Like all writers, Lloyd has a lexicon: words that he favours which run a seam through his text. As I read and re-read his book, his favourite adjectives – 'transactional', 'dependent', 'inauthentic', 'representative', 'counterfeit', 'colonised', 'refracted', 'indebted' – began to form a pattern. I don't think he uses the word 'parasite', but that is what I spotted winking at me from his pages: an organism 'that lives on or in an organism of another species (its host) and benefits from deriving nutrients at the other's expense', to give the dictionary definition, while 'the host does not benefit from the association and is often harmed by it'. This exactly describes Mangan's approach to his 'host poems' and it conjured up for me the image of him taking up residence in the poetic bodies of Schiller, Tieck, O'Hussey, etc. and, more obliquely, in the bodies of his critics.

This Parasitical Mangan is unable to conceive of any relationship – with government, parents, friends, editors or the poets he translates – except in transactional terms, where there are losers and winners, beggars and benefactors, debtors and creditors, victims and chastisers, colonisers and colonised, hosts and parasites. At an age when most children are dependent on their parents, Mangan became the financial support of his, and from this dependency he was never to escape. He didn't follow the usual pattern of growing up, leaving home and starting his own family. He could never rid himself of the burden of his father either financially, domestically or psychologically. The complex co-dependency that ensued – his father was dependent financially but continued to dominate him psychologically – left Mangan helpless to escape but with a preternaturally sophisticated understanding of the nature of transaction and dependency, which deepened as he grew older because of his condition as a colonised subject within an empire that wasn't delivering.

Growing up in the Liberties, Mangan experienced first-hand the failure of the Act of Union to uphold its promise to improve the condition of the country. Just as his domestic situation made a mockery of the truism that parents support their children, the regional and national situation made a mockery of the official line that Britain was looking after Ireland and had its interests at heart. His awareness of all this, at conscious and unconscious level, gave him a particularly lethal insight into the nature of translation. Dryden, still the most influential theorist of translation when Mangan was writing, might view translation as an equal partnership in which the translator 'maintains' the character of the original, and that might seem reasonable from the secure shores of Britain where the creators of the new world order conversed on equal terms with their counterparts in the ancient world, the Greeks and Romans, but as an Irishman translating German* translations of Persian, Mangan knew different. Transparency and parity are utopic ideals since there is no way that a translation can be exactly equivalent to the original – in all transactions, someone loses and someone gains.

Those living in a stable, bourgeois state might have confidence that an original text can be authentically translated, but for Mangan – coming from an unstable state losing its native language and subject to constant political and legislative reworkings – the whole idea of authenticity and fixed identity is bogus, and the translator's role is to draw attention to the inauthenticity. Mangan fulfils this role by producing multiple translations of the one poem, radically mistranslating whole verses, carelessly reassigning poems to different poets, 'fathering on other poets the offspring of his own brain' and generally making a mockery of the process. The recreated poems are like costumes reassembled from an earlier outfit and the idea that one of these assemblages is truer or more real than another starts to seem ridiculous.

As the re-creator and coloniser of the text, the translator seems to hold all the cards and this is how Mangan generally frames it, with the translator cast as the aggressor – 'knouter', 'matador', 'ornamentor', etc. – but he knows that the translatee, seemingly

---

*In Mangan's time, there was no imperial Germany, rather a collection of small states vulnerable to annexation by France, Russia or Austria.

so passive and plundered, wields ultimate power because the translator cannot exist without him. The translator, though coloniser and dominator, is also and fundamentally a parasite surviving off the host text. If Mangan occasionally framed his relationship to his hosts as mutualistic – he calls some poets his 'debtors' since he has improved their work – he knows that the source poems can exist perfectly well without him whereas he can't create without them.

In human societies the word 'host' often carries a sense of dominance and control since hosts entertain in their own homes, with guests in a supplicant position, but this positioning is undercut when we turn to the natural world since it is the parasites who choose the host who is helpless to eject them. As an Irishman, Mangan understood this complex interplay of dependency: Britain 'hosts' Ireland within its empire but is also a parasite living off the body of Ireland. Where most translators act scrupulously by the text that they're transforming, constantly checking back to see if they're staying true to the original, Mangan is high-handed and indifferent – the host poems are his to abuse, or improve, as he wishes. This seems a classic instance of the victim re-enacting the treatment meted out – the scolded child hitting her doll.

This is the seditious, parasitical Mangan who fizzed at me from Lloyd's pages (although the above is a riff, not a paraphrase of his book) and if I recognised him, it's because I had encountered him before. Far from 'starting from scratch' and 'purging' the past, the parasitical trickster is in many ways a reversion to the past: he resembles *The Comet*'s 'mystifier and humbugger', *The Nation*'s abominable joker, the *Wake*'s 'pseudostylic shamania', and the sly spirit behind the annotations to the *Collected Works*. He is now the Mangan of our times. Despite Shannon-Mangan's best efforts to resuscitate the suffering saint, it is as a seditious parasite that Mangan entered the twenty-first century.

*

After Lille, I stopped making wild excursions to conferences in the hope of running into Lloyd but in January 2017, I heard he was in Dublin. Someone gave me his email and when I contacted him, he suggested a drink in Café en Seine on Dawson Street. Café en Seine is a large, art nouveau-styled café-bar, which seems to fit into a tradition of Dublin Orientalism, like Bewley's Oriental Cafés and the bazaar in Joyce's story 'Araby' and the Turkish baths on Lincoln Place which Leopold Bloom goes into, and like, of course, Mangan's poems. It is maximalist burlesque, a riot of patterned tiles and waving palms and hanging lamps and marble counters and wrought-iron balconies and coloured glass and is not considered in good taste. Neither my hipster Tenters friends (whose aesthetic is mid-century Scandi) nor Frank (eighteenth-century Georgian) would be seen dead going in, and the coffee isn't good enough, but I've always liked its space and light, and I was admiring that Lloyd, who hadn't lived in Dublin for decades, should have such an unerring instinct for the Manganese.

In my mind he had become my mother's description of Denis Donoghue in her UCD tutorials in the 1960s – formidably long, thin, icy and dismissive – but the man sitting on the stool at the burnished copper counter wasn't like that at all. He was small, warm, sweet and friendly, and as we had one whiskey, and then another, he was revealed as Mangan's man – slightly haunted, slightly vulnerable, humorous, and with a great 'first encounter' story.

'I'm from Dublin but I didn't go to school here – I'm Protestant and my parents didn't want me to have to learn Irish, so they sent me to boarding school in Belfast. I was called "a dirty Fenian" by East Belfast boys and that's when I defined myself as a Republican. My sister wasn't sent to boarding school, she stayed here, and it was in her school textbook that I read a poem of Mangan's, it was the 'Vision of Connaught', and it haunted me.'

This is poignant – the exiled Republican reading the nationalist poem that would have been his birthright had he been allowed stay home – and also uncanny because here again is the elusive sister who goes in and out of tales of Mangan. When it came to choosing a subject for his PhD in Cambridge, Lloyd remembered Mangan, but he met with a lot of resistance – 'In Cambridge, no one was interested in nineteenth-century Irish literature; Joyce would have been fine, or Beckett or Yeats.' He had misgivings himself, which he describes in an essay: 'Writing on JCM in the late 1970s and early 1980s, I was often overtaken by a sense of haunting, of possession perhaps. Despite my frequent misgivings about the achievement of the poetry I was reading, misgivings amplified by the widespread assumption that few of Mangan's poems were worth critical consideration any more, the work refused to let me go. It was as if from beyond the grave the poet compelled attention.'

In person, he described this haunting more graphically: 'Mangan's long, bony arm kept reaching up from the grave to grasp me.' If he didn't shake himself free as his professors wished it's because he couldn't – the grasp of rigor mortis – and because he 'was desperately excited by the idea of applying post-colonial theory, which no one was doing at the time' and he had found in Mangan the perfect subject for this application. But the resistance to what he was doing continued:

My thesis [submitted 1982] didn't create a stir at all. I couldn't get a publisher and Denis Donoghue spoke against me for a Fellowship in Cambridge. I was about to join the European Commission as a translator – yes, I was going to become a poet-translator! – but then Berkeley [the University of California] Press said they'd publish my thesis in their New Historicist Series. The book did cause a stir when it came out and that's when I moved to the States where they got what I was doing much better.

Thence the stellar academic career.

This was a longer way round than I'd realised and was less a narrative of meteoric success than one of heroic prevail: he'd had to fight not only disinterest in Mangan but suspicion of post-colonial theory and it showed true courage to plough his lonely furrow for so long. Donoghue's berating of Irish critics for not taking up the challenge was, I now realised, the flagellant's whip turned in on himself: he was the one who had failed to assimilate Lloyd on first reading and had lost him for Cambridge.

At this drink – the only time we ever met, we parted on the friendliest terms, but then he disappeared, ignoring my emails, which I didn't much mind since it preserved his enigma – I got closer to the antagonism between Lloyd and Chuto, which had puzzled me because in many ways their work is complementary and they obviously share a grudging mutual respect for each other's contrasting skills. I would have thought they could have agreed to disagree on what type of translator Mangan was. And they probably could have but their contrasting views came to a head over the editing of the *Collected Works*.

*

Both Chuto and Lloyd present Mangan as a prankster, but with a key difference: where Lloyd's Mangan is inveterately critical and parodic, Chuto's is 'protean', to use Mangan's own self-definition, meaning versatile and shape-shifting. Chuto's Mangan is sometimes scoffing and mocking and using translation as a critique, but he is also capable of behaving like a conventional translator: acting in good faith by the source poet and trying to render a version as close to the original as possible.

Chuto is anxious to emphasise Mangan's proficiency in faithful translation because he wants Mangan to be accorded his due: he regrets that Mangan isn't recognised, like Ezra Pound, as a great poet-translator and doesn't feature in world anthologies of translation. If Mangan is positioned as purely anarchic, transgressive and parodic, then anthologists might have an argument for refusing him status as a major translator. Chuto wants to broaden Mangan's scope and the critical terms of reference. To borrow Mangan's pedantically obsessive parsing in an essay, the seditious, parodic joker is, for Lloyd, the Mangan in *the* Pack, whereas for Chuto he is a Mangan in *a* Pack.

This is a substantive difference, which flared into the open over the editing of the *Collected Works*. For Lloyd, the *Collected Works* presented a brilliant opportunity to recast Mangan and do something new in the history of poetry editing. He feels the poems are inextricable from the essays in which they first appeared, and that Mangan was engaged in a cohesive enterprise – at once an analysis of the nature of translation and a criticism of German Romanticism – which in its indirection, wrong-footing and undermining has all the hilarious subversion of Swift's 'Battle of the Books'. For Lloyd, many of Mangan's poems have little meaning outside the context of the essay in which they appear and to present them as stand-alone poems is to invite ridicule (people will point out that they're poor) and to depart from Mangan's purpose in writing (he knows they're poor, that's the point! he is trying to show up the original poet). For a century and a half, readers had only encountered the poems as stand-alone in anthologies. Lloyd saw in the projected *Collected Works* a chance to redress this: he asked that the poems be reprinted as they had first appeared, embedded in the text of the essays.

Chuto refused. To the usual reasons – it would seem strange and potentially off-putting for the general reader and where do you stop, do you also print poems from *The Comet, The Nation, The Irish Penny Journal* and all the other papers that Mangan contributed to within the columns in which they appeared? – there was the fundamental disagreement as to what kind of poet Mangan is. For Chuto, Mangan is quite often translating as accurately as he can and doing what all poets do, 'stringing sweet sounds together', and to present the poems embedded within the essays is to reduce them to a critical exercise, to deny them their discrete aesthetic identity.

There is no reconciling these viewpoints. I'm not impartial – I share Chuto's view of Mangan as all kinds of poet, not just one kind – but I do have sympathy with both. In every journal that Mangan's work appears in, sooner or later, you find him attempting to subvert its culture/politics: he did it in the almanacs by smuggling in serious verse under guise of acrostics and rebuses; he did it in *Dublin University Magazine* by taking the piss out of scholarly learning; he did it in *The Nation* by sending in comic verse when he knew Duffy wanted solemn, patriotic fare. And his creativity is reactive: it feeds off his reading and his poems are frequently a coded commentary on what other contributors to the journals are up to, which is why my own research insights came from returning to the original journals and contextualising his poems against others published there and even their positioning on the page.

To reprint the poems the way they were first published is to clarify what can otherwise be mystifying – why is Mangan producing such a damp squib of a verse? Why the note of savage suppressed glee? – and it forces the reader to consider the historical context, which is essential to understanding any poet. And presenting the poems in their original setting would be something new and attention-grabbing; it would send out the message that the critical discourse has moved on from evaluative and hierarchical bourgeois arbitrations of taste towards an understanding of poems as socio-economic, cultural-historical texts.

As against this, I don't buy into Lloyd's view that Mangan is engaged in a comprehensive exercise in criticism and that he's always using translation as a mode of criticism. He sometimes is, but what I detect isn't a methodical critic, detached and disciplined enough to deliberate on German romanticism and make this the whole point of his translations, but someone more haphazard and solipsistic who is frequently using the source poem as a springboard to perpetuate his own preoccupations and obsessions.

Lloyd might answer that whether Mangan is being critical or solipsistic, the essays still throw light on the poems and should be reproduced, but if the essays don't amount to a comprehensive, deliberative exercise, if Mangan is sometimes just being haphazard and expedient – he was, after all, paid to fill pages – then there is less argument for giving the prose full billing with the poems. Mangan submitted the same poems to multiple publications, hoping to get paid double for them. When he slips a poem into the *Dublin University Magazine,* having previously featured it in *The Comet,* is it really worth piously reprinting his factitious reasons for this expedience? And in the absence of other poets' work appearing in the context in which it was first published, isn't singling out Mangan making too high a claim for his exceptionalism, and doesn't it suggest that his work isn't good enough to stand alone? And publishing the poems as they first appeared, embedded in the essays or the newspaper columns even, does risk alienating the general reader and condemning Mangan to academic interest rather than widening his readership (although it's true that the elusive 'general reader' isn't rushing out to buy the six volumes of the Irish Academic Press).

These are the arguments. No halfway house is possible. Chuto considers that the extensive annotations, which provide the context and reproduce phrases from Mangan's commentary, are enough for the intelligent reader to work out what is going on. 'As editor,' he called it. Two decades later, Lloyd, still bitter, described it to me as 'a travesty'.

A brilliant creation?

Frank liked to call people he liked 'brilliant creations'. The first time he said this about my father's best friend, to whom I had just introduced him, I bristled at what I took to be a slur on the friend's sincerity, as if he were being accused of imposture. Frank cut off my spluttering protestations with the impatient and enigmatic remark: 'Oh, we're all creations.'

This sounded more Wilde than Frank and I hardly knew what to make of it. I've known people who were obvious self-creations – there was the girl in our clubbing years who renamed herself after a character in Greek myth (or an American city, I was never sure which) with such compelling humourlessness that we all fell meekly into line and never called her by her birth name again; and there was the boy at school who mutated into a minor member of the Brat Pack by changing his clothes, accent, movements and gaze (it was too strictly imitative to be inventive – I don't think Frank would have called it 'brilliant' – but we were only fourteen). But the idea that we're *all* creations, including me, including Frank, confused me because I had no sense of having created myself – except in the matter of clothes and that's just female rite of passage, what Hollywood calls 'the Makeover' – and Frank always seemed to me so invariably himself in every situation that I was convinced he'd walked out of the womb in suit, cufflinks and cigar, scanning auction catalogues and discussing Joyce, and this seemed borne out by photos of him as a child with shrewd, ironic eyes and by his accounts of obsessive childhood philately and of storming back into Uncle George's pet shop behind Clery's to complain that he had been sold a dead (rather than a hibernating) tortoise. That child is so much father to the man I know that I was sure he had simply expanded into his given character rather than, as he appeared to be claiming, creating himself. But when I read his book, *The Parnell Split*, the descriptions of Parnell seemed familiar, as if I'd known his character already, and after a while I realised that what was familiar was that they could be descriptions of Frank. Of course this could be an instance of Parnell 'becoming his admirer' but Frank sticks very close to the sources and all the quotes are from Parnell's contemporaries, so I don't think that's what was going on. I think that in whatever space is left to us after our genes and upbringing have done their worst, Frank filled with his idea of his hero. This hunch was confirmed in the most obvious, e.g. the most visual, sense by the Parnellite beard he sported in his youth, and by the magnificent Parnellite frock coat he wore on our wedding day.

There was never any question about whether Mangan created himself. Like Jay Gatsby and Marilyn Monroe and Marilyn Manson and George Eliot and George Orwell and everyone else who successfully renames themselves, he wasn't born of his parents, but of his idea of himself. Through executing this idea, he elided his origins. I think his manifest success in ceasing to be James Mangan, scrivener and part-schooled son of a bankrupt Liberties grocer, and becoming the romantic poet Clarence Mangan, master of exotic tongues, goes some way to explaining the puzzling lack of sources for his early life: he had no interest in keeping records of his unpromising past, and his contemporaries, invested in the idea of him as an exotic mystery, had no incentive to collect the facts or solicit the recollections that would confirm his mundane beginnings. I remember telling an eminent historian that Mangan was Catholic and getting a sceptical look. From his hazy knowledge of early nineteenth-century poetry and exceptional knowledge of Irish history, this historian was pretty sure that Clarence Mangan, contributor to the *Dublin University Magazine*, translator of German and Persian, copyist in Trinity College library, must be Protestant because how could a Catholic of that era, a *poor* Catholic, have learnt those languages and found his way to that journal and that library, and anyway whoever heard of a Catholic called Clarence?

Being James Mangan was a dead end that he had to escape. How did he do it? All self-invention works off models and the zeitgeist: we create ourselves through what we read and watch and listen to, and who we hang out with. My 'makeover' came, like everyone else's in my generation, via films, TV, magazines and whatever turned up on the street and the dancefloor. But Mangan came of age in the depressed and over-surveillanced Dublin of the 1810s and 20s. The aristos had packed up their houses and departed the capital, taking their flamboyant clothes and expensive tastes from the streets; the theatres and concert halls had closed, and there were no public art galleries. Even the Church wasn't awaft with wine and incense and glittering with icons and stained glass, as in France or Italy; it was a re-purposed storehouse down a side alley. All Mangan had for self-invention was books. He couldn't afford these either and there were no public libraries until O'Connell set up the Repeal Reading Rooms in the 1840s, but a few prominent booksellers (Spottswood, Jackson's, John Archer's) established circulating libraries, with membership by subscription. Someone – his father or uncles? – must have paid Mangan's subscription because books became his 'refuge', as he writes in his memoir, and eventually the springboard to becoming Clarence.

I imagine I know what it was like for him to escape into his books because I was a little bibliomaniac myself of the most obsessive kind and – in what I now recognise as incipient fan fiction – would send myself to sleep earnestly counselling Isabel Archer not to marry Gilbert Osmond and worrying that Cat had suffered too much early trauma to be a good Chrestomanci, showering all the empathy and concern on these fictional characters that I withheld from people around me. But if I compare our circumstances, I realise that my escape into reading was the palest echo of Mangan's: I was born into a happy family in a prosperous liberal democracy in the late twentieth century, which means that I was always being taken to the park and the beach, the circus and the zoo, ballet lessons and summer camp, parties and playdates (or whatever we called them then, something less creepy) and holidays to far other lands and other seas, and even though I blanked a lot of this for books, I was being continually distracted from the page, whereas the 'desultory rambles', which were all Mangan had by way of alternative, were no competition for the *Arabian Nights*; nor could the power of my books to shock and inflame compete with his.

Here's what came out when he was in his teens: Byron's 'Childe Harold's Pilgrimage', 'The Giaour' and 'Don Juan'; Shelley's 'The Cenci' and 'The Mask of Anarchy'; Mary Shelley's *Frankenstein* (anonymously); Thomas Moore's 'Lalla Rookh'; Coleridge's 'Kubla Khan' and 'Christabel'; Maturin's *Melmoth the Wanderer*; De Quincey's *Confessions of an English Opium Eater*. These are some of the most electrifying things ever written, exploding with sex, drugs, blasphemy, satanism, dandyism, liberty, individualism and Eastern exoticism. We know that Mangan read these, and every other romantic text he could get his hands on, because he quotes liberally from all the above works in his essays. And when I try and think what it was like for this Jesuit-schooled boy from the Liberties, who has never been outside Ireland and is afflicted with the low self-esteem of Catholics in the penal era, to read this stuff, I find I have no personal point of comparison. I can't compare it to my teenage reading though I read some pretty steamy stuff, but what I read was old, its shock blunted by bearing the fingerprints of generations of readers, or if recently published, had a deadened, static feel because it had all been said already.

The closest I can get to the teenage Mangan reading incendiary romanticism proclaiming free love and the end of organised religion, which contradicted everything he was being taught by the Jesuits and revealed a world which bore no relation to how people around him were living, is Joseph Brodsky 'pseudo-poet in velveteen trousers' reading Auden in the USSR, or the teenage Greta Thunberg reading about the imminent threat to the planet while everyone around her carries on as if nothing has changed. I think existential terror is exactly what Mangan got from romanticism – the revelation that there is no anthropomorphic God blew his mind – but he was luckier than Greta: he got other stuff as well and it was just what he needed for re-invention.

Romanticism gave him his poetic themes of death, love, roses, nationalism and the Orient, and it gave him his poetic mood, which he mocks in an early poem as 'that air of mystery, / That unimaginable moodiness, / That something inexpressibly profound / No living mortal bears the power to fathom', and it gave him his name, Clarence, which came via the Romantics' idol, Shakespeare.* He is very obviously a romantic creation; is he also a 'brilliant creation'?

Choosing the right themes and name and striking the right attitudes isn't proof in itself because there were any number of

---

*It was romantic thinkers, starting in Germany and spreading to France and England, who put Shakespeare on the pedestal that he still occupies today. Hamlet's riposte to Horatio – 'there are more things in heaven and earth than are dreamt of in your philosophy' – became the Romantics' answer to neoclassical rationalism, and Shakespeare their chief example of what Keats called 'negative capability' – the ability to be receptive to all aspects of existence, the state in which 'man is capable of being in uncertainties, mysteries, doubt, without any irritable reaching after fact and reason'.

romantic wannabes wandering Europe at the time, sporting red waistcoats and writing poems to death and the nightingale, and some of them even killed themselves, poor things, in imitation of Goethe's Young Werther, and you wouldn't call them brilliant; you'd call them sad. Maybe self-creation only becomes 'brilliant' when it goes beneath the surface? Reading *The Parnell Split*, I think that the most important thing Frank took from Parnell wasn't his beard or frock coat or even his aloofness, though he could wrap himself in that very effectively when he needed to; I think it's his loathing of public sanctimony. Frank's vast tolerance of what people get up to in their private lives may seem in the twenty-first century like an affront or an anachronism and I warned him this could get him cancelled, dismissed as an entitled male guarding the privileges of the patriarchy, but I don't think that explains his provocative tolerance. It's because he is thinking of Parnell. When the voices go strident against sexual misconduct, he hears Healy in Committee Room 15 and the bishops on the pulpit, and Dante in Joyce's Christmas dinner scene, excoriating Parnell's morals. I think that at a formative age he was so affected by what happened to Parnell that it shaped his understanding of the world, and withholding judgment became organic to him.

Nobody ever knew Mangan like I know Frank, which makes me sad. Nobody ever tried to penetrate his pose to find out what it meant. It would have been very hard, it's true, and maybe impossible, as he brag-laments himself: 'What cared I if those who attempted to break down, with their feeble fingers, the adamantine barrier that levered me from a communion with mankind, perceiving the futility of their enterprise, retired from my presence with disgust and despair?' But the answer to this rhetorical question is that, of course, he cared very much, and though he sounds categorical, he provides, as always, a small wistful escape route – because if someone with firm, rather than feeble, fingers had tried, then perhaps … And in one of the saddest, if still bravely tragicomic, passages he ever wrote, he implies that all they had to do was ask:

> Indeed the very circumstance of a man's walking about and perspiring under such a peculiar Cloak ought alone to have been sufficient to convince him that there was a mystery of some sort connected with the perspirer; and had he only trundled up to me and put the interrogatory – 'Man in the Cloak, art thou He?' – I would have responded to his sagacity by nobly and without all disguise flapping my side-wings in his physiognomy.

*

It is the job of the critic to 'trundle up to [the text] and put the interrogatory' in order to unlock the 'mystery connected' to the writer's 'disguise'. It was a challenge I thought I was up to because I had another pressing reason to interrogate Mangan's reading: I was trying to airlift him out of Ireland. I had started to notice that almost all his critics and biographers explain him through Ireland: Joyce ('Mangan is the type of his race') follows Mitchel ('his history and fate were indeed a type and shadow of the land he loved so well'), and it was with a kind of shocked déjà vu that I realised that Lloyd's excitingly different-looking Mangan is *still* trapped in Ireland – he can't escape 'his excluded position as a colonised subject', which is surely exactly the same as being 'the type and shadow of the land'. The impact of Ireland is different in all three cases: for Mitchel, the suffering heroic country creates the lyrical nationalist; for Joyce, the 'narrow and hysterical nationality' irreparably damages the sensitive genius; for Lloyd, colonialism produces the mordant postmodernist. Different outcomes but an identical influence: Mangan is always explained as a product of Ireland. I am not free myself from this pervasive tendency - I also pin him forcibly to the Liberties and to Irish history – but this collective insistence that he is the product of his environment seems to deny him his agency as a brilliant creation and his remarkable feat in remoulding unpromising raw material into something rare, exotic and thrilling.

And the overwhelming emphasis on Ireland ignores that this boy who invented himself through his reading, and *only* through his reading, wasn't reading much that was Irish, since he couldn't speak or read Gaelic and the tradition of Irish writing in English was only getting going and was in any case co-opted into the British mainstream – writers like Swift, Sterne, Edgeworth, Moore and Maturin were seen as part of the British comic tradition or the European romantic tradition. Some of what they wrote was distinctively Irish-themed and located, for instance 'A Modest Proposal', *Castle Rackrent*, and *Moore's Melodies*, and this certainly gave Mangan a sense of literary lineage, but he doesn't cite them, or any Irish author, nearly as often as he does Shakespeare or Byron. The first nationalist poem he ever wrote, 'To My Native Land', was inspired by a satire of Byron's, 'The Irish Avatar', which says it all, really. Until the Famine, Mangan mostly avoided writing about, or engaging directly, with Ireland. Physically and emotionally, he was trapped where he was born; intellectually and imaginatively, he got as far away as he could. Given his heroic efforts to read his way out, to master German, to translate the *Sturm und Drang*, to appropriate orientalism, it seems terrible that we won't let him out of Ireland. I can hear his claustrophobic howl of anguish at 'being shut up in the cavern'.

I wanted to find out how reading the English Romantics and translating the German Romantics affected, or infected, him at a deep level and I wanted to know what he himself contributed to the movement. Fired up, I plunged blithely into the study of Romanticism. This was a really terrible idea, which cost me months and months of my life, and just the memory of it now triggers panicky feelings of bewilderment and resentment. I read one book, and then another, and another, and another … and by then I was lost in the dark wood, in a thick mist, with no way through … I couldn't even get a working definition of romanticism, let alone figure out how it might have influenced Mangan. I would land on a definition which seemed applicable but when I tried to fit it, everything would begin to dissolve and shape-change. For the longest time I thought this was Mangan's fault and roundly cursed him for being so slippery, but then I read Isaiah Berlin's *The Roots of Romanticism* and I realised that the problem goes way beyond my poor poet, and he may be a symptom, not a cause.

'The subject is by no means easy' begins Berlin silkily and proceeds to frame the problem by quoting any number of 'countervailing' definitions of Romanticism from e.g. Goethe ('romanticism is disease, it is the weak, the sickly,'), Nietzsche ('it is not a disease, but a therapy'), Taine ('a bourgeois revolt against the aristocracy'), Friedrich Schlegel ('a feverish longing to break through the narrow bonds of individuality'), Stendhal ('the romantic is the modern and interesting, classicism is the old and dull'), Ruskin ('a contrast of the beautiful past with the frightful and monotonous present'), Ferdinand Brunetiere ('it is literary egotism, the opposite of self-transcendence') and so on, and so contradictory. Without drawing breath, Berlin then plunges his befuddled readers (or audience rather, the book began as lectures) into a seasick ride:

> Romanticism is the primitive, the untutored, it is youth, the exuberant sense of life of the natural man, but it is also pallor, fever, disease, decadence, the *maladie du siècle*, La Belle Dame Sans Merci, the Dance of Death, indeed Death itself. It is Shelley's dome of many-coloured glass, and it is also his white radiance of eternity. It is the confusing teeming fullness and

richness of life, Fülle des Lebens, inexhaustible multiplicity, turbulence, violence, conflict, chaos, but also peace, oneness with the great 'I Am', harmony with the natural order, the music of the spheres, dissolution in the eternal all-containing spirit. It is the strange, the exotic, the grotesque, the mysterious, the supernatural, ruins, moonlight, enchanted castles, hunting horns, elves, giants, griffins, falling water, the old mill on the Floss, darkness and the powers of darkness, phantoms, vampires, nameless terror, the irrational, the unutterable ...

And on and on and on – through pages and pages, Berlin piles up well over a hundred marvellous 'countervailing' examples of what Romanticism is ('it is also dandyism, the desire to dress up, red waistcoats, green wigs, blue hair ... It is the lobster which Nerval led about on a string in the streets of Paris' etc.), culminating with the magnificently bathetic: 'It is perhaps not very surprising that, faced with this, A.O. Lovejoy, who is certainly the most scrupulous and one of the most illuminating scholars who ever dealt with the history [of romanticism], approached a condition nearing despair.' *Perhaps not very surprising ...!* The bathos is perfected by the sublime mismatch of the poor despairing critic's name. I felt for Lovejoy. I felt *like* Lovejoy. Months and months into my season of hell in romanticism, and I was no closer to finding out how his reading infected Mangan.

To make it worse, through all my miserable confusion, my 'condition approaching despair', I was picking up an alarming note, faint but unmistakeable, of *failure* around Mangan's romanticism. Joyce was the first to sound this note when he compared Mangan unfavourably to Blake and traduced Dark Rosaleen as a mad, abject, dying queen, which is to say a travesty of the romantic muse. Joyce blamed Ireland and its 'bloody crimes', 'madness' and 'narrow, hysterical' nationalism for Mangan's failure to be as great a Romantic as Blake: Romanticism can't flourish in the hostile, stony Irish soil and that's not Mangan's fault (except insofar as he didn't transplant himself elsewhere). Subsequent critics took up the theme of Mangan as a warped/failed romantic but were less inclined than Joyce to exonerate him and blame Ireland. In a 1968 review of the longer memoir, the young Eavan Boland wrote impatiently: 'The melodrama and morbidity of this fragment would be more arresting were they not also so unoriginal. The fact is that they draw heavily upon a posture of self-destruction which by the 1840s, when this account was written, had become a stereotype of romanticism.' It is presumably with Joyce and Boland in mind that Lloyd writes of 'Mangan's writing being read as a falling off from the romanticism it seeks to continue'. (Even without a definition of the 'romanticism it seeks to continue', I understood that 'falling off' cannot be a good thing.)

Then I came across an essay which does define romanticism, and which stood out from the pervasive slipperiness around the subject for the succinct clarity of its argument and the bracing dismissiveness of its judgment, signalled in the title: 'James Clarence Mangan and the Romantic Stereotypes: "Old and Hoary at Thirty-Nine"'. The author, Jean Andrews, takes her definition of romanticism from Mario Praz's classic, *The Romantic Agony* (1933), the first book to expose what was previously only whispered about or sampled as a guilty pleasure: romanticism's dark underbelly – the torture scenes in Maturin and Delacroix, the homosexual, sadistic fantasies of Lautréamont, the dreams of Gautier 'where all the most unbridled desires can be indulged and the cruellest fantasies take concrete form', the crime, damnation, incest in Byron and Shelley, etc.

Praz's book is electrifying with wonderful chapter headings like 'The Metamorphoses of Satan', 'The Shadow of the Divine Marquis', 'La Belle Dame Sans Merci', which Andrews briskly distils into what she calls the 'sex-death-devil nexus'. In her reading of Praz, a Romantic must be unashamedly transgressive, ever ready to plunge into erotica, blasphemy and nihilism, and she constructs from this premise a Mangan as memorable, if less critically influential than Mitchel's suffering angel and Lloyd's sly postmodernist. Her Mangan is a kid from a troubled home who gets punch-drunk on the romantic Kool-Aid; strikes attitudes drawing on Byron and Werther; projects an air of melancholic intensity, leavened by the occasional opaque joke designed to keep people out, not draw them in; renames himself via Shakespeare; lets it be thought that in some mysterious way he has mastered Turkish, Persian, Coptic, Gaelic; sits alone in pubs scribbling in multi-coloured inks, as if each ink corresponds to a different language or a different mood; develops a secretive opium habit and teases the rumour mill by alternately boasting and denying it; 'disappears' his income through gambling and drink; establishes a persona, the Man in the Cloak, and retreats into it more and more, 'shunning all and shunned by all in turn', until he becomes a self-fulfilling prophecy, a public disgrace whom people wring their hands over, and then, quite suddenly but entirely predictably, dies aged forty-six.

And this may seem like a Romantic life and death but when you look at the work, he's no Romantic; he's the opposite, an inhibited Catholic, terrified of sex ('At a time when the erotic was as important to poetry as to Gothic fiction, Mangan's work is unique in its lack of a sexual awareness' writes Andrews, stingingly) and uncomfortable with blasphemy ('the best that can be said of [his Faustian tale, *The Thirty Flasks*] is that it is Gothic horror tale subverted by its own humour'). Only in the last branch of the nexus does Andrews allow him some success, grudgingly admiring his treatment of 'the wasteland' which she terms 'the romantic trope corresponding to death or inner despair', but this isn't enough to save him. Turning his own pet word, 'wasted', against him, she writes scathingly that he 'wasted his gifts trying to live out an impossible literary role' – which is to say that if he hadn't come under the influence and distorted himself into romantic attitudes, he would have led a more sociable life and his talent would have developed more easily and naturally. Her final paragraph is stinging:

> Mangan's religious orthodoxy prevents him being admitted to the inner circle of Romanticism. With his innocence and child-like belief, he could never have fathomed the darker depths of Romanticism, although he assumed its outward trappings. [He] was himself 'old and hoary at thirty-nine' because of a tragic commitment to Romanticism he never fully understood.

This Mangan is certainly self-invented but he's not a 'brilliant creation', he's a pathetic creation, a romantic poseur, a wannabe – just like Eavan Boland's Mangan 'leaning heavily upon a posture of self-destruction which has become a stereotype of romanticism'. (Andrews doesn't mention Boland and is unlikely to have read her short review written two decades earlier; it unnerved me that these two witheringly succinct women had found their way separately to the same conclusion.) I admired Andrews for her clarity on a subject, Romanticism, which seems to melt everyone's mind, and I got a transgressive thrill from her readiness to call Mangan out as an artistic failure because aesthetic evaluation isn't something Eng. Lit. people do any more (I can still hear, or feel, the silence that burst on my undergraduate seminar, like the popping of a balloon, when I protested of *The Color Purple* 'but it isn't any *good*', and the follow-up sound, which sealed my sense of being a small unruly child, the polite clearing of the professor's throat …). But mostly her essay devastated me: I recognised her romantic poseur very well; I was always meeting him out and about; I just never thought he was Mangan.

*

When my sister and I first came to Dublin to go to college, we plunged in as enthusiastically and blindly as I would later plunge into the study of Romanticism. We'd come from an international school in Brussels, which we enjoyed – it would be hard not to enjoy this school of many nationalities and no uniform with its atmosphere of an American high school – but we had an inarticulate sense of something missing. The surface multiplicity of different languages masked a deep conformity since everyone's parents worked at the EU institutes or NATO so that when we read *Brave New World* in class, I was struck by the passage describing how the children are divided into groups of Alpha, Beta, Delta, Epsilon etc., according to their programmed ability. We were all, I felt, good little Betas, indistinguishable from each other. Instead of expressing the distinct cultures that our parents had come from, we seemed to merge into one ersatz culture, internationalist, peace-loving and feel-good, but lacking in specificity.

It was perhaps the wish to escape conformity that attracted us in our first year in college to flamboyant people on the fringes who liked to strike attitudes (though it was also because it is easier to befriend outsiders than infiltrate the impenetrable cliques of Dublin schools). There was the boy who had 'Byron de Sade' stencilled on his zippo and wore only black and consumed a cocktail of drugs but gave off a certain squeamishness so that if you had asked him whether he whipped his sexual partners or slept with his sister, as his stencilled heroes did, I think he'd have fainted … And there was another who lived his life by The Diceman, which meant if he rolled the die and it came up 1, he had to go to the library, but if it came up 5, he went to the bar … And there were the drawling dope-smokers who drove us mad because every time we tried to pin down an arrangement, they told us to chill and release ourselves from the tyranny of the clock ... And there was the Carlos Castaneda enthusiast who wanted to abandon civilisation, or at least urbanism, and live the simple life of a nomadic tribe, apparently unaware that Castaneda had been unmasked as an imposter ... And there were all the boys in nightclubs and in kitchens after parties, who probably didn't quote Blake, 'the road of excess leads to the palace of wisdom' but may have quoted 'Seize the day' or 'Carpe diem' or just 'Live in the moment', and whichever it was, the meaning was clear: *have sex with me right now and if you don't, you're frigid*, which perhaps because it rhymes with my name but also because I'm Generation X, seemed like absolutely the worst thing I could be ...

I could go on – maybe I could pile up as many examples as Isaiah Berlin (no one led a lobster on a string through the streets but one guy did tell me solemnly that the best way to gate-crash a club or party was to arrive at the door carrying a lobster in each hand; I feel sure he's right) – and after my long day's journey into the dark night of Romanticism, I can now recognise all these poses as romantic derivatives, although at the time I'd have pointed to the more obvious influence of 1960s free love and 70s punk, not realising that the 60s and 70s and 90s were decades of romantic revivalism. Berlin called Romanticism 'the largest recent movement to transform the lives and the thought of the Western world' and it has gone on exerting its influence into the twenty-first century.*

If I call these friends Romantic poseurs, I don't mean it as an insult – a pose in your twenties can be a good thing, a means to free yourself from your parents and teachers and their expectations

---

*Although I feel like its long reign, from Blake to Pete Doherty, may finally be coming to an end and the backlash beginning – the millennials' insult of 'okay Boomer' is an attack on romanticism's narcissistic cult of the individual, its seedy bohemianism presenting as glamour, its self-indulgent excess presenting as enlightenment; something much sterner, more ethical, more communal and more puritanical being required in an age of climate catastrophe.

of you, a step on the way to becoming a 'brilliant creation'. You're allowed to discard it when it's no longer fit for purpose, which is what most of our friends did when they got down to the serious business of building careers and raising families. Their poses didn't 'ruin their lives' or 'waste their gifts' and there was nothing 'tragic' about their 'commitment to romanticism' (perhaps because they weren't deeply committed). They are not what Andrews accuses Mangan of.

But a few didn't get away so easily. They fell 'through the pit abysmal' – or 'fell into hell' as Shane MacGowan rephrases it – and if it's simplistic to blame their addiction on their pose, because addiction will out, it's reductive not to interrogate the interplay between the two. When I think back to sitting in the car with Tim, listening to the stripped snarl and raging nihilism of the Velvet Underground, Hole, Nirvana and the Lemonheads, I know that the magnificent soundtrack is endorsing his choices and making him feel part of something significant, and that without it, the ride to meet his dealer would be very bleak indeed. Romanticism (or its derivatives) gave him the excuse he needed not to get clean, and maybe that excuse is the difference between life and death, so if Romanticism didn't make him an addict, maybe it stopped him from stopping … The whole question is a bit Yeats after 1916: 'Did that play of mine send out certain men the English shot?' which Yeats answered with another question: 'Was it needless death after all?' suggesting that inflaming the young was maybe worth it for the romantic goal of Irish freedom. Kurt Cobain and Amy Winehouse might say the same thing – their deaths were worth it for *Nevermind* and *Back to Black* – and their superfans might agree (although their families wouldn't, obviously). It's the wasted lives – the wasted *wasted* lives – that haunt us. How do we make the argument that those deaths weren't needless?

Andrews's portrait of Mangan is wretched because she won't accord him the status of Cobain and Winehouse. In my desperation to disprove her and claim Mangan as a true ravaged romantic, I deployed Isaiah Berlin because if romanticism manifests in multiple guises, then you can't reduce it to Praz's nexus, and there must be any number of 'countervailing' examples as authentic, if less glamorous, than the blasphemous voluptuaries. And even if you accept Praz as the determinant, then Andrews isn't right that Mangan fails at blasphemy: the long memoir casts the father as the Devil who wrests his son from the paradise of schooling and plunges him into 'sulphurous' offices, while the well-meaning priests bleat useless warnings.

I did recognise, as I frantically piled up arguments, that my efforts were out of all proportion to a single article by a young post-doc. Yes, Andrews gathers up all the mutterings about Mangan as a Failed Romantic into a succinct and cogent case, but she didn't change the critical landscape like Lloyd; there was no rational reason to be devoting so much time and attention to her. Why was I getting so het up? I had to admit that she had hit a nerve. My agitation reminded me of the student at Joyce's lecture, who recognised the 'mad', 'narrow and hysterical' Ireland that Joyce was depicting but didn't want to admit that he did, so displaced his rage onto different targets. If I follow this logic, then my own howl of fury came about because I recognised something personal in Andrews's attack on Mangan but didn't want to admit it.

What was it I recognised? If I were Chuto who, as the young father of young children, spent what sounds like a dangerous percentage of his salary on gambling, I wouldn't have to dig too deep to uncover my bond with Mangan, but it wasn't so easy to see myself in her description. Even with all Berlin's multifarious examples of romanticism to pick from, I couldn't find any that applied to me. I couldn't claim to be melancholic, pantheistic, pansexual, iconoclastic or any of those exciting things. But since I couldn't deny that Andrews's essay had touched a nerve, I bravely poked and prodded till I discovered the humiliating truth: I'm a romantic-by-proxy, which is to say, I displace/transfer my need for romanticism onto my partners.

I was always irresistibly attracted to addicts so that my sister used to sarcastically call me an enabler (she got the whole addiction-to-addicts thing out of her system by the time she was sixteen, but then she was a teenage dirtbag and I was a late developer). My list of ex-boyfriends, or ex-flings, would fill the Priory (or somewhere less expensive) and should I ever wish to write an enabler's memoir as a kind a subset of the addiction memoir genre, I'd have more than enough material. Apparently, people who go with addicts are suffering from 'a saviour complex' or 'white knight syndrome' – they (*we*!) are moral masochists who get off on putting others' needs before their own; or they/we are closet narcissists who want to be the ones to redeem the sinner, so that people say solemnly 'he would have died without her!' But I don't think I ever wanted, or tried, to sober up my addicts. It was the intensity of their existence that attracted me – their refusal to weigh consequences or rein themselves in, their willingness to go for it with no thought of tomorrow, their complete absorption in me for the brief, heady period when I seemed like the answer to their deepest needs and our love the manifestation of all that's right in the universe, before, abruptly, it shrivelled. For this 'I cannot help returning like the moth to the flame' though I'm not proud of being an addict's groupie.

So I can't deny what first attracted me to the addict James Clarence Mangan, not given the nature of our first encounter – in a lock-in, on MDMA, in the company of Ireland's most famous addict. I could argue in my defence that if it was the seedy glamour of his life that drew me, it was the lure of his work that kept me, but you can't separate the work from the life. You choose as your biographical subject someone who fascinates you and the reasons that attract you to an addict in real life – the glamour of the highs, the pathos of the lows, the recklessness of the self-destruction, the flurry of distractions that prevent you getting to the heart of the person so that you are always seeking, never at rest – continue to hold true in the research life. This isn't surprising since you've entered into a relationship with your subject, which bears obvious similarities to a love affair: there's the same inbuilt obsolescence (it's going to end someday) and the same mutual parasitism (the biographer is building a reputation through the subject, who is escaping oblivion and neglect through the biographer) and time spent with an addict, whether in life or research, is thrilling and infuriating because the addict is on a kind of grail quest, restlessly seeking the clarity of the lost high when life seemed explicable and meaningful, and at some level you must believe in this quest, or you wouldn't stick around.

If I'm drawn to Mangan because of his addictions, and if his addictions were fanned by his Romanticism then this implicates me in Andrews's scathing evaluation and she has me in a double bind: if the object of my displaced romanticism is himself a poseur, then I'm wasting my life on someone who wasted his life: I'm wasted-by-proxy. This is so obviously mortifying – like being a fangirl to a tribute act – that it explains why it became my mission to prove Mangan was 4 Real, carved in the blood of Romanticism.

Seven divers shades of concealment

A phrase of Lloyd's was nagging at me: 'Mangan's sartorial eccentricity is thus doubled in his stylistic mannerism.' This comes near the end of the book, so by the time I got to it, I had already read the chapter 'Veils of Salis' in which Lloyd quotes some of Mangan's sartorial metaphors. I hadn't made a note of these when reading but they must have lodged somewhere because as I turned over Lloyd's doubling of sartorial and stylistic mannerism in my mind, I found myself making another of my obsessive lists, which I titled 'Cloaking Metaphors'.

This list would take up more pages than anyone wants to read. Mangan cannot seem to go many lines without spinning, winding, folding, curtaining, shrouding, garbing, vesting, canopying, and everything else you do with cloth. Here is the briefest sample:

- 'The darkly over-curtained / And mysterious doom of man'
- 'This dim dell which gloom and cloud / and death-black mists forever shroud'
- 'Avert thine eyes from woman's face when Twilight falls and she unveils'

- 'When Heaven's dim veil uprolled, the starry heaven gleamed'
- 'Our prelates and our priests they uncassock'
- 'Woollen plaids would grace herself and robes of silk her child'
- 'Cloaked in the Hall the Envoy stands, his mission unspoken'

And so on, and so on. When you check back to the original source poem, you generally find that there is no clothing metaphor, which is proof – if the sheer quantity isn't enough – that we're dealing with a pathology because you can always tell Mangan's obsessions by what he adds to his translations, and his inhibitions by what he takes away. When reaching for cover, he seizes whatever woven material is at hand but also structures like bars, cages, walls, and he draws down the whole natural world of cover: twilight, clouds, shadows, branches, leaves, trees, etc. He is always anthropomorphising nature with the language of the draper – 'a pall funereal curtains the kingly glory of the sun, / And robes the melancholy earth'.

What you will never find in his poems: a naked girl in an open field at noon on a cloudless summer day. Instead, the girl will be veiled and placed in a convent that is hidden behind trees. Her lover, donning penitential haircloth, will make his way through difficult terrain to approach at twilight under clouds; he will strain his eyes through the dying light to see through the leaves and branches to the decaying convent walls, until she appears at a window in her nun's veil and raises the lattice, giving him the briefest glimpse of her face before she disappears from sight. This is the scenario of Mangan's version of Schiller's 'The Knight of Toggenburg', a wistful and elegiac poem about courtly love, which, in Mangan's hands, becomes almost comical as you count up the barriers placed between the knight and his girl.

The Man in the Cloak cloaks his poems! This revelation landed, for me, like the purloined letter hiding in plain sight in Poe's short story. And it opened a valve. Suddenly wherever I looked, in his life and work, I spotted him running for cover. For a start, his pseudonyms, of which there are very many: Drechsler, Selber, Terrae Filius, Vacuus, HiHum, Whang-Hum, Mark Anthony, Peter Puff Secundus, A Mourne-r, An Idler, Monos, A Yankee, Lageniensis, Herr Hoppandgoön Baugtratuer, Herr Popandgoön Tutchemupp, Solomon Dryasdust, Dr Berri Abel Hummer, etc. Surely these are cloaks? And wasn't his proficiency in writing riddles and acrostics because these are built around hidden answers? And what is translation but a new outfit, or disguise, for the source poem? Mangan suggests as much when he deploys clothing metaphors to describe his role as translator: 'We must see if it be not practicable to exhibit the Ottoman Muse in apparel somewhat more attractive than which decorates her here'; 'We have (for no base purposes) disguised [these poems] to the best of our poor ability'.

Then there are the descriptions – or rather sightings – of him from contemporaries. He is never spotted in open terrain in broad daylight; it is always shadows, walls, twilight, gloom, recesses. I originally thought this was a romantic trope but now I think maybe it was more strictly observational and that, like a bat, Mangan waited for cover of twilight.

And the way he deploys God – or rather GOD, like that in capitals, whom he wheels out to close down a poem when it is threatening to become too dissolute or nihilistic. This is why Andrews dismisses him for his 'religious orthodoxy' and 'child-like belief', but I don't think the capitals spell faith and assurance. They suggest to me a panicked run for cover. His poem 'Melancholy' is a meditation on misery which is closed down abruptly with a cheery injection: 'GOD IS LOVE!' but there is no chance of this cliché, double-wrapped in capitals and exclamation mark, shifting the mood of the poem. Mangan's GOD feels to me like the fig-leaf in medieval paintings of Adam and Eve: all you can think of is what he's seeking to hide.

And his humour. The phrase 'hiding behind jokes' is so wellworn that it has fed into a named psychological disorder, Sad Clown Paradox, which is described as 'the contradictory association between comedy and mental disorders such as depression and anxiety'. Obviously Mangan suffers from this: he is like all the famous depressives who make us laugh to distract us (and themselves) from the pit of despair, but the jokes of his that rivet me most are the hidden and opaque ones.

In the literary essays in the *Dublin University Magazine* that accompany his translations, he spends a lot of time praising and denigrating different poets and apologising for his 'inadequate translations' of 'beautiful pieces'. The tone is frequently pompous, sententious and simpering. You regret the false modesty and wince over the parade of knowledge which seems embarrassingly typical of the autodidact. Only when you read the annotations to the *Collected Works* do you realise that he is praising poets for poems they never wrote and castigating himself for poor 'translations' of his *own* original compositions.

The pompous language turns out to be a cruel parody of academese. Behind the avatar of an insecure autodidact trying to prove himself, is a savage satirist wreaking revenge. Sectarianism and discrimination impoverished him and prevented him from going to university and now he is using the country's most learned journal to perpetuate a joke on its unionist editors, contributors and readers. Like the two tailors in 'The Emperor's New Clothes', he is getting them to nod along in warm agreement to nonsense rather than admit their ignorance of German poetry.

Mangan had plenty of models for narrative disruption from his reading of Irish and German authors, but the disruption isn't what I find remarkable; it's that he chose to hide it. Reading Sterne's *Tristram Shandy* or Hoffmann's *Prinzessin Brambilla*, you know from the first page that you are in for a wild ride. But in Mangan's literary essays for the *Dublin University Magazine*, no banner of fiction unfurls to signal that you are entering a hall of mirrors. Instead he lets you think you're in the familiar if dull and intimidating environment of academia so that when you glaze over in boredom and confusion, you feel guilty for not following the argument, even while you're picking up on some kind of instability which you can't quite put your finger on, like being in a group of people who appear to be sharing a joke, but when you ask to be let in on it, they smoothly change the subject …

For the longest time I thought that Mangan was ploughing a lonely furrow, but now I think that maybe he was channelling the major figure in German Romanticism, Friedrich Schlegel. In his youth Schlegel was extremely radical – he later became a conservative bore, like Wordsworth – and wanted to tear down society. He spotted in the subversions of Swift and Sterne a way to disrupt narrative realism and social orthodoxy but realised that if the disruptive techniques were too overt then they would be named and categorised and that would simply bring about new orthodoxies and new rules. To avoid this, Schlegel suggested being covert and secretive about the subversion, but he was himself so covert about counselling covertness that he would only do so obliquely in articles so allusive that a late nineteenth-century English critic attempting to explain 'romantic irony' (Schlegel's name for his method), abandoned the field, pronouncing it not very *'eingehend'* (thorough).

It's not only the critics. Schlegel's own literary disciplines, Tieck and Hoffmann, failed to pick up on his oblique message to remain oblique – their narrative disruption shrieks at you. The person who did, I think, get what Schlegel was getting at, was Mangan, though

I have no way of proving this since Mangan was too Schlegelian to cite his influence, but he was steeped in German romanticism and it seems likely that he got the steer from Schlegel, though I guess it's not impossible that he came up with the approach himself. Anyway, he perfected the method and if Schlegel had been alive and radical in 1835 (instead of six years dead and, prior to that, twenty years a conservative bore), he would have been entranced at the way Mangan launched his demurely subversive assaults from the *Dublin University Magazine*, the citadel of Unionism.

By perpetuating a paradox on the Sad Clown Paradox – hiding his melancholy behind a joke that no one knows is a joke – Mangan sealed his place as one of the greatest romantic ironists in the English language and in so doing proved Andrews wrong: if he hides his romantic credentials, he can't be a poseur.

I wondered was he as opaque in his conversation as in his writing. There are no real descriptions of his conversation, but I recalled that my favourite anecdote of him dodging the guests at the party in Summerhill has a reference to his 'brilliant talk'. When I went back to re-read the story in O'Donoghue's biography, I discovered this remarkable line: 'Carleton proceeded to look for the poet, whom he eventually found hidden under cloaks, coats and wraps in one of the rooms.' The Man in the Cloak cloaks his poems *and* hides under cloaks and coats! The scene has vast comic potential – the bullying comedy of *Looney Tunes* or Hanna-Barbera, where large predatory animals, cats, coyotes and bulldogs, chase small fleeting animals, mice and birds. Picture the faint movement under the bundle of coats that alerts the predatory Carleton to the hiding place, and imagine him, whiskey tray balanced in one hand, rooting in the pile to extract from its centre, a wriggling cloaked and hatted Mangan, who is propelled back to the guests to perform. With all eyes on him, what can this pathological escape artist do to disappear? He can't run back to the coats, or take cover behind a chair, or blow out the candles to plunge the room into darkness, and yet the tale ends, like all his tales, and like Tom and Jerry or Roadrunner, with escape: he 'gladly leaves'.

How did he do it? Reading back over the anecdote, I realise that although he seems exposed, he had the cover of whiskey. One of the draws of alcohol is that it allows you to be someone else and a key way to diagnose an alcoholic, as against someone who simply likes a drink, is that they change personality. A brochure from an addiction centre explains the metamorphosis: 'Alcoholics frequently begin to experience significant personality changes when they are drinking. Some may become "happy drunks", while others may become "mean drunks" or simply withdraw. The person you "used to know" before they became addicted begins to disappear in front of you as they drink.'

Mangan wasn't a 'happy' or a 'mean drunk' but the descriptions from Gavan Daffy and Mitchel suggest he could be a loquacious drunk. We know that in order to 'disappear here' in front of the guests at the party, he started to talk, and Carleton describes this monologue – it certainly wasn't a conversation – as 'brilliant'. When I picture him forced back to face the guests, I imagine him drawing down all his covers: telling jokes, relaying dreams and visions, spinning similes and double negatives until his listeners were so discombobulated that when he gladly left, they were glad he'd left.

The arrows connecting what Mangan wrote and how he behaved were now falling fast and furious: attire → metaphors → addiction → humour → hugging into the walls. I drew all my lists into one list, which I would have liked to keep to seven because it's the magic number – 'seven divers shades of ink' and Empson's 'seven types of ambiguity' – but I couldn't stop it proliferating. When I hit thirteen, the dirty dozen, I stopped adding to it:

1. Clothes
2. Darkness/shadows/walls
3. Drunkenness/opiates
4. Humour
5. Pseudonyms
6. Riddles/acrostics
7. Translation
8. Cloaking metaphors
9. Double negative
10. Digressions
11. GOD
12. Dreams
13. Writing badly

The list moves from material, physical and narcotic cover to linguistic and psychological. The proliferation is astonishing. If he had deployed just the first few modes of concealment on the list, if he were just Clarence, aka the Man in the Cloak, who creeps out at twilight and composes under cover of translation and seams his work with clothing metaphors and makes opaque jokes and can only socially interact when drunk, that would be proof enough of pathology, but there's more and it gets stranger.

Take the double negative, his opaque method of saying something positive. It is not in him to be cheerful but sometimes the translation demands it. In those instances, he hides behind a flurry of double negatives. He will write 'I travelled unfainting', or describe a face as 'undefaced by time, undimmed by tears', and a cypress tree 'beneath whose yet undarkening shade'. What these lines are saying is positive – the traveller is robust, the face is young and happy, the day is new – but you have to unscramble to work it out. The first time I read this line: 'Such are the sufferings unfelt where love can be avowed', I felt mournful until I unpicked the negativity and realised that he's saying that there is no suffering when love is declared openly.

And take writing badly, an accusation that is always being made against him. From the start, his critics were confused and irritated that a poet who could be so sublime could also be clotted, rhetorical, lazy and careless. Irritation with him flashes across Mitchel, O'Donoghue and Joyce, and gets louder in the twentieth century. I'm guilty of this myself. Lots of Mangan seems pretty bad to me – diffuse, portentous, indistinct, generalised, over-elaborate. I find only a handful of his poems brilliant from start to finish although, equally, only a handful are uniformly rotten. Mostly he reverberates: the poem might begin brilliantly and run out of steam like 'A Vision of Connaught' or have just one marvellous stanza embedded in dross like 'To Childhood', or maybe just a few lines, or maybe just a phrase.

Yeats called him a writer of 'electric shocks', which carries the suggestion of aftershock, exhaustion and slump. Comparisons to the stately Yeats show him up as particularly erratic, undisciplined, inchoate. Certainly, he lacks stamina and cohesion, but he made, I think, a virtue of his flaw and turned bad writing into another mode of concealment, a way of protecting, enclosing, and secreting the few wonderful lines. When you've read enough of him, you start thinking there's something slick, showy and unwise even about turning out consistently honed verse. It begins to seem both more natural and more exciting to wade through the dross to earn the startling image.

Boredom is part of the experience of reading great novels. Martin Amis called *Don Quixote* 'bristling with beauties, charm, sublime comedy; also, for long stretches (approximately about 75 per cent of the whole), inhumanly dull'. We race over Levin and his serfs to get back to the fervour of Anna and Vronsky; we push on through the parodies in the maternity hospital to earn Molly Bloom's soliloquy; we submit to incarceration in *The Prisoner* to be released to *Time Regained* – but if someone were to offer us these novels with all the dull bits excised, would we take them? I'm an impatient reader, and in the race to the finish I cheat by skimming the boring bits, but even with this dishonest way of reading, the rhythm comes through, and I know that if those long tedious stretches were removed, the novel would thin out, lose pace, and begin to lie. Life is boring as well as great. Nothing displays the courage of the great novelist so much as the willingness to bore us stupid.

A poem isn't a novel. A novel is democratic, vulgar and inclusive, where a poem is elitist and rarefied, a distillation of a profound experience. In the slightly chilling description we got at school, a poem is 'the right words in the right order'. An epic like *Beowulf* might be allowed its turgid passages but poetry gave up on length centuries ago and now we go to it for a quick hit – 'a shot of espresso', says Jeannette Winterson. So Mangan doesn't get away with his languor and his evasions; he puts readers off.

Only if you sit down and read everything he ever wrote do you grant him some of the latitude we give great novelists. Then his fits and starts settle into a kind of pattern; then you grow intrigued, concerned, finally tender over his neurotic burrowings and sneaking evasions; then you discipline yourself to sit calmly through the smoke and rhetoric to wait for the sudden rustle, the flash of life, the glimpse of Keats through a thicket.

*

The moment you realise that Mangan's appearance exactly matches his language, behaviour and psyche is the moment he moves from being a real-life, historical person who once existed, to becoming a fictional character – one of those memorably eccentric cameos in Shakespeare, Dickens, Gogol or Flann O'Brien, who slips on and off the page or stage, looking exactly the way he speaks. Only in fiction do people achieve such perfect coherency between the ego and the id, which is why Janet Malcolm, with her Wildean feel for subverting cliché, claims that real life is 'by no means as coherent as the world of fiction, and peopled by characters by no means as lifelike as the characters in fiction'.

When I was twenty-one, I went out with a Romantic ironist of advanced order, though of course we had never heard of Romantic irony, so no one called him that. He was known and admired, as well as feared and shunned, for the extraordinary mordancy and opacity of his wit, and for his refusal, or inability, to make ordinary decent small talk. He didn't affect emotion that he didn't feel and what he felt, he didn't let on. He had an ear for falsity and cliché which was frankly terrifying. When I first knew him, I found him impossible to talk to since he didn't chat or gossip or respond to conversational gambits except to swoop down on isolated phrases to ridicule them (not cruelly; the attack was on the language, not you personally). He was always being compared to the great twentieth-century comics, Spike Milligan and Peter Cook and Flann O'Brien, but it seems no coincidence that in his thirties he moved to Berlin and although he had previously shown no particular aptitude for languages, mastered German with nonchalant ease as if his neurotically subversive and scoffing mind had been waiting all along for the language of Tieck, Hoffmann and Kafka.

He is the most Mangan-like person I have ever known but he only ticks two of the items on my list: opaque humour and booze. He didn't wear layers of clothing, or adopt a pseudonym, or talk in sartorial metaphors, or deploy the double negative, and when he went to parties, his conversation bemused people, but he didn't hide under coats. I've met or heard of people who ticked other items on the list: other Dublin peripathetics under their forty coats, and addicts who hide behind drink or drugs, and obfuscators who use convoluted language to distant or distract their listeners, but I've never met, or read about, or heard of, anyone who ticked all thirteen items on my list. Mangan may be the most secretive person who ever lived. Why was he like that and what was he hiding?

After the effort, so exhausting for me and perhaps also for the reader, of chasing Mangan down through his modes of concealment and breaking through his defences, one by one, I felt as coarse and brutal as Carleton stalking him through the rooms with the whiskey bribe. Paul Durcan has a strange and moving poem called 'The Death by Heroin of Sid Vicious' which, perhaps because it opens like Mangan's great poem 'Siberia' in an arctic death-camp and deals obliquely with opiate overdose, has always reminded me of Mangan. But in earlier readings I missed how much it's about pursuit, breaking for cover, capture:

At daybreak – in the arctic fog of a February daybreak –
Shoulder-length helmets in the watchtowers of the concentration camp
Caught me out in the intersecting arcs of the swirling searchlights.

There were at least a zillion of us caught out there –
Like ladybirds under a boulder –
But under the microscope each of us was unique,
Unique and we broke for cover, crazily breasting
The barbed wire and some of us made it
To the forest edge, but many of us did not

Make it, although their unborn children did –
Such as you whom the camp commandant branded
Sid Vicious of the Sex Pistols. Jesus, break his fall:
There – but for the clutch of luck – go we all.

Durcan identifies with the pursued, counting himself among the 'us caught out there'. I don't feel like I can throw my lot in with the maimed and pursued seeing as I'm not marginalised, or an addict, or homeless, or depressive, or a poet. I can't really claim to feel 'caught out' below the watchtowers but, equally, it would be posturing to identify myself with the camp commandant because icy indifference, or outright sadism, is not what I feel when I turn the searchlights on Mangan and chase him down through his modes of concealment, cutting off his escape routes one by one, until I get him, wriggling and protesting, under the microscope. I feel a tender protectiveness towards his pathological need for concealment, and an awed respect for his ingenuity in finding so many ways to take cover, and I would gladly let him go, except that overriding my natural human sympathy is the merciless researcher's thirst to find out *why*. Though this thirst isn't the anger and hate of the camp commandant and it doesn't seek Mangan's death but only his secrets, it is still a deadly sin: avarice, which Mangan called 'covetousness' and, in a marvellous poem of that title, identified as the translator's sin.

Down the rabbit hole

One afternoon I called into my friend who owns the Solomon Gallery in Dublin city centre and was amazed to find a picture of Mangan on the walls.

He was naked, which was a shocker, and gazing at a woman plumped down on cushions on a divan, her dress rumpled up to expose her ass. You don't expect to find Mangan in a boudoir but, having pitched him into this improbable scenario, I felt that the artist had got his presence there exactly right: in the picture he is in profile (as he is in every image) with his back to the viewer and the sense of him shrinking into his nudity is compounded by him being stood in a pint glass, immersed in liquid to the tip of his nose. The glass and liquid seal him off as successfully as his cloak and hat, so that he is of the scene but not in it, which exactly describes his relationship to life. I was in awe of this artist's bold imagination. Forcing the celibate into confrontation with sex was a brilliant starting point and I was moved to see Mangan rendered in his own words: 'shrined like gas in glass'.

My friend listened politely to my outpourings and then pointed out that it wasn't Mangan; it was a self-portrait of the Meath-born

artist, Michael Farrell, peeping from his pint glass at one of the most famous nudes in art history: Francois Boucher's homage to the fifteen-year-old Irish courtesan Marie-Louise O'Murphy, a painting that so excited Louis XV that he demanded to meet 'La Morfi' and promptly made her his mistress. Apparently when Farrell moved to Paris in the 1970s and saw the Boucher in the Louvre, he became obsessed and began riffing on it in numerous sketches and prints, where he plays up the Morfi Bottom, although none of his prints or sketches is remotely sexy. Instead, they bristle with jokes and ideas. In some, the girl's body is labelled as meat – *Fourquarters, Rump Steak, Gigot,* etc. – in a very Manganese pun on Boucher (French for butcher) and an overtly feminist comment on the way that history and the art canon have reduced the Irish girl to the king's piece of ass. Another version is captioned THE VERY FIRST REAL IRISH POLITICAL PICTURE and according to the art critic Aidan Dunne, 'Farrell is clearly equating Ireland with the courtesan; he's also implying that she is exploited and abused.'

This observation is so Manganese that instead of feeling chastened that the Man in the Glass wasn't Mangan, I congratulated myself on my perspicuity and began busily noting the similarities between poet and artist: just as Mangan re-translates sensual oriental verse, Farrell 'translates' Boucher, converting erotic European art into what Lloyd would call a 'secondary image'. Boucher's rococo brush transfigured the real girl into an erotic pin-up and Farrell transfigured Boucher's curves into witty pop art, by which stage we have no idea what the real Miss O'Murphy looked like; her identity has been effaced, just like the Oriental poets whom Mangan rendered into English from the German. And like Lloyd's Mangan, Farrell is notably postmodern and avant-garde: decades before the now ubiquitous phrase 'the male gaze' was even coined, he inserts it as commentary on the erotic European canon – the Male Gaze as Peeping Tom, what a brilliant image!

I was now in a state, well known to researchers, of seeing connections to my work everywhere. This state, which you could call the 'research high', is something like the Baader–Meinhof phenomenon or red-car syndrome but where that feels random and aimless – you hear about someone/thing and suddenly it's cropping up everywhere – the research high feels active and significant. You're not just passively noticing something you've never noticed before; you're actively seeing patterns and confirming personal discoveries. Everything you see, hear, read and dream confirms whatever it is you've just discovered or 'proved' in your research. You're mesmerised that you're only seeing all this now, and astonished that no one else has ever put it all together.

In this state, you feel great – of course, you do, you're high. There are many kinds of high – the research high, the hallucinogenic high, the religious ecstasy 'higher being' high, the manic/bipolar high – and what unites them is pattern perception: the sudden awareness of signs and validations, invisible to others, which suggest an underlying structure that explains the world.

If you're on acid, or you're manic, or in a cult, or a conspiracy theorist, the people around you will freak out and stage an intervention and you will be sectioned/medicated/removed from fellow cultists. This doesn't generally happen with the research high but I've frequently woken up through the night to scribble stuff down on scraps of paper by my bed, convinced that the precious insight in my racing mind must be preserved, only to read it back over in the morning and find a few sentences of gnomic banality. Some truly bonkers books have been written by scholars who disappear down the rabbit hole and don't come back up, resulting in reviews that remark starchily that the book is 'in need of a good editor' which is code for 'someone should have staged an intervention'. On the other hand, if you don't disappear down the rabbit hole, at least for a while, your research won't take off and you might give up on it, since, without the high, research is a slog and can seem arid, exhausting and pointless. The high is what exorcises the spectre of Casaubon that haunts all researchers.

It was after I'd turned the searchlights on Mangan and flushed him out of his hiding places and put him under the microscope that the research high came over me. I became obsessed with knowing why he so obsessively seeks cover. Trying to crack his pathology as though it were a mathematical code wasn't working, so I decided to go with my research high and let it throw up comparisons to anything and everything, including to recent stuff that Mangan couldn't have encountered. I had plenty of reservations about this approach but since I couldn't stop making connections, it seemed repressive to set my mind against them, and I had as my excuse that Mangan loved to deploy similes and metaphors himself and that the Romantics favoured the ambiguity and polysemy of metaphor and simile over the hard empirical certainty of definition and categorisation. I felt that my amorphous hovering was putting me in a state of Keatsian 'negative capability' – the ability to be receptive to all aspects of existence, 'capable of being in uncertainties, mysteries, doubt, without any irritable reaching after fact and reason', which struck me as perhaps the only way to approach Romanticism without losing your mind. And this is exactly the state of mind in which Joyce wrote *Finnegans Wake*, the whole text one long river of analogies swimming into each other, as if Joyce had spent the seventeen years writing it on a high of pattern perception. Mangan is woven into the pattern of the *Wake* and intertwined with writers born long after his death.

Anyway, once I gave my mind permission to float, suspended in 'uncertainties, mysteries, doubt', I began to spot Manganese modes of concealment everywhere. I found them in Kafka – in the paranoia and slipperiness of *The Trial*, the way the prosecutors deploy bureaucratic, legal language as a screen behind which there is no named concrete offense, and in the zoomorphism of *Metamorphosis* where humans are concealed behind animals. And I found them in *Macbeth*, the most cloaked world besides Mangan's that I know of (and perhaps not coincidentally one of Mangan's most quoted texts).

When we studied *Macbeth* in school, our teacher had us make a list of all the clothing metaphors (this is possibly the source of my obsessive lists, now I come to think of it) and in this way, drew our attention to daggers 'breech'd in gore' and skin 'laced in golden blood' and sleep 'knitting the ravelled sleeve of care' and numerous other clothing images, including a mixed metaphor – 'was the hope drunk wherein you dressed yourself' – which would normally be a Bad Thing but in this instance isn't, because obviously Shakespeare is making some kind of point although it took hundreds of years for someone (the critic Cleanth Brooks in a seminal essay, 'The Naked Babe and the Cloak of Manliness') to work it out. The cloaking metaphors create a world where everyone must proceed with subterfuge, since to be direct and honest and appear nakedly as yourself, is to risk death. The scions of dangerous bloodlines flee under cover of darkness, and then return with a whole army disguised as a wood. Nothing is as it seems and nobody can be trusted, but at fleeting moments, another world is glimpsed, a world of transparency, openness and honesty symbolised by 'the naked newborn babe'.

For the atmosphere of *Macbeth*, Shakespeare drew on the Elizabethan England that he grew up in, with its network of spies and priest hunters, plots and conspiracies, secret masses and priest holes. In this world where reckless language could lead to death or imprisonment, it was madness to write or say what you actually believed. Mangan's childhood was less viscerally savage, but it carried a pervasive atmosphere of risk: the fortified barracks at Corn Market loomed over the Liberties like a watchtower; the press was heavily censored and on the rare occasions that unfiltered words made it to the page, retribution was swift with editors and journalists arrested, fined or forced into hiding. Emancipation in 1829 initiated a thaw and people began to write freely, even recklessly. But after the 1848 revolutions in Europe, the mood darkened, and editors and journalists began being jailed again and exiled. Mangan was never in danger because he didn't write about politics directly. In his perception of risk, he was smarter than his colleagues because he was that bit older and remembered the pre-Emancipation days and because he was innately fearful and secretive. His inveterate cloaking and veiling metaphors function as aide-memoires to keep his guard up. Evidently, Shakespeare got it right: when people feel under surveillance, they do start speaking like drapers and set designers.

The research high brought a buzz to art exhibitions: instead of wandering round, giving a bored thumbs up or thumbs down, I now had a purpose.

At an exhibition of Celtic Art in the British Museum, I stopped excitedly in front of a shield. The caption explains that 'Two birds are hidden in the swirling decoration' – if you float your gaze, you can make them out – and the phrase exactly describes what Mangan does with his best lines. On the next display, of a sword mast, the caption explained that 'strange faces and fantastic beasts are often hidden in early Celtic designs' and 'people may have believed that hidden designs protected the owner or gave them strength'. This recalls the Book of Kells, and its astonishingly intricate calligraphy and designs, the constant knotting and lacing which spirals so protectively around and around the Word of God, suggestive of nothing so much as warding off the Evil Eye. (Mangan worked for a few years as a copyist in Trinity Library so, unlike most people

in Ireland at the time, he actually saw the Book of Kells.)

And one desultory afternoon in London I followed Frank into the Royal Academy to see the work of an artist called Joseph Cornell, whom we had never heard of. Spread out around the room were boxes – wooden-framed, glass-fronted, about the size of large shoe boxes – with different stuff displayed inside: cuttings, collages, found objects. Pausing in front of a box in which small glass medicinal jars were neatly stacked, each containing different *objets trouvés* – butterflies, tiny eggs, a shell, paper clips, rubber bands, brown sediment, blue liquid – I was struck by the particularity of glass behind glass, which recalled the Mangan line 'shrined like gas in glass'. It was whimsical, and Mangan isn't whimsical, but it was also kind of humorous and definitely neurotic and pathologically protective, and it wasn't creating from scratch, it was montage, using other people's things to assemble something new, which is exactly what Mangan does. When I came to a box called 'Towards the Blue Peninsula' I whipped out my phone to take a picture:

This has four protective coverings: the main box-frame, and

behind that, the slim horizontal barriers/levers, top and bottom, behind those the grille; behind that the picture frame which serves as a window onto the distant prospect of cerulean blue – the 'blue peninsula' of the title, and the only painted art in the box. This seemed to me an exact visual representation of what Mangan does: hiding the object of desire under layers of protective covering and posing it just beyond reach. This is the Knight's glimpse of the veiled girl behind the walls and bars in the forested convent.

When I googled Cornell, his character and biography turned out to be gratifyingly Manganese: born in New York in 1903, he was the eldest of four children, whose father died young and indebted, so the family had to downsize. Joseph attended, but never graduated from art school, and earned his living as a wholesale fabric salesman (*fabric!*) to support his mother and disabled brother. He suffered migraines and stomach aches, never left New York State and never married. Although fixated on beautiful women, whose iconic images filled his boxes, he was probably gay, according to critics.

I found it freaky that these eldest sons, thrust too early into providing for their families by the bankruptcy/death of the father and forced to take on grinding uncreative jobs, should have responded almost identically to the stress: with psychological ailments, reclusiveness, sexual repression, and a preoccupation with the exotic and far-flung that they only experienced at a remove through the images/poems of others. I imagined Mangan's mordant smile on the similarity of their initials: J.C. and J.C.M.

Cornell was an eccentric autodidact, but he had a gallery, art world contacts, a disciplined approach, and a sophisticated understanding of the canon, so he isn't considered an outsider artist, though, as with Mangan, there is intersection. Outsider art – or to use the German word, *geisteskranke* art, which I prefer because it contains the word ghost – is the art of mentally ill people who lack formal art training. It is frequently characterised by coils, spirals and recurrent patterns suggestive of paranoia, the mind turning in on itself, obsessive-compulsive rituals, entrapment and aversion, as in the work of the Swiss artist Adolf Wölfli, who spent his adult life in an institution after an abusive childhood, and filled his elaborate pictures with lines, dots, music chords, leaving no space un-patterned.

The same obsession with filling every inch of the space is

apparent in the work of outsider artist Ian Pyper, full of watching eyes and waving hands.

These images suggest to me Mangan's fear of the empty page, his constant 'plaiting and plastering', his looping twists and onanistic hands. They recall in particular the long memoir, with its games of scale and cyclical recurrences, its images of hunting, constriction and contagion, of small, sick animals being hounded, swallowed, poisoned and infected, its watching eyes that peer at the narrator from every turn.

But when I look at outsider and *geistekranke* art – which has the quality, like children's art, of timelessness, being so unfettered by artistic trends that it can't be dated to any historic period but seems to emerge straight from the id – I can also see Mangan's essential difference. It is not just that he is highly professional and even vogueish so that his style, technique and themes date him to the early nineteenth century, it's also that, although he is hemmed in, he is not locked in. His trellises, leaves, dusk, veils, clouds aren't impermeable; they let in shafts of light and air. An early poem opens in a prison – 'Chains, bolts, and bars, and massive doors, / Impervious walls, and roofs, and floors' – but just when you think he has sealed himself in, he concedes 'Gratings where day-light rarely pours / A flickering ray / To disunite the lingering hours / Of night and day'. He wrote these lines when he was nineteen and that ray continued to flicker across his work until the end. Like Cornell's patch of blue, the ray is the escape from being locked/boxed in and explains, I think, why we are happy to linger in 'The Vision of Connaught' and 'Towards the Blue Peninsula' but start to feel claustrophobic in outsider art.

*

The many Mangans who flickered at me as I flicked through my deck of comparisons are very different, but they have in common that they are all taking cover. Eventually, I organised them into three piles. In the first pile, which I called Masking, I placed Michael Farrell. In the next pile, Fear, I put Kafka, Macbeth and the *geistekranke* artists. In the third pile, Ray of Hope, I put Celtic shields, the Book of Kells, and Joseph Cornell. This trinity – Masking, Fear and Hope – provides, I think, the explanation for Mangan's pathology of concealment.

The Masking suggests that Mangan adds dreams, masks, jokes, similes and cloaks into his poems to create an atmosphere of artificiality, inauthenticity and metafiction. If naturalism and realism are ways of rendering experience as directly and artlessly as possible in order to insist that 'this is how it happened' then Mangan's 'plaiting and plastering' moves so far from naturalism that the implication must be that 'this didn't happen'. Other translators don't point up the unreality of their enterprise by layering masks, jokes and dreams into their work, but other translators are willing us to suspend disbelief and pretend that what we're reading is the author's authentic lived experience. Mangan won't indulge us, or himself. It's part of his paradoxical honesty that he will trick and veil to prevent us relaxing into the security of believing that anything he writes happened in the way it claims to. His continual multiplying of texts (numerous versions of the same poem) turns him into a kind of proto-Warhol. By refusing the original work its status as the ur-text, he calls into question the whole idea of authenticity and sincerity in art and in life. Ingenious, playful and slick, this Mangan of the Masks has seen through everything, and it is all a joke.

To turn from this to the second pile is to move from scoffing to terror, from concealment as a knowing pose, to cover as a desperate protection against fears which are both rational and irrational – and the more I considered the images in the pile, the more the division between the two blurred. Macbeth and Joseph

K are genuinely threatened by external forces, but they are also paranoid and plagued by invisible terrors, and the fusion between outer threat and personal delusion is what gives these works their power. When we ask where Kafka got his unforgettable images, we talk about his innate neuroticism, his overbearing father, and being Jewish in an antisemitic environment – which is to say genes, upbringing and environment. Similar pressures produced Mangan's pathology of concealment: an abusive childhood, mental instability perhaps inherited from his father, being Catholic in a Protestant supremacist society, impoverished when there was no welfare safety net, gay when homosexuality was a crime and a sin. It seems impossible to separate out these pressures which combined to produce an art that is always taking cover.

It was a relief to turn from the dark suspicions of the second pile to the Ray of Hope in the third pile, and to realise that Mangan's pathology of concealment is not just fear-based, it is also protective and what he wants to protect is joy in all its transient fragility. The exquisitely delicate lettering of the monks serves to both protect and convey what is holy and fragile. Cornell lacks their gossamer delicacy, but you get a similar sense in his boxes – which rather resemble the shrines you see at the side of the road in the Mediterranean – of him striving to protect and suggest something intangibly precious. This essence is what the German Romantics called *sehnsucht* ('inconsolable yearning') or the blue flower, and what the medieval Christians called the holy grail, and the ancient Greeks called *elpis* – it is the sliver of hope that Pandora glimpsed in the horrors streaming out of the box.

Intrinsic to *sehnsucht*/the holy grail/*elpis*/the blue flower is that it is always suspended just beyond reach – it is something lovely, fleeting, mysterious and withheld. Cornell's box is called 'Towards the Blue Peninsula', after an Emily Dickinson poem, which does a beautiful job of floating and aching towards, without ever reaching, the fleeting joy that it seeks:

> It might be easier
> To fail – with Land in Sight –
> Than gain – My Blue Peninsula –
> To perish – of Delight –

I think Mangan glimpsed the blue peninsula and had the same protective instinct towards it as Dickinson, Cornell and the Celts. That he found a way to convey it is, for me, the final proof that he 'fathomed the depths of romanticism'. His most amazing, if his most demented attempt, to convey the 'flickering ray' is the bravura two-page paragraph that opens his essay on the poet Ludwig Tieck. The reader has to make their way through ever more ingenious metaphors of concealment – shadows, scales, clouds, the stumbling-block, the snare, pitfall, maze, labyrinth, the triple blinds, the mirage, the opaque spreadsheet, etc. – to reach the final sentence, itself a series of analogies suspended on a simile, to earn Mangan's marvellous metaphors for this precious, intangible thing that makes life worth living but which we can never quite grasp:

> As a man in a dream, entering a well-known house to gaze on 'old familiar faces' finds himself all at once in a foreign habitation, an enchanted pile; and astonished, alarmed, and confounded, but unreflecting, roams from chamber to chamber, encountering sphynxes, hippogriffs, talking birds and walking statues, and yet still pursues his wanderings, hoping to the last to meet those he is in quest of, so we, while wondrous fancies flit before us, and undefined shapes multiply around us, and all the phantasmagoria of the morbid intellect crowd about us, explore page after page of the mystic volumes that present us with them, and still expect to discover in the end the secret soul

of all – hidden, perhaps, in some unsuspected nook, like the soul of the licentiate Pedro Garcias, in the preface to Gil Blas, or diffused over the entire surface of the writer's imagining, like star-light over a deep flood – a subtle gas, with whose peculiar properties our faculties could become intimate only after we had been breathing it so long as to forget our ordinary atmosphere, as the eyes of a man who passes from a bright room into a dark one must learn to accommodate themselves to the change before the haze that rests on surrounding objects can be dispelled.

In this passage of almost Proustian sensation, Mangan finds two metaphors for what he terms 'the secret soul of all': it is 'a subtle gas' and 'star-light over a deep flood' – not moonlight which throws a comparatively strong glow on water, but the barest flicker that reflects celestial bodies so far away that we see them not as they are, but as they once were. This is a rather wonderful metaphor for the elusive joy or hope that enables us to go on living in a world of pain. Mangan wrote this passage in 1838, around the same time that he donned his cloak. As he entered the 1840s, he had all his defences in place to keep danger out and protect the fleeting joy that constantly eludes us. He would need to be prepared. The catastrophe that he had been anticipating all his life was on its way.

Part Three: Famine ghosts

Zeno's paradox

By early spring 1846 the potato blight was back, the news from the south-west was unremittingly bad, and Mangan was a mess. The humiliations heaped on him are like a parody of the Irish misery tale, a tragicomic passage in *An Béal Bocht:* he was an alcoholic and an opium addict, a barfly and a hobo, estranged from his relatives and increasingly distant from friends, except when he wanted a loan; his father was dead, his mother was dying, his surviving brother was shiftless and violent. He was still producing good poetry, but it was more of the same, German and Oriental translations, which nobody was getting too excited about or even reading much since they appeared in the rarefied *Dublin University Magazine* and not in the country's favourite paper, *The Nation.* Trinity College Library was growing increasingly fed up with his 'irregularities' and by the end of the year they would 'dispense with him' (though John O'Donovan says it was Mangan's moustache, not his drinking or his lateness, that got him dismissed). He was an object of fascination and censure to the people of Dublin. Joseph Hudson, writing in *The Shamrock* in 1875, recalled meeting him in a 'free-and-easy' in the neighbourhood of Camden Street' (perhaps The Bleeding Horse):

The company was chiefly composed of tradesmen, scribes, counter assistants, and the better class of the labouring population … In the midst of this jolly assembly might be seen one silent, solitary individual, generally seated near the fire – so near as to make one suppose that the faded colour of his brown coat was scorched from its heat … A young man of the company sings one of Moore's matchless melodies, followed by rounds of applause. Mangan applauds not: he gazes on the ceiling as though his mind wandered far away from the scene around him … He declined to sing but repeated with great delicacy of feeling the words of an old German song, 'All my Riches are my Songs'; then, pointing to his glass, said in sad tones, 'You found me poor and have kept me so …'

After getting from Mangan a promise to 'conquer his every social weakness', Hudson and his friend left him and the next day the friend received from Mangan a poem in his handwriting: 'Farewell to the sparkling wine-cup! The brain-deceiving wine-cup! The cup that slays a thousand ways, / The soul-degrading wine-cup' etc. Hudson and his friend weren't the first or last to extract the promise of sobriety from Mangan – his combination of astonishing talent and deceptive meekness seems to have brought out the proselytiser in people. Although Hudson emphasises the poor company that the genius is keeping – 'tradesmen, counter assistants, the better class of the labouring population' – he paints an innocent scene. Mitchel suggests much worse company and much fouler dives: 'There were two Mangans, one well known to the muses, the other to the police … Nothing gives so ghastly an idea of his condition of mind as the fact that the insane orgies of this rarely-gifted creature were transacted in the lowest and obscurest taverns, and in company with the offal of the human species. From this thought one turns away with a shudder.'

Meehan makes the same point obliquely: 'Waywardness and irresolution were strongly developed in Mangan, and despite words of encouragement and gentle attentions, he would, at intervals, be missed for weeks and months from the little circle in the attic, none knowing whither he had gone.' The 'whither' functions like Mitchel's shudder – it is the veil drawn over the unmentionable scene (though the reader, revolted by the patronising 'encouragements and gentle attentions', cheers Mangan on for abandoning the creepy 'little circle in the attic'). O'Donoghue castigates Mitchel for being 'unnecessarily brutal' and for putting 'the facts very crudely' but doesn't disagree that they are facts, which 'cannot be disputed in so far as they refer to the period subsequent to 1845 … I myself was told by some who used to see him that the forlorn condition of the poet was a heart-rending sight.'

What was this condition exactly, and what were the 'irregularities' that got Mangan dismissed from Trinity, and where was it he went when he ditched the little circle, and who were the 'some who used to see him' and what did the police pick him up for, and what 'orgies' did he 'transact' in 'obscure taverns'? On first reading these suggestive asides with their odour of sanctity and thrill of horror, I thought it was mostly nineteenth-century snobbishness over a poet frequenting taverns and consorting with labourers and I felt confident that in our more egalitarian age we would have taken Mangan's irregularities in our stride, whatever they were, but then I remembered getting sight of a weird and deeply unsettling clip of Pete Doherty and Amy Winehouse from I think 2008, shot with a jittery handheld camera, in a bare-walled, windowless room with bleak bluish artificial light, and they are both slurring and Amy's eyes (you never see Pete's) are pinned and she has a little shoebox of white mice, just born, and when she picks them up, they are the size of her fingernail, hairless and blind with long attenuated ghostly little limbs that never stop scrabbling, which Pete calls 'wiggly wibble', and Amy points one at the camera and puts on a little mouse girl voice and says: 'Blake, please don't divorce Mummy, she loves you ever so,' and then she takes up another and has him say, 'I'm only a day old, I don't know what I'm doing, but I know what love is,' which could be a line in a song, and Pete just keeps saying '*awww*' as in *awww*, so sweet (baby mice) and *awww*, so sad (divorce), and watching this, I'm torn between wanting to keep watching because it's mesmerising, and wanting 'to turn away with a shudder' because it's private and it's two people unravelling, and I don't want to be like some J.G. Ballard character getting off on watching car crashes … And now, remembering this and other lurid clips showing troubled celebs, I realise my reaction to them is exactly that mix of sanctity and thrilled horror that I accuse Mangan's commentators of, so maybe the 'shudder', 'whither' and 'irregularities' were the only ways of adverting to, without dwelling on, whatever strange, unsettling stories were going round Dublin about Mangan. There is no way he was having 'insane orgies' in the sense that we understand the term, but he could have been doing some pretty weird stuff that would shock us as much as it did his contemporaries. It's a fallacy, though we all fall into it, to think our age is any more liberated or tolerant than preceding ones.

Anyway, my point is this: Mangan in 1846, three years before his death, was like poor Amy in 2008, three years before her death: inducing feelings of pity, guilt and frustration in fans. A few still reverently hope for a miracle, but experience says there is no coming back from these desperate situations. In some of the last words he ever wrote, in his impersonal memoir, Mangan found a telling metaphor for the desperation: 'When a fly is rapidly sinking in a glass of water, and not a soul in the house besides himself, it is difficult for him to forbear conjecturing that he must go to the bottom.' The first time I read this line, I formed the impression that the fly sinks to the bottom, but writing it out now, I see that I'm wrong: the fly *conjectures* that he must hit bottom, but whether or not he actually does, is left open. It is Zeno's paradox – the fly, like the arrow, is suspended in motion, even while our minds, which crave finality, hasten it on its course.

In spring 1846 it was difficult for the people of Dublin to forbear conjecturing that the rapidly sinking Mangan must go to the bottom. That he found a way to defy gravity and reverse his downward propulsion, is the source of his fame. All his biographers and critics are mesmerised by this moment. Here is D.J. O'Donoghue:

> From the opening of the year 1846, when the fearful shadow of an impending famine was cast over the country, Mangan, though he did not change his own habits or mode of life, almost entirely forgot his mannerism, and assumed the character of an almost inspired prophet … Hitherto he had been contented with the name of 'poet', he now appeared as the great national poet of Ireland – the most splendidly endowed with imagination and keenness of vision of any Irishman of his time.

And here is Robert Welch, a stringent twentieth-century critic otherwise withholding in praise of Mangan:

> He had the misfortune to live through one of the most chilling periods of Irish history. What is extraordinary is that he tried, for a few months, to measure up to it, and in doing so became something of a spokesman for the afflicted and starving. Unlike most of *The Nation* poets he became national, even nationalistic, without failing as a poet as well.

And Shannon-Mangan:

> Mangan was now forty years old. If he had stopped writing altogether or if he had died at this point, he would be remembered as a very interesting, quirky minor poet and translator of considerable promise and international tastes in literature … However he did not stop writing and he did not die. Instead,

as a middle-aged man, he went on to achieve an intensive run of fine work including his greatest poems – an unprecedented accomplishment in the history of Romantic poetry.

And Eavan Boland, also generally critical of Mangan:

It was at this moment that JCM drew upon himself the lightning of an old culture in search of a new form. That he did so is due to the coincidence between his own dilemma and the circumstances of the country. For Mangan was as passionate and outraged as Irish history. His mind was plagued by a formless sense of loss, his personality verged always upon dissolution.

None of them quite manages to convey how extraordinary the moment was, or to explain how Mangan managed to overcome his situation and 'measure up'. O'Donoghue and Welch peddle pieties that miss the point – it's not 'though he did not change his own habits or mode of life', but *because* he did not change them that Mangan was able to express the national suffering, and far from it being his 'misfortune' to live through such a 'chilling period', in terms of his poetry (the only thing that counts for him and his readers), it was the greatest possible *good* fortune. Eavan Boland does better – she picks up on the lightning that flashes through 'Dark Rosaleen' ('there was lightning in my blood / Red lightning lightened through my blood') to convey the sense of Mangan's meteoric rise from the gutter, but 'coincidence' feels too weak for the fatal convergence between his personal circumstances and the country's.

The person who best conveys the miracle is Mangan himself. It came to him in a dream in June 1846, right in the middle of the wondrous 'few months' that Welch refers to, when the masterpieces were pouring out of him. He recounted the dream in a letter to Duffy:

I had a singular dream a few nights back. There was a light and a throng – not the 'livid light and trampling throng' of Coleridge, yet quite as impressive. In other words, a monster moon shone in the firmament, and a crowd of people were beneath, with whom I held, as I suppose, a long conference. I say, 'as I suppose' for all that I distinctly remember was that, turning away from them, I found myself on the verge of a precipice, with these words of St John in my mouth – 'and none of you asketh me, Whither goes thou?'

The words from St John's gospel are spoken by Jesus to his disciples just before the crucifixion: 'But now I go my way to him that sent me; and none of you ask me whither goes thou' (John, 16). Mangan is dreaming himself as Christ addressing his followers ahead of the lonely 'precipice' of death.

Four decades later Oscar Wilde would make the same overt link of his fate with Christ's in a famous passage in *De Profundis*:

On November 13th, 1895, I was brought down here [Reading Gaol] from London. From two o'clock till half-past two on that day I had to stand on the centre platform of Clapham Junction in convict dress, and handcuffed, for the world to look at … Of all possible objects I was the most grotesque. When people saw me they laughed. Each train as it came up swelled the audience. Nothing could exceed their amusement. That was, of course, before they knew who I was. As soon as they had been informed, they laughed still more. For half an hour I stood there in the grey November rain surrounded by a jeering mob.

This, like Mangan's dream, could read like lunatic grandiosity, but both writers get away with linking themselves to Christ because posterity has validated them: O'Donoghue referred to 'My Dark Rosaleen' as 'a national apotheosis' and in gay iconography, Wilde is the Christ figure who, through the horror and injustice of his punishment, set free future generations. Of Wilde you might say, as Shannon-Mangan does of Mangan, that had he died on his fortieth birthday, he would be remembered as a dazzling drawing-room wit and an interesting dramatist of clever comedies – but he didn't die, he stood trial and went to prison. It was the extraordinary fate of Mangan and Wilde to become the emblems and voices of the tragedies that befell countless voiceless others.

Wilde's account, like everything in *De Profundis*, is highly deliberated, emotion recollected after the event. I find Mangan's account more striking because he dreams it *as it is happening*. The moment that Mangan found a way to respond to the Famine has the narrative power, lustre and unlikeliness of a Hollywood movie. It is not like Yeats writing 'Easter 1916' immediately after the Rising, or like Heaney publishing *North* in 1975 in response to the Troubles because a masterly response to crisis are what readers expected from these magisterial poets at the height of their powers who, from the start of their careers, have positioned themselves as national poets. There isn't a gulf between people's expectations of Yeats and Heaney and their achievement – which means there isn't a Hollywood story.

The narrative of the downtrodden and humiliated hero suddenly igniting in response to catastrophe, to save the day is the stuff that Hollywood is made of – it is Dean Martin in *Rio Bravo* mastering alcoholism to reclaim his youthful title of 'best shot in the west' or an overweight Shelley Winters in *The Poseidon Adventure* putting her all into one last swim to save her companions or Mel Gibson in *Braveheart* withstanding gruesome torture to cry freedom. There would be no film if the hero didn't come back from disaster – it's the first rule of screenwriting, but life doesn't generally happen like the movies. Humiliation, addiction and poverty destroy ability and ambition. Writers can live romantically hand-to-mouth when they are young, but to continue producing good work into middle age, they need security and stability, a room of their own, with heating and regular meals; Woolf wasn't wrong.*

Where other Manganistas hone in on his deathbed as the scenario for their plays and scripts, it is the apotheosis I am obsessed with. How did it come about? How did he suddenly pick himself up from the gutter and start producing masterpieces? I know how Hollywood would tell the tale:

Dublin 1846. The sky is overcast. The colour is grey. Crowds of filthy ragged desperate people beat on the gates of the workhouse. They look something like the famous Famine sketches from the *Illustrated London News* or the *London Pictorial Post*:

THE IRISH FAMINE: SCENE AT THE GATE OF A WORKHOUSE.

---

*I can think of others who wrote from the gutter, e.g. Bukowski, Jean Genet and Hubert Selby Jr, but I still think Mangan is unique because while these defied the odds by producing in squalid circumstances, their work is cumulative; they didn't suddenly ignite in response to national calamity and shift into a new and startling register. With Mangan, the stakes are higher.

In a hovel, James Clarence Mangan wakes fully dressed in coat and cloak. He reaches for a bottle, stumbles to his feet and makes his way through the streets, where he doesn't seem to notice the hordes of people, clearly migrants from the west (they are speaking Irish where Dubliners speak English). In a smoky tavern, he sits morosely alone and behind his back, people shake their heads and whisper, 'You'd never guess but he used to be a genius.' Leaving, he scuttles into a pharmacy, and then he is back in his digs measuring laudanum into a glass. He sinks back on his filthy rags as a vision of the East comes over him – generic orientalist images of sun, minarets and turrets, but some idiosyncratic images too, a man bestriding a rhinoceros … Where Dublin is in shades of black and grey, the Eastern hallucination is in the colours of an oriental carpet so that when he comes out of the vision, the contrast with his shivering, grey existence is unbearable.

Then something happens. I'm thinking late one night, he stumbles over a freezing, emaciated child in an alley who clutches to him, whispering in Irish, which he doesn't understand and then a shawled old woman appears, like the symbol of Ireland in *Cathleen Ní Houlihan*, and takes the dying child from him and says 'Can you write about this?' and a drunk passes by and sneers, 'He can only write that oul German stuff,' and he stumbles back to his room and measures out his drops of laudanum but the vision that comes on him isn't of the East but of Ireland in full Celtic kingly glory, in the shapes and colours of the Book of Kells, and then the scene darkens to a winter's battle scene in a rural landscape, snow falling on exhausted warriors, and then he is back waking up in his squalid room, and he is not quite sure, and neither is the viewer, were the child and women part of the vision, and he gets up and stumbles into a bar and, ignoring the jeers, retreats to a corner and dips his quill into green ink and writes 'I walked entranced through a land of morn ...'

Okay, the script needs a bit of work, but its central tenet, that Mangan's apotheosis comes about through contact with a real, dying Famine victim, is what the biopic genre demands, and I think it is how I initially pictured Mangan's environment in 1846 – contagious, starving migrants pouring into the Liberties from the west and overcrowded workhouses and food riots. I pictured him writing his masterpieces out of an apocalypse so huge that you could not leave your house without being plunged into its full horror. As a child of the eighties and Live Aid, I think I saw the Famine as Ethiopia in the Rain and Mangan's masterpieces as a direct response to the sights, sounds, smells and feel of death.

It was reading David Dickson's *Dublin, the Making of a Capital City* that first disrupted my sense of what it was like for Mangan and other Dubliners. It was one sentence that pulled me up short: 'There was a rapid deterioration of the urban environment in the bitter winter of 1846/7 when crisis migrants poured into Dublin, reducing the roads to heaps of mud ... for a mile and a half ... as vast numbers of country beggars mingled in the traffic.' This was the exact scenario I had been imagining, Dubliners brought face to face with the horror, but I was very familiar with the timetable of Mangan's apotheosis, and the few months in which he produced his unbroken run of masterpieces spanned April to October 1846. I knew that he didn't go west during this period, or at any time ever. If, as Dickson was suggesting and as I confirmed through other sources, there were few or no signs of the crisis on the streets of Dublin until December 1846 then Mangan wasn't creating his masterpieces through personal experience. He was getting the story from the media.

*

The first time that coronavirus moved from the outer to the inner reaches of my awareness was on 23 January 2020 when I was watching the news of the Wuhan lockdown. We gazed at the vast empty boulevards flanked by blank skyscrapers and the processions of eerie grey figures wrapped in protective gear, carrying what looked like fire extinguishers, moving slowly and intently like columns of ants, with what purpose I hardly knew – to wipe the whole vast city clean? 'Everyone in the world will get this,' said my older brother decisively. He is a hypochondriac. I was impressed that he'd been paying so much attention to this mysterious illness on the other side of the world, and sceptical that he was right.

Six weeks later, on 12 March 2020, the government announced the closure of schools, colleges and museums until the end of the month 'at the earliest'. I was chiefly concerned that I mightn't be able to get married at the end of May, as planned, but my mother said it would probably be over by then and I thought so too. Two and a half months seemed a terribly long time. Nobody I knew knew anybody who had been diagnosed with coronavirus, as we were still calling it.

We retreated into Zoom and FaceTime and the eerie beauty of empty streets under limpidly blue skies, weather so unprecedented for Ireland in March and April that it seemed another signal that something extraordinary was happening. When I would meet up with a friend for socially distanced but still clandestine walks (beyond our 2km), she would drive me mad by shooing me away, with flapping hands rubbed red and raw from constant sanitising, every time I breached the 2 metres she was imposing between us. Perhaps because half my family are hypochondriacs, my default position on illness and infection is blasé and nonchalant, covered by the vague 'it'll all be grand', but she is the opposite and in her mind a horror show of creeping contagion, sickness, and death was unfolding that might claim her stepmother, her mature students, her elderly neighbours, our friend undergoing chemo. I realised that she saw herself as a walking vector, potentially spilling virus wherever she went, leaving it on surfaces and hanging in the air to infect vulnerable people. And because I'm constitutionally argumentative and this was all still new, the salad days of the pandemic, and I hadn't yet learned that pronouncing on the direction of the virus makes you a hostage to fortune, I would start to denounce what I saw as the excessive rigour of the lockdown, and she would retaliate with opposite arguments, both of us coming from a place of ignorance, being neither parasitologists nor epidemiologists. It was a queer feeling to know that all around the country and all over the world, people were having the same argument, and in places like Wuhan and northern Italy and New York the argument was sharpened by the raw fear of personal experience, but in Ireland in the first lockdown, the fear was at once concrete (the virus definitely existed and was definitely killing people) but abstract (there was nothing yet to see on the streets or even in the hospitals).

As I gazed in riveted horror at the apocalyptic images streaming into my screens from Italy and New York of patients unrecognisable beneath ventilators, doctors and nurses beyond exhaustion having to choose whom to save, and army trucks moving through the empty streets bearing bodies to distant crematoriums – I thought that this was a quintessentially 21st-century-way to experience a crisis. To know so much about something far away, to be sitting safe at home, suspended in a state of hypothetical fear, gazing at what might be your future, seemed like something only the technological genius of our digital age could deliver. It was only later – perhaps after we got married in an almost empty church, its doors locked to the street so that Frank exclaimed, 'It's like the penal laws!' triggering a memory of Mangan's christening in a repurposed warehouse – that I realised that, except that he was reading newspapers, not watching screens, this was exactly how it was for Mangan in the first year of the Famine when he was writing his masterpieces.

Shoring against the ruin

In 1846 anyone who was interested and literate in Ireland could keep themselves informed about the progress of the Famine. If anything, there was information surplus rather than deficit, which makes the Famine a very modern catastrophe. By the 1840s almost every county in Ireland had a few local papers and the bigger papers like *The Nation*, *Cork Examiner*, *Belfast News Letter* and *Freeman's Journal* syndicated snippets from the smaller regional papers and from British papers, giving their pages something of the reach of today's press agencies. The amount and quality of information and the diversity of opinion, coming from even the remotest regions of the country, was impressive. Dubliners could follow the debates in Westminster, printed in full across numerous columns, almost in real time, and they could read about events in Killarney, Wexford, Tuam within a few days of their occurrence, which meant that they were well informed about regions they had probably never visited.

As every Irish schoolchild knows, the Famine began in autumn 1845 when the potato blight reached Ireland, but no one in 1845 knew this. Ireland was used to the potato crop failing periodically and regionally. When the potatoes were dug out in mid-October

1845, the extent of the blight did cause panic but Mangan's editors on *The Nation* were among those counselling calm, predicting, wrongly, that only half the next crop would be lost. It is from early 1846 that 'from almost every county in Ireland come reports of more and more urgent alarm and terror as the earthed-up potatoes are uncovered and found masses of loathsome rottenness' (*The Nation*, 14 February 1846). This is when Mangan starts to engage.

To read through the reports that he was reading is to be floored by the undertow of restrained emotion in even the shortest news items: 'Not later than yesterday, we are told Mrs Gerrard dispossessed not fewer than 447 wretched beings – turning them upon the world and raising their huts to the earth. A poor man whose family were lying in fever implored to have the walls of his cabin left up in order to shelter them – but to no purpose' (*Roscommon Journal,* 14 March 1846); 'In Killarney, we are told that in the lanes and alleys, with a population of 1,100 human beings, three-fourths are living in filth and wretchedness; they have one meal of half-rotten potatoes sold at 5s. a peck; they have no fuel, nor bedclothes.' (*Cork Examiner,* 15 April 1846). The artists' sketches in the *Illustrated London News and the London Pictorial Post* have defined the look of the Famine but, perhaps because they are now so familiar, they do not, for me, wrench the heart like these anonymous news reports with their cautious restraint: 'we are told …'

I wondered what Mangan pictured when he was reading these reports. He had never seen 'the lanes and alleys' of Killarney, nor 'the cheap lodging houses' of Dungarvan where 'beggars squat, the number of destitute amounting altogether to at least 1,000 souls' (*Cork Examiner,* 6 February 1846), nor the market at Castlebar 'where provisions which hitherto were considered reasonable rose to an alarming height and turf can scarcely be had at any price' (*Connaught Telegraph*, 8 April 1846). The furthest he got from Dublin was his uncle's prosperous farm in Meath and in this he was typical of Dubliners. Before the rail tracks were laid down in the 1850s, travelling to the southwestern seaboard meant a horse-drawn coach journey of between thirteen and twenty hours to the main cities, and as long again out to smaller towns and villages. It was with a sense of disconnect that I realised that when Mangan and other Dubliners were following the progress of the Famine in spring 1846, they were reading about places far more exotic and unknowable to them than Milan or Bergamo were to us in spring 2020. The exoticism, or what we would now term the 'othering' of the victims, was played up by some of the papers, for instance the conservative *Kerry Examiner* in its account of food riots in Carrick-on-Shannon (21 April 1846):

> The town is in a horrible state. The populace rose and broke into all the meal and provision stores and afterwards into the shops generally. Unfortunately, our excellent Resident Magistrate was absent from town on some necessary duty – and there was no local Magistrate to bring the military out. They had it all their own way – and the town is just as if it had been sacked by an army of Sikhs.

Examined up close, the Famine, at least in its first year, does not follow the unremitting, remorseless downward gradient that history has assigned to it. Tracked day by day and region by region, the graph peaks and troughs, fizzes and sputters like the Dow Jones on a jumpy day. Every fresh potato crop brings fresh hopes: on 5 January 1846 a correspondent to the *Cork Examiner* gives thanks that 'Providence in mercy to us has stayed the potato cholera' but within three weeks the same paper is 'regretting to say that those who, a short time since, ridiculed the idea of the existence of any serious disease in the potato crop are day by day becoming converts to the belief that the disease has not been exaggerated, that scarcity is certain'. Five months later, the *Derry Sentinel*

(20 May 1846) has some hopeful news: 'We are gratified to learn that the early planted potatoes are doing well. We have made careful inquiry in different parts of the country, and we find that, in all cases where due attention has been paid to the seed in its proper selection, and where the ground in which it has been planted has been sufficiently dry, the result has been highly favourable.' This 'careful inquiry' seems as neurotic as the decision of the 'gentleman from Castlemartyr' to send a package of rotting potatoes into the *Cork Examiner* (8 June 1846), with this note:

> *You* will be sorry to perceive by the accompanying parcel, that the destructive disease, which so much affected the Potato Crop of last year has again visited us. I have about three roods of those potatoes, and up to *Sunday* last, they were the admiration of all who saw them, nearly closing in the drills. They were planted whole, the first week in February, on ground that grew turnips last season; and now they present but a sickly, burnt up appearance, in place of the beautiful luxuriant aspect they bore last week – this is a bad beginning so early for this year.

Sending a package of blight into a newspaper seems like the display of stigmata to doubting Thomas, and this is what the litany began to suggest to me: a kind of stockpiling of hard evidence to persuade the authorities that the country is in crisis and action is needed. The government does act, shipping Indian corn (maize) to Cork in February 1846, but it doesn't act cohesively; the Treasury, ideologically opposed to state intervention, sets onerous regulations around how the corn can be distributed. When Dr Dominic Corrigan publishes in February his devastating pamphlet *Famine and Fever as Cause and Effect in Ireland*, which concludes, based on detailed analysis of past crises, that 'if Famine be permitted to take place, pestilence may be expected to follow', the government is panicked enough to set up a Board of Health and appoint Dr Corrigan a member. Astonishingly, though this Board agrees that 'many circumstances favour a major epidemic', it assures the government in the summer that an epidemic will *not* occur, because 'the next potato crop will be normal, as had been the case in previous blights'.

To be reading during the Covid lockdown of 2020 of the perpetual false dawns of 1846 gave me an eerie sense of déjà vu. The same voices seemed to echo to each other across the centuries: the Cassandras and Pollyannas, the scientists and amateurs, the realpolitikers and magical thinkers, the pragmatists and conspiracy theorists, the handwringers and Malthusians. I had become habituated to these from living through a global pandemic and was astonished to find them assembled back in the Famine, like a perpetual commedia dell'arte of crisis responders. What was amazing to me was that Irish people in 1846 had patchy knowledge of science and medicine but extensive lived experience of famine and epidemic, whereas in 2020 it was the reverse: a huge amount of scientific knowledge but no experience of a global pandemic in living memory. The fact that reverse situations two centuries apart should trigger similar popular responses implies a kind of atavistic crisis reflex, which kicks in irrespective of scientific knowledge or lived experience.

Anyway, by spring 1846 the grim stats and the horror stories were building up, and with them the hydra's head of competing narratives around what was happening and how it should be dealt with. Reading back over the papers now, the sense of chaos and confusion is overwhelming, and I could only imagine how it must have been for people then, who had no idea how it would turn out and must have tormented themselves with the usual terrible questions: how bad is this – as bad as the doomsayers are claiming, or just another regional famine in remote localities? Do I need to keep away from crowds? Is it right that we are still exporting grain when people are hungry? But if we don't keep up exports,

the farmers will get no income, and won't that make things worse?
Should we be preparing to emigrate? If, when, how … the questions
challenged poets as well as politicians. Mangan's colleagues on *The
Nation* did their best to find answers, or at least to set the scene, but
their best was mostly terrible:

> Striding nearer every day,
> Like a wolf in search of prey,
> Comes the Famine on his way –
> Through the dark hill, through the glen,
> Over lawn, and moor, and fen,
> Questing out the homes of men.
> And a Voice cries overhead
> Rend your hair – the hot tears shed
> Ye shall starve for want of bread.
>
> (by 'Heremon', 7 March 1846)

Even for *The Nation*, this is thrillingly bad (it reads like the
inspiration for Evelyn Waugh's famous parody of purple prose
in *Scoop*, 'feather-footed through the plashy fen passes the
questing vole', though casting the Famine as a questing beastie
is beyond satire). It is so bad, so far beneath the elegant pathos of
the anonymised news reports, that it conveys nothing except the
exaggerated reverence accorded to poets in the nineteenth century.
The words don't seem to emerge out of the crisis in Ireland – the fens,
lawns and moors belong to the English, not the Irish, landscape
– and this serves to distance the horror, which was perhaps the
unconscious intent of writers too inept and frightened to bring it
home.

This is what Mangan was reacting to when he began engaging
with the Famine in early 1846. His immediate response was to
launch what Shannon-Mangan calls his 'hate cycle', an excellent

description for the clutch of furious poems that appeared between 28 February and 18 April. These include three translations of rabble-rousing 'Lieder von Hasse' ('songs of hatred') by minor German romantics, which are not much good as poetry but are highly revealing of Mangan's state of mind: after years of refusal, he is finally submitting to Duffy's demand for insurrectionary verse. More interesting are the two original poems that top and tail the 'hate cycle' which – as if in riposte to the bland distancing of the other *Nation* poets – are aggressively local and contemporary in their referencing.

'The Rye Mill' (21 February) deals with the decay of a 'once merry mill' in Leixlip. A surface sheen of punning jocularity dissolves into helpless rage as the narrator lashes out at everyone he holds responsible for the decay: the laissez-faire theorists 'Mill, McCulloch and Ricardo', the 'absentee rackrenters' (i.e. landlords), 'curry-powder Norfolk' and 'the Chancellor himself? A mummy in a wig' – direct references to a notorious speech by the Duke of Norfolk advising that the Irish eat water flavoured with curry powder, and to the vocal support for eviction of the Chancellor, Lord Brougham. Evidently, Mangan was following the news.

He closed the cycle on 18 April, with his hottest and best piece of hatred: 'To the Ingleezee Khafir, Calling Himself Djaun Bool Djenkinzun' claims to be a 'particularly genuine Persian poem' by 'Meer Djafrit' but readers recognised it as an original composition by Mere Chaff Writ addressed to John Bull Jenkinson, i.e. England. Beginning 'I hate thee, Djaun Bool / Worse than Márid or Afrit, / Or corpse-eating Ghool. / I hate thee like Sin,' the poem is an expletive of curses from an 'Old Moslim' on the 'vile Ferindjee', Djaun Bull. The second verse opens 'I spit on thy clothing' and the whole poem is like a rage-fuelled gob of spit, a piece of burlesque with an undercurrent of Swiftian rancour, the crystallising of Mangan's bitterness over the British response to the Famine.

In another notorious speech by British aristocracy, the Queen's uncle, the Duke of Cambridge, had told an agricultural society in Leicester in December 1845 that the Irish should eat 'rotten potatoes and seaweed, or even grass [because] we all know that Irishmen could live upon anything'. This was casting the Irish as scavengers capable of subsisting on putrefying matter, with the subtext that they are vultures and hyenas scrounging off the British Lion. By equating John Bull with a 'corpse-eating ghoul', Mangan is subverting this trope and channelling Swift's 'A Modest Proposal' and its depiction of the British as cannibals feasting on Ireland (although the poem now reads like scary prophesy, because in the later years of the Famine people did eat grass and seaweed and there were dark rumours of cannibalism).

'To the Ingleezee Khafir' is Mangan's zenith of rage, which buckles beneath the weight of its anger and the bitter knowledge that words are inadequate to bring about the gigantic effort – political, financial, logistical and psychological – required from British rulers and administrators to avert catastrophe. This rage is a welcome corrective to the scoffing and whitewashing of the Tory press, but it also feels impotent because railing against the inhumanity of the royal dukes was spitting in the wind and even if readers had risen up to 'blast' the 'despots' from earth, as demanded in one of the 'Lied von Hassen', they couldn't have averted the crisis. It had gone too far. This wasn't a corrupt patent, which might be removed by Swiftian invective; it was a tsunami and inferno. There could be no saving the day and Mangan seems to have realised this because he dropped his inflammatory rage as suddenly as he had embraced it and moved into a completely different register.

In the same edition, Saturday 18 April 1846, as 'To the Ingleezee Khafir', a poem entitled 'Siberia' appeared in the news section, printed immediately after a thunderous editorial entitled 'We Can't Starve' and signed, unusually enough with its author's name: James Clarence Mangan.

In Siberia's wastes
The Ice-wind's breath
Woundeth like the toothed steel
Lost Siberia doth reveal
Only blight and death.

Blight and death alone
No Summer shines.
Night is interblent with Day.
In Siberia's wastes alway
The blood blackens, the heart pines.

In Siberia's wastes
No tears are shed,
For they freeze within the brain.
Nought is felt but dullest pain,
Pain acute, yet dead;

Pain as in a dream,
When years go by
Funeral-paced, yet fugitive,
When man lives, and doth not live,
Doth not live – nor die.

In Siberia's wastes
Are sands and rocks.
Nothing blooms of green or soft,
But the snowpeaks rise aloft
And the gaunt ice-blocks.

And the exile there
Is one with those;

They are part, and he is part,
For the sands are in his heart,
And the killing snows.

Therefore, in those wastes
None curse the Czar.
Each man's tongue is cloven by
The North Blast, who heweth nigh
With sharp scymitar.

And such doom each drees,
Till, hunger-gnawn,
And cold-slain, he at length sinks there,
Yet scarce more a corpse than ere
His last breath was drawn.

What was it like for readers to move, in the space of a few pages, from the hot rage of 'I hate thee, Djaun Bool' to this icy numbness? The poem seems to have emerged out of the psyche onto the news pages, which is perhaps why for a century and half no one realised that it is a translation. In the original, by Ernst Ortlepp, each stanza begins with the refrain 'In Siberia, in Siberia'. The repetition and even rhyming creates a rhythmic jauntiness and the references to the prisoners as Polish ties the poem to a specific historical time (the 1830 Polish uprising). Mangan removes the refrain, lengthens the lines, breaks up the rhythm, and untethers the poem from its historical setting – his Siberia is a metaphysical wasteland, timeless and non-specific, whose inhabitants aren't given a nationality or reason for their imprisonment.

Mangan always plumbed 'waste' for every possible meaning – 'I have wearied with my plaints / the unending wastes of air' he wrote in 1835 (that is 'wastes' as in 'expanses' and 'extraneous'); 'the very soul within my breast is wasted for you, love' he writes in 'My Dark Rosaleen'

'Wasted' as in 'wasting away' and 'squandered'); 'a ruined soul in a wasted frame' he writes in his autobiography ('wasted' as in 'destroyed', 'lost potential' and prefiguring our sense of 'high on drugs'). Long before T.S. Eliot, Mangan understood the wasteland as both a physical and a psychological space, a barren zone, timeless in the most chilling sense, where no moment is counted because no moment matters. That line 'years go by / funeral-paced, yet fugitive' tick-tocked through my mind during the Covid lockdown when the weeks crawled by because nothing happened and we couldn't escape our neighbourhoods or see anyone new, and yet, once passed, these weeks, so agonisingly slow to move through, were wiped clean from my memory, leaving no trace. My brother, who has volunteered in refugee camps, says this is the way time passes in the camps where inmates have no respite from the monotony of their surroundings and nothing to plan for. As humans, we mark time through distinctive happenings and changes of location and planning for the future and without these, the hours creep by funeral-paced, but the repetitive non-events are fugitive in the memory, gaining no foothold. I think this is what Thomas Mann is saying in *The Magic Mountain*, his meditation on time and incarceration, set in a sanatorium. In *Finnegans Wake*, Joyce makes a variegated pun on the names of the two authors and the disease that links them and the way that time drags in their works: 'a collera morbous for Mann in the Cloack' (the clock hidden in the cloak is very good).

With its short lines, its tonal restriction, its air of dragged-out exhaustion and its rhythms that don't quite scan, 'Siberia' is Mangan's masterpiece of waste and his first great artistic response to the Irish Famine – which never mentions Ireland.

*

When Mangan moved from the hot hatred of naming and shaming and calling for insurrection to the icy numbness of the wasteland, he moved from the Hollywood scenario of Saving the Day to another scenario which is also a universal trope, if less melodramatic. In this scenario, there is no way of preventing the destruction. The task is more modest: to bear witness and/or salvage something to survive into the future; to shore fragments against the ruin. What is witnessed/ shored/ salvaged is a kind of memory capsule, but it goes deeper than that – it enables a better future to unfold. The ur-salvaging myth is Noah building the ark to preserve enough animal species to regenerate the postdiluvian world. Noah is in a race against time: he has to build the ark and gather the animals before the tsunami hits. I think Mangan in spring 1846 had the same sense of having to shore his fragments/poems before he is swept away by the disease and hunger that are sweeping 'nearer, nearer' from the west (and that will eventually claim him).

The creation and survival of the Book of Kells has become another Salvaging/Shoring Myth, channelled in Cartoon Saloon's animation of *Brendan and the Secret of Kells* in which a young monastic apprentice races to complete and hide the Book before the Vikings ransack the Abbey. The narrative plays on the actual conditions in Ireland in the ninth century and on the peregrinations and miraculous survival of the Book of Kells, not only against the Vikings but centuries later, against Cromwell's army, and perhaps owes something to the possibly apocryphal story of the Franciscan monks, the 'Four Masters', retreating to a cottage in Donegal in 1632 to chronicle, in Gaelic, the annals of Irish history, in a last-ditch attempt to preserve their culture against the ruin that the Plantations and the Reformation were wreaking on it.

The *Book of Kells* and *Annals of the Four Masters* are generic images of salvage and bearing witness. It is frequently artists and scholars who are charged with this task. Anna Akhmatova's account of the creation of her masterpiece, 'Requiem', about the Stalinist purges, which claimed her husband and imprisoned her son, is highly conscious of taking on this role:

During the frightening years of the Yezhov terror, I spent seventeen months waiting in prison queues in Leningrad. One day, somehow, someone 'picked me out'. On that occasion there was a woman standing behind me, her lips blue with cold, who, of course, had never in her life heard my name. Jolted out of the torpor characteristic of all of us, she said into my ear (everyone whispered there) – 'Could one ever describe this?' And I answered – 'I can.' It was then that something like a smile slid across what had previously been just a face.

She could describe it – but she was afraid to write it down. Terrified throughout the years of composition of being incarcerated herself in the gulag, Akhmatova, together with a few friends, committed the 'Requiem' to memory, and it was only published after Stalin's death. The poem, its own survival an act of memory, sanctifies memory as a sacred duty and its message that you cannot move on to the next phase (of your own life or the nation's life) unless you keep alive the memory of suffering is close to Santayana's famous maxim that 'those who cannot remember the past are condemned to repeat it' and anticipates *vergangenheitsbewältigung* – the 'working through the past' undertaken by Germany in the decades after the Holocaust.

'Could one ever describe this?' – Akhmatova's simple, direct answer, 'I can,' is alien to Mangan, who is rarely simple and never direct. But in his own indirect way he did for the Irish Famine what she did for the Stalinist purges. He shored against the ruin. If he was able to do this, alone among writers in Ireland, it was because he was prepared. Since childhood he had been waiting for something terrible and when it happened, maybe he felt the vindication of Spike Milligan: 'I told you I was ill.' Now the man who could never look straight at anything had found the subject that can't be looked at.

Le Soleil ni La Mort ne se peuvent regarder fixement. You cannot look straight at death or the sun. In Greek myth, Athena gives Perseus a brightly polished shield so that he can refract the gaze of the Medusa. She is Death: to look at her is to be turned to stone. Huge national traumas are like Medusa, Death and the Sun: if you gaze straight at them, you will be petrified or burnt. Mangan instinctively sidestepped the trap that other *Nation* poets fell into. They tried to find literal words to describe the devastation, and 'turned to stone', or to pebbles, seems a fair description of their lifeless verse, so risible is the mismatch between their buoyant thumping rhymes and the scale of the tragedy: 'Fainting forms, hunger-stricken, what see you in the offing? / Stately ships to bear our food away, amid the stranger's scoffing.'

Mangan was never going to nursery-rhyme his way through a national calamity but it's not only that he knew to avoid the thumping beat; he knew to avoid directly evoking the tragedy. All his life he was like a kind of manic Perseus, holding up his mirrors – his veils, masks, metaphors, jokes, double negatives, shadows, clouds, cloaks – to avoid looking at a theme directly. This was because he was terrified, seeing danger approaching from every direction, and because he was innately protective; his instinct was always to shield what he loved, not highlight it. His pathology of concealment can come across as neurotically over-protective, but in the face of vast tragedy it begins to look like the only fitting response, both morally and aesthetically.

After the horrors of the early twentieth century, Beckett issued a directive 'to find a form that accommodates the mess, that is the task of the artist now'. His implication (backed up by his plays) that the 'form' will not be overt was taken up enthusiastically, if not always successfully by other writers. Norman Mailer's 1967 novella about a hunting trip in Alaska entitled *Why Are We in Vietnam?* channels the indirect approach but the constant nudging – hey, this story about shooting a grizzly is really about Nam! – is irritating and since Mailer isn't pathologically secretive, the effect feels strained and opportunistic. This isn't what you get from Mangan's choice to write about rye mills and Siberian prisoners and ruined medieval abbeys – anything except Famine in Ireland. Indirection is what he has always done, and just as the deliberate mannerism of his early 'love' poems was paradoxically honest in signalling to the reader that the scenario is a construct, so his metaphorical approach to the Famine shows up the crudeness of the other *Nation* poets' attempts to imagine themselves into a suffering which is, in fact, unimaginable. His subtlety and delicacy, the respectful restraint with which he hovers at the threshold of horror, seems to prefigure Primo Levi's insight that the true story of the Holocaust can never be told because the most vulnerable perished, voiceless, in the camps.

A theatre director today, looking to stage the Famine, probably wouldn't attempt a literal recreation because simulations of evictions, riots and soup kitchens are impossible to stage and wouldn't work for today's sophisticated audiences. Primed by the stark minimalism and austere metaphors of Beckett, Bergman, Tarkovsky and Peter Brook, contemporary theatre-goers prefer to see despair conveyed through the empty stage and debris of the wasteland: rags, bins, tree stumps, gnomic jesters. Mangan grasped all this before the great twentieth-century masters of theatre and the play of his life shouldn't directly depict the Famine.

The final Act could open on a biting monologue of hatred, at once blackly comic ('I spit on thy clothing') and deeply disturbing ('We have all had more than enough of love, now for a spell of hatred') and then, in a grotesque but oddly uplifting moment, a ragged mob troops on stage brandishing pathetic weapons and singing a bellicose song, until the lights dim, they fall silent and distance from each other, huddling to the extremities of the stage, and all the lights go out except on the Mangan actor's mouth which moves rapidly but no words are coming out … and then the spotlight fades, and the stage is left in deep gloom until, from the wings, a ghostly light appears, a kind of phosphorescence, in which the audience can just make out a flowing, almost floating, female form with long hair in tendrils – or perhaps all that is needed is a faint light and a sibilant whisper to suggest the aisling.

'Siberia' hardly cold on his pen, Mangan had found another metaphor for the Famine: the seventeenth- and eighteenth-century Gaelic 'poems of the dispossessed'.

Quarrying in the bowels

All decisive acts acquire a sense of inevitability. When Frank and I broke up and got back together again that became the story of our relationship, our eventual togetherness made contingent on our having suffered distance. The stories we tell ourselves (as individuals and nations) work backwards from the decisive moment – the wedding, the break-up, the military victory, the revolution – to illuminate the path that took us there. But that's not what it feels like as events are unfolding. I know that when I was walking around the Liberties muttering Verlaine, I thought it was truly over with Frank and couldn't see a path through, but this effort to recall the instability of that period is like swimming against the warm current of my memory, which knows how things actually turned out. Most books and films progress in a focused way towards a conclusion which seems foregone because in these narratives character is plot and actions have consequences. This model of storytelling seems to be hardwired into us and nearly impossible to break. In 'The Road not Taken' Robert Frost tries to get us thinking of contingencies but fails because our lives are littered with hundreds of these forsaken roads and I don't believe anyone ever selects just one to cry grandiloquently 'oh, the difference now to me', plus the poem is so binary that it reinforces rather than disrupts the model. The only text I know of that captures the randomness and disconnectedness of moving through the present is Jane Bowles's *Two Serious Ladies* and the sense in that novella that anything might happen from one page to the next and that the two ladies on their 'deadbeat odysseys' through New York and Panama are reacting haphazardly to each new situation with little reference to past behaviour, is unnerving despite, or because, it is so like life and so unlike any other novel.

Mangan's decision in summer 1846 to engage obliquely with the Famine by riffing on the Gaelic 'poems of the dispossessed' did so much to seal his legend that it quickly acquired the sheen of inevitability. In the telling, this catastrophic situation, the Famine, is crying out for these poems of catastrophe, with Mangan, catastrophic survivor of catastrophes, their only possible interpreter. The three lock together in a kind of trine of necessity. It's obviously far too late for me in this book to try and reproduce the random disjunctions of Jane Bowles but I would like to try and get across just how unlikely the whole thing was, how sparse was the landscape and understanding of literature in Irish and how high the odds against anyone, especially a Dubliner who knew no Irish, coming upon these poems.

The greatest Irish scholar of Mangan's age, John O'Donovan, called himself 'a mere quarryman digging, from the bowels of antiquity materials, for the future poets and historians of Ireland'. That word 'quarrying' brings to mind the aftermath of an immense disaster like Pompeii or the Aleppo earthquake or Krakatoa eruption, an event so cataclysmic that it buries a whole world beneath it. The image seems extravagant and was not how I felt about the Gaelic world, about which I had a hazy but more or less coherent and chronological sense. Since I didn't pick this up in a formal school setting, I felt I must have absorbed it from the air, just by living in Ireland, or inherited it as a kind of birthright (the tales of Fianna and Cuchulainn whispered into my cot perhaps).

But then I came across a set of dates, which jolted my sense of continuity with the past and of connecting to things that had always being there: the first publication of Brian Merriman's *The Midnight Court* in Irish (1850) and English (1897), and of Eibhlín Dubh Ní Chonaill's *Caoineadh Airt Uí Laoghaire* in English (1892) and Irish (1896). Both poems were composed in the 1770s (and survived until publication through the oral tradition and in lone manuscripts) but Mangan, born just a generation after their composition, knew nothing about either. I'm not sure why I found this so hard to get my head around. Perhaps because both are now so famous that they have spawned secondary industries so that even people who aren't interested in Irish or poetry have a sense of them through the Merriman Summer School, the Druid Theatre productions, *At Swim-Two-Birds*, *A Ghost in the Throat* ... Or perhaps because Mangan was so close to them in time and space – in Clare and Kerry in his day people were reciting those poems – and we are so far. How could he not know then what we know now? It was like discovering that Heaney knew nothing about *The Playboy of the Western World* or McGahern about *Dubliners*.

These dates opened the floodgates. I realised that this not-knowing was so endemic and pervasive that it would be easier to count what Mangan did know than what he didn't. It's not just that he didn't know the poems we all now know – 'Amergin' and 'The Hag of Beare' and 'Pangúr Bán' and 'Donal Óg' and 'Anois teacht an Earraigh' – he barely knew the myths and legends of the Tuatha de Danaan and the Fianna and the Red Branch. He would have known about the Children of Lir from *Moore's Melodies* and maybe he read John O'Donovan's translations of medieval manuscripts which began appearing in the 1840s, but he had no real clue of the amazing world of gods and heroes which Samuel Ferguson, Yeats and Lady Gregory would reveal to later generations.

All this was somewhere out there when he was there, but it was lost, buried or ignored. The manuscripts from which these poems and legends would eventually be published were scattered to the winds – Charles O'Conor of Belangare's extensive collection of manuscripts was in Stowe estate in Buckinghamshire (and subsequently acquired by Oxford's Bodleian Library); 'Cúirt an Mheain Oíche' was in Cambridge; the 'Caoineadh' was in the O'Connell family papers; the Egerton collection of sixteenth-century legal manuscripts was in the British Library; other manuscripts were in Belgium, where Franciscan monks had fled after 1601. Trinity College owned the most valuable collection of manuscripts but lacked the scholarship to make sense of what they had – in 1836 John O'Donovan was asked to compile an analytical catalogue of their holdings; four years later he was only halfway through the job, and the annotating, contextualising and translating had to wait for future generations. When George Petrie bought the second volume of the *Annals of the Four Masters* at the sale of a private library in 1831 and passed it on to the Royal Irish Academy, it was only the fourth Gaelic manuscript in their holdings, although the Academy had been founded to 'promote and investigate science, polite literature and antiquities' in Ireland.

Surveying this blasted heath, I thought that my sense of an immense disaster was accurate after all since no other explanation seemed possible for the burying and dispersal of so much of value, and for a rupture in learning so violent that much of what was uncovered could not be understood. Máire Mhac an tSaoi's observation that 'all Irish men of learning before the advent of modern linguistic science [in the 1880s] were largely ignorant of Old and Middle Irish, and both unaware of the extent of this ignorance and reluctant to admit its effects' is a devastating gloss on O'Donovan's wry self-portrait as 'a quarryman digging in the bowels of antiquity'. He doesn't know that he lacks the right tools; he doesn't know what he doesn't know …

The epicentre of the disaster was back in the long seventeenth century, in the Tudor and Cromwellian plantations, the flight of the Earls, the Williamite Wars, but the aftershocks continued on for centuries through the Penal Laws and the mass emigration and epidemics which affected the rural poor, ergo the Irish speakers, disproportionately, so that by 1829, the year of Emancipation, little was visible from the wreckage, at least in Dublin. In the Irish-speaking regions beyond the Pale, it was a different story thanks to a still robust oral tradition. Here Gaelic culture was not so much buried as hidden, to use Daniel Corkery's famous phrase. I think this 'hidden Ireland' counts as yet another Manganese mode of concealment although a reflexive mode since Mangan isn't the concealer here, but the concealee. After he met John O'Donovan in 1832, he would have got a sense of a whole lyrical world hidden from him, and maybe he also got this from his father, who as a hedge-school teacher in Shanagolden in the 1780s presumably spoke and taught in Irish. Those from whom things are hidden become secretive in their turn and if Mangan was secretive for all the personal reasons I'm suggesting – childhood trauma, homosexuality, opiate addiction, revolutionary views, etc. – he was also just generationally secretive like everyone his age in Dublin and the Pale who had to negotiate the world through absence. Of all the gaps that echo around Mangan, this gap of two millennia of native language, history and culture is the most vertiginous. If it seems extravagant to compare him to 'Mao's children' in the Cultural Revolution, I suspect that as an adolescent, he knew as little or less about the history, culture and language of his country than Chinese students in the 1970s did about theirs. Perhaps Hilary Mantel gets closer to what it was like: growing up in England with Irish grandparents, she had little sense of Irish language or culture until as an adult she came across Corkery's *The Hidden Ireland* in a bookshop. Its account of the wreckage of Gaelic culture following the plantations 'nearly broke' her heart:

> I felt a keen deprivation, and a dismay: if (in some Variety of Religious Experience) I were to meet one of my foremothers, then maybe she would speak that language, and I this, and – though I admit such a meeting is unlikely – it would be a kind of disgrace, a neglect. Though odd, my feelings were not sentimental; I simply became aware that all my life I had been living in a room with a door I'd ignored, while trying to climb out a narrow window. My efforts to learn Irish didn't come to anything. I soon realised that knowing the language wasn't the point; the point was knowing what I didn't know, and listening for the music inside the silence.

This is eerily like Mhac an tSaoi's comment on Gaelic scholarship and gets across the trauma of not knowing what you don't know, of not recognising the door as a door. All of Mangan's generation in Dublin grew up with this sense of 'deprivation … dismay … disgrace … neglect'. Emancipation, which relaxed the political environment, softened the climate for Irish scholarship and in the 1830s the emissaries between the 'two Irelands' could start their quarrying: antiquarians like George Petrie who didn't speak Irish but revered the past; amateur enthusiasts like James Hardiman and John O'Daly who began collating and translating poems; bilingual scholars like John O'Donovan and his brother-in-law Eugene O'Curry who became the first professional scholars in Irish language and literature when they were hired by the Ordnance Survey, the Royal Irish Academy and Trinity College to begin the mammoth task of annotating, contextualising and translating the culture. Their efforts would lead, by the 1860s, to the establishment of Irish departments in universities, but in the 1830s and 40s the terrain still resembled, as O'Donovan characterised it, an archaeological dig: a few stunning finds survived intact but, with most of the material scattered and buried and without the requisite scholarship, these couldn't be linked, contextualised or elucidated. Absences gaped and meanings remained mysterious and tantalising – Mangan's ironic pun on his condition on his deathbed, 'unhoused and un-annalled', describes the condition of Gaelic literature during his lifetime. And his sense of this literature wasn't only fleeting, it was 'false and perjur'd'.

In the 1760s the Scottish writer James Macpherson had published poems that he claimed as translations from a third-century Gaelic bard, Ossian. They took Europe by storm – Goethe put them into *The Sorrows of Young Werther*, and Melchiorre Cesarotti's Italian version was a favourite of Napoleon's – and unleashed the biggest literary row of the century. The scholarship of Charles O'Conor of Belangare and the polemics of Samuel Johnson eventually exposed Macpherson as a fraud, his 'sagas' made up. The episode was double-edged: it hugely popularised Gaelic literature across Europe – Thomas Moore owed his success to Macpherson – but it brought an atmosphere of fraudulence to Gaelic scholarship and translation, which made it easier to dismiss the real achievements of the culture. In the course of dispatching Macpherson, Samuel Johnson characterised Gaelic culture as oral, peasant and folkloric. It would take O'Donovan and O'Curry decades of painstaking research to establish that it was also documented, professional and sophisticated, and they had barely got started during Mangan's lifetime.

In theory, Irish people were getting an introduction to their heritage through the translations that started appearing intermittently from the late eighteenth century, beginning with Charlotte Brooke's *Reliques of Irish Poetry* in 1786, but these were so few and so poor that the only comparison I can make is to people in the Soviet Union watching shaky projections of poorly dubbed and damaged cuts of Hollywood films, and that doesn't quite convey it because even the worst-quality footage is more approximate to the original film than this line 'The various emotions that sway me / A lover alone can impart' is to 'Trí ní a chím tríd an ngrá / an peaca, an bás is an phian'. If Mangan read this translation of a folk poem which appeared in dual language in the anthology *Irish Minstrelsy* (1831), he couldn't have known, since he had no Irish, that it bore no relation to the original (which Thomas Kinsella translates as 'Through love I have seen three things / evil and pain and death') but I bet he suspected, given his insight into translation, that the original had suffered terrible damage crossing languages, moving from those short stabbing words and arresting repetition into languid imprecision. I think he had a shrewd sense that what he was getting from these translations was as false, if not as perjur'd, as the Ossian sagas.

The first door that opened into the past, as Mantel would say, came in 1834 in an incendiary review by Samuel Ferguson, in the *Dublin University Magazine*, of *Irish Minstrelsy*. This anthology was a labour of love for its editor, James Hardiman, a one-eyed native Irish speaker from Mayo who worked in the civil service but had wanted to be a priest. He had spent years gathering poems and songs, dating from the 5th to the 18th centuries, and finding translators for them, and in a defiant introduction, he made the case for Gaelic Ireland as a great classical civilisation, comparable to Greece and Rome, with a world-class literature written by professionally trained bards. Colonisation had severely ruptured this civilisation but even after the plantations and the Reformation, the bards continued to produce marvellous poetry which Hardiman terms distinctively native – the bards 'fought and spoke and wrote in Irish', he claimed, and were 'invariably, Catholics, patriots and Jacobites'.

This incensed Ferguson, a young Belfast Unionist who had recently started studying Irish. His review pulls no punches: Gaelic culture was folk and peasant, not classical and sophisticated, and 'the tardiness, not to say retrogression, of civilisation and prosperity in Ireland' wasn't down to colonialism but to the 'excess of natural piety' which made the Irish cling to Catholicism rather than embracing the Reformation: 'The question is not whether more whiskey was drunk in Ireland before, or after, the time of Cromwell ... but whether the moral intemperance, the mental dissipation and habitual idleness which characterise the Irish were more the consequences of *our penal laws or of their own savage customs.*' (The italics are Ferguson's; note 'our' penal laws and 'their' savage customs.) Only the 'rustic naivete' of its folk poetry, 'wild, mournful, incondite, yet not uncouth', redeemed this savage society and it is the 'simple sincerity' of the amateur poets – those desperate outlaws', 'rustic lovers' and 'pining friars' – that Ferguson wants to see celebrated, not the 'artificial pedantries of the professional bards'.

Read from this distance, their quarrel is poignant: two Irishmen fighting for ownership of their heritage – in Hardiman, you mark the anxiety of the Connaught Catholic to have his dignity restored and the greatness of his culture recognised; in Ferguson, the anxiety of the Belfast Protestant not to be disenfranchised from that culture. If Hardiman's classicist claims for Gaelic culture seem insecure and over-egged and his conflation of Irish with Catholicism depressingly narrow and exclusivist after the pluralism of the United Irishmen, Ferguson's tribal superiority is obnoxious, his defence of colonialism outrageous (and not just for us reading now but for them then – the Penal Laws had never recovered from Swift's *Modest Proposal* and *Draper's Letters*) – and he is plain wrong about the quality of the professional bards, as he would admit tacitly when he began translating from them himself a few decades later. And yet he emerges as the victor in this contest because he aces what counts most: the translations.

The five translators whom Hardiman had found for his *Minstrelsy* followed the received wisdom that poetry in translation should approximate to the rhythms and metres of English poetry. Since Gaelic metre is nothing like English and since none of Hardiman's translators was much of a poet, their efforts were stilted and artificial. Ferguson demolished them in a scathing footnote – 'the majority of these attempts by the fierce invaders of the barrenness of Irish literature ... are spurious, puerile, unclassical – lamentably bad' – and followed up with an astonishing lesson in how to preserve 'the barrenness' of the Irish language. Adhering to what he calls 'the strict severity of literal translation', he abandoned rhyme, metre and scansion to inaugurate the direct, curt, barren, unrhyming mode of translation which is, still today, the preferred way of translating from Irish into English. Here is the version of 'Torna's Lament' in the *Minstrelsy*, translated by John D'Alton:

> O, let me think in age
> Of years rolled by
> When in the peace of infancy,
> 'mid all the ties of holy fosterage
> The future Lords of Erin's doom,
> With smiles of innocence and unambitious play
> Passed the rapid hours away;
> The royal children of my heart and home
> Nial the heir of hundred-battled Con
> And Corc, of Eoghan More, the not less glorious son.

And here is Ferguson, translating the same passage in half the words:

My two foster-children were not slack
Nial of Tara and Corc of pleasant Cashel
(Nial) of the mighty race of Owen More
(Corc) worthy descendant of Con of a hundred battles.
They conquered Ireland – great was their valour.

It doesn't have to sound like English poetry. By now, we're so used to this way of translating from Irish, and so familiar with free verse generally, that we don't even notice Ferguson's radicalism. Aged just twenty-four, and new to the study of Irish, he severed translation from English poetic metre and idiom to produce versions, which, according to Mhac an tSaoi, were 'so far in advance of the taste of their time that the author himself is constantly defensive of them and protective towards them'. It was an astonishing achievement, which still reverberates.

The row is seminal in the history of translation – and not just translation in Ireland but everywhere. It reads like a gloss on a famous text of romanticism, Johann Fichte's 'Addresses to the German Nation', whose message that a distinctive native culture deserves de facto an independent government was hugely influential on romantic movements in Europe but took longer to land in Ireland, perhaps because O'Connell's attitude to the Irish language obscured its politicising potential. Inspired by the Enlightenment rather than Romanticism, O'Connell judged indigenous language and culture an impediment to political independence and his case for repeal of the Union depended on demonstrating that a progressive, English-speaking, modernising Ireland was capable of running its own affairs.

It wasn't until the launch of *The Nation* in 1842 that the Fichtean argument began gaining ground in Ireland – preparing the way for the Gaelic League's rallying cry 'Not free merely but Gaelic as well' – but I'm pretty sure that Mangan, with his sophisticated grasp of romanticism and translation and his Young Ireland dislike of

O'Connell, realised that Ferguson's victory in 1824 was pyrrhic. I think he spotted the irony in Hardiman claiming superiority for Gaelic culture with terrible translations and Ferguson patronising the culture with brilliant translations, and was covertly amused at Ferguson walking into a trap which Hardiman didn't even know that he had set. He didn't comment on the row at the time but four years later, he was granted a ring-side seat on these questions of politics and culture when he found himself employed in the inner sanctum of Gaelic translation: the Ordnance Survey.

*

The Ordnance Survey of Ireland was established in 1824 following 'a clamor from landowners for a new map of Ireland that would update and standardize land valuation and taxation'. Inaugurated against a background of violent agrarian upheavals, it was overseen by the British Army's Board of Ordnance. Whether it was a military tool is disputed among historians, but it was certainly 'an exercise in colonial management – an effort to gather information to allow the effective control and administration of the colony'.

In 1824, the Irish countryside was minutely named, right down to significant rocks and tiny streams, but, except within the inner Pale, the names were in Irish and had developed haphazardly and organically over centuries. Now the Survey wanted them translated and described at speed. Since Irish wasn't an academic discipline, there was no agreed system of orthography or philology to draw on. The task was huge and for the original employees of the Survey – British officers and engineers – impossible.

In 1828, Thomas Larcom, an English lieutenant with the Royal Engineers, was put in charge. Formidably organised and ambitious – he would eventually be appointed under-secretary of Ireland – he realised the need for local experts. The team he put together was remarkable and included the country's leading antiquarian (George Petrie), native Irish speakers and hedge school teachers (John O'Donovan, Eugene O'Curry), a teenage artist (William Wakeman) and a revolutionary poet (Mangan). These formed a separate section within the Survey, known as the topographical, orthographic or historical section, which met in Petrie's house in Great Charles Street in north inner-city Dublin, with a mission to 'collect every possible information, antiquarian or topographical, about [every] portion of the country'.

For eight or nine years, 1833–42, Petrie's house was the headquarters of Celtic studies in Ireland, its front parlour 'hung with mahogany cases, which contained the most valuable and unique collection of Celtic antiquities to be found in the kingdom' and its back parlour 'a mess of dusty, worn old books and documents, ancient and modern'. To this office, O'Donovan and O'Curry would return from field-trips round the country, bearing back place-names and topographies to be translated and described via an orthographic system which, being pioneers, they had to devise as they went along.

The Ordnance Survey now functions as a signifier for the colonising project in Ireland and beyond. This has been the case since the first performance of Brian Friel's play *Translations* in Derry in 1980. The scenario – the arrival of English surveyors to a Donegal village in 1833 – can be transposed to any region where there is a colonial invading language and an indigenous precarious language; the play has been successfully performed in Cardiff, Barcelona, Minsk and Kyiv.

Friel put the Survey on the literary map, but he didn't invent its exciting tensions. In an excellent recent study, Cóilín Parsons makes the case for the Survey as inherently paradoxical in design and execution, negotiating a series of contradictions: it imposed the English language on the Irish; it brought the tools of modernity (mapping, cataloguing) onto pre-modern agrarianism; by documenting a culture under siege, it 'preserved on paper' what was being 'destroyed on the ground' and concurrent with this 'paradox of the archive' was a paradox of staffing: the success of the project depended on native speakers gleaning local information which meant, in practice, that the men employed by the British Army to 'translate' Ireland for the purpose of land registration and colonial administration, were Catholics and nationalists.

Where Friel was fascinated by the tension of English surveyors going into the rural villages,* I am fascinated by the inherent tension of the office in Great Charles Street. I imagine O'Donovan and O'Curry, like characters in *Translations*, switching between conciliatory English to Larcom and Petrie, and sarcastic politicised Irish to each other. We know there was a political edge to the discussions in the house because a whistleblower staff member wrote anonymously to the government, signing himself 'A Protestant Conservative' to complain that the other staff members were Catholics and nationalists who 'carried their bigotry and politics to all parts of the kingdom … taking down the pedigree of some beggar or tinker and establishing him the lineal descendant of some Irish chief, whose ancient estate they most carefully mark out by boundaries'.

Into the tension, paradox and polyglottery arrived in 1838 the most paradoxical and polyglot writer in Ireland. It was an astonishing moment in Mangan's, and the Survey's, life. Did the Survey's inherent paradoxes sharpen his approach to translation, or did his own seditious approach colour the project? I'm guessing a delicate interplay, but the significance can hardly overstated: we wouldn't have Mangan's Famine masterpieces without the Survey.

At first, he was a backroom boy, arriving late each day, sipping from his tar-water and keeping to the background, but in 1840 he

---

*The play is historically inaccurate: in 1833, the Survey wasn't sending out British officers but native Irish speakers like O'Donovan and O'Curry.

acquired a starring role in one of the Survey's cultural off-shoots when Petrie launched, from his house, *The Irish Penny Journal*. The nervous editorial which Petrie penned for the first issue of this short-lived but influential journal goes straight to the heart of the Survey's paradox:

> *The Irish Penny Journal* will be in a great degree devoted to subjects connected with the history, literature, antiquities and general condition of Ireland. All subjects tending in the remotest degree to irritate or offend political or religious feeling will be rigidly abstained from, and every endeavour will be made to diffuse sentiments of benevolence and mutual goodwill through all classes of the community.

The two sentences form an oxymoron: Petrie is trying to block out the truth self-evident from the atmosphere in his own house that 'history, literature, and antiquities' will always 'irritate or offend political or religious feeling'.

It was a few months after the launch that Petrie had a job for Mangan. He wanted a translation of an earthy comic poem, 'Bean na Trí mBó'. Through the correspondence and memoirs of other team members, we know how this came about: O'Curry provided a prose translation into English which Mangan turned into poetry.

William Wakeman, the teenager sketch artist, claimed that 'I verily believe the composition did not occupy [Mangan] half an hour'. The result did not meet with Ferguson's 'strict severity of literal translation' – the English is twice as wordy as the Irish:

> O woman of three cows, agrah, don't let your tongue thus rattle
> O don't be saucy, don't be stiff, because you may have cattle
> I have seen – and here's my hand to you, I only say what's true –
> A many a one with twice your stock not half so proud as you.

It was however a triumphant rendition of Hiberno-Irish. The editors of the *Collected Works* observe shrewdly that Mangan 'objectifies the piece into a dramatic monologue, evoking a persona reminiscent of characters in English-language Irish novels of his own time', e.g. *Castle Rackrent, Traits of the Irish Peasantry, The Collegians*.

Mangan's version of 'Woman of Three Cows' appeared, unsigned, in *The Irish Penny Journal* on 29 August 1840, alongside the original Irish. Over the next months, he produced three more translations from the Irish for the journal, not comic folk poems but great bitter seventeenth- and eighteenth-century laments, which he hibernicised through the elegiac evocation of place names and 'the bitter word' – the line 'vassal to a *Saxoneen* of cold and sapless bones!' seems calculated to 'irritate political feeling' and must have made Petrie nervous. Hibernicising was a departure for Mangan (his German translations don't sound Germanic); he was presumably influenced by Ferguson and the discussions in Great Charles Street.

The Irish Penny Journal lasted a year, folding in June 1841, which doesn't explain why Mangan produced no more translations from the Irish. *The Nation*, which launched in 1842, was constantly begging for them – Duffy eulogised Mangan's 'power of making his verses racy of the soil' and begged that 'he would lend his help to an Irish ballad history'. This prompted a jealous response from O'Curry: 'Mr Mangan has no knowledge of the Irish language, nor do I think he regrets that either … It was I that translated those poems from the originals.'

People were fighting over ownership of his poems but Mangan himself wasn't that pushed. He refused all of Duffy's appeals and didn't pitch to the *Dublin University Magazine*. It seems like he only did those four poems in *The Irish Penny Journal* as a favour – O'Curry's note to O'Donovan in August 1840 suggests as much:

'Mr P is working, on Mangan's back, for the life, on the P.J.' Mangan's relationship with O'Curry was poor. Described by O'Donovan, as 'exceedingly jealous-minded ... and cannot bear to be set right', O'Curry was tetchy and difficult. He was irritated by Mangan getting all the credit for the poems, called him 'a schemer', and took his share of payment. But Mangan could have collaborated with someone else or drawn on other translations. He didn't, perhaps because he always preferred what was distant and exotic, and liked the challenge of solving 'untranslatable' poems. Maybe turning English prose into Hibernicised poetry – in half an hour, if Wakeman was right – didn't seem like much of a challenge; plus, he disliked Duffy's propagandistic nationalism, and liked teasing him ...

Whatever the reason, for five years Mangan resisted all pleas for Irish verse, until in May 1846, he found his way back to it.

I can scale the blue air

The Famine was a cold time. Blight leads to penury, which leads to eviction, which leads to hypothermia, which leads to death. This sequence was well understood in Ireland, and during the gathering storm of spring 1846, the papers were full of cold and the threat of exposure. *The Kerry Examiner* (7 April 1846) reporting on 'nine poor families evicted from their tenements', emphasised that 'the day was particularly wet, cold and inclement, more in fact like a mid-winter than a spring day'. *The Leinster Express*, a conservative paper, reported that 'on Tuesday last we had the Sheriff and 12 policemen from Abbeyleix, turning out four families near this town, on property belonging to Mr. Fitzgerald of Ballyroan – the poor creatures are *living behind a few sods*; without any covering from the weather'. O'Connell in his speeches put constant emphasis on 'the turning out of the naked, the unfed and unclothed poor of Ireland' (*Cork Examiner*, 15 April 1846) and this was echoed by his MPs, who spun a distressing narrative in the House of Commons: 'Fancy an Irish peasant ejected from his hovel, which has sheltered him and his family for generations. His roof-tree thrown down upon him; the very walls levelled; his land taken away; he, his wife, his children, his aged father and mother, driven out in hunger and wretchedness, without shelter on the cold road, to die of fever or famine in the ditches' (*The Nation*, 11 April 1846).

After a public works labourer, Jeremiah Hegarty, died in a ditch in the Mizen peninsula of Cork, the inquest in November 1846 reported that 'want of sufficient nourishment was the remote, and exposure to the cold, the direct cause of death'. The testimony of Hegarty's daughter reveals the cumulative deprivation that led to hypothermia: her father's bed, she said, 'was a little straw scattered on the ground and some packing for his covering' and the rain was 'down through the house'; the family had no turf for the fire 'because they had no food for the people that would be required to cut it' and her husband's greatcoat and a quilt, which might have warmed her father, 'had just been pledged in order to help pay for the manuring of the garden'.

As a thin, malnourished peripathetic who didn't take steady meals and lived in draughty tenements, his layers of clothing as much a bulwark against the cold as an artistic statement, Mangan had the tramp's intimate knowledge of rain, wind and cold and he felt these reports to the bone. It was the 'killing snows' that had drawn him to 'Siberia' and his version is a rebuke to Ortlepp's inadequate understanding of what it is to be cold. He knew German Romanticism couldn't provide the shivering misery that the papers were reporting on, and that he would need to find other texts to work off. Maybe, though he couldn't understand Irish, he could hear – from listening to O'Donovan, O'Curry and John O'Daly – that it *sounds* cold. The Irish language isn't soft and yielding and liquefying. It is all hard edges; a point Seamus Heaney makes brilliantly in an essay on early Irish nature poetry:

> The authentic chill of winter and the bittersweet weather of a northern winter pierce into the marrow of the quatrains [of 'Scél lem dúib']. I can think of only a few poets in English

whose words give us the sharp tooth of winter anywhere as incisively … It almost seems that since the Norman conquest, the temperature of the English language has been subtly raised by the warm front coming up from the Mediterranean. But the Irish language did not undergo the same Romance influences.

I think it was the 'sharp tooth' of the wintry Irish language that brought Mangan in 1846 back to the seventeenth- and eighteenth-century laments that he had translated six years earlier and which resonated so eerily with the current situation: 'Long they wander to and fro, proscribed alas! and banned / Feastless, houseless, altarless, they bear the exile's brand.' Starting with 'The Dream of John MacDonnell' on 16 May, he published twelve translations over the rest of the year, reworking existing versions in English – all of them appearing in *The Nation* except for three, which featured in an anthology in October (allowing for printing schedules, they were probably written in summer).

The critical and popular response was immediate – on 10 October 1846 *The Nation* gushed that 'there are some translations which for intrinsic beauty we would scarce exchange for any poetry in the English language – chief among these is Mr Mangan's Dark Rosaleen' – and the fame of these translations continued into the twentieth century. Nobody questioned the staggering achievement. But then the backlash began, slowly and slyly. It was death by a thousand cuts rather than a hatchet job, but by the start of the twenty-first century, the deed was done: Declan Kiberd's compendious *Irish Classics* (2000) opens with the seventeenth-century bard Seathrún Céitinn and ends with Patrick Kavanagh and in between there are chapters on everyone you would expect in both languages, O'Rathaille, Swift, Goldsmith, Merriman, Ní Chonaill, Edgeworth, Carleton, Wilde, Yeats, Joyce, Synge, Ó Cadhain, etc., a roll call of the classics, but no chapter on Mangan who gets just five mentions, all fleeting. Every previous scholarly attempt to assemble a canon of Irish classics had included Mangan, not necessarily admiringly, but his historical significance was always noted. The omission from *Irish Classics* is the final consummation of the Mitchel trope of Mangan the Unknown. I can imagine Mangan taking 'diseased gratification' in the fulfilment of his prophesy of 'unfelt, untold, unknown', but I would like to make the case for putting him back into the canon. To do that I have to start with why I think he has been taken out and this involves a confrontation with 'my own frequent misgivings about the achievement of the poetry I was reading', as David Lloyd characterises his own doubts.

*

As a bilingual scholar, Kiberd moves easily between the two languages and his creation of a dual-language canon feels right but I don't think his fluency in Irish is incidental to his decision to leave Mangan out of his *Irish Classics*; my hunch is that Irish speakers have had a lot to do with booting Mangan from the canon. I got an intimation of this very early in my research when I told my father's best friend who I was working on. I was expecting excitement and encouragement from this magnificent man – the 'brilliant creation' adored by Frank – who was brought up in the Cork Gaeltacht, speaks four or five languages and loves poetry in all of them, and loves especially O'Rathaille, but instead, I got an impatient and dismissive snort, something along the lines of 'Victorian rhetoric!' I was taken aback but thought no more of it until, sometime later, a writer and editor from a Belfast Protestant background who had taken the trouble to learn Irish and was close to Irish-language poets, confided in me, by email, that Mangan fills him with 'horror victorianorum – horror of the Victorians, which even Irish people could not escape' and pointed me to 'a nice straightforward translation of Róisín Dubh' by Thomas Kinsella: 'You can see how Mangan has puffed it up!'

It was the recurrence of Victoriana that got me suspicious because Mangan isn't a Victorian. His last decade of life coincides with the first decade of Victoria's reign, but she was barely a Victorian herself then and, in birth, formation and influence, Mangan belongs to the Georges and the Romantics. I felt that Victorian was code for stuffy, imperial, un-Irish. My sense that my father's friend and the editor hadn't really read Mangan but were repeating received opinion was sharpened when I turned to books by Irish-language scholars. I may be guilty of confirmation bias – primed by the sneers of these two men, maybe I went looking for more sneers – but except for Desmond Ryan in *The Sword of Light* (1939), I couldn't find any Irish-language scholar in the twentieth century with much good to say about Mangan.

Introducing his own translation of 'O'Hussey's Ode' for an article in 1921, Osborn Bergin, professor of early and medieval Irish in UCD, notes that 'Mangan did not know Irish; his original was an inaccurate prose rendering by Ferguson … and the details are all wrong … Mangan's poem must be judged on its own merits.' Three years later, Daniel Corkery in *Hidden Ireland* (1924) launched a paean to O'Rathaille's masterpiece 'Gile na Gile', which depends for its rhetorical effect on rubbishing Mangan. The passage builds to the bathos of the last line:

> 'Gile na Gile' resembles some perfect movement of a Mozart sonata, compact of brilliancy, spontaneity and poise. It is flawless, as secure in its magic when heard for the thousandth as for the first time. Mangan, translating it, makes a slow-paced, dull-voiced attempt to reproduce its rhythm and melody, but every single phrase of the original surpasses in music, ease and swiftness the corresponding phrase in the English. How

different is 'flashing dark-blue eye' from 'gorm-risc, rinn-uanie'! … Phrase after phrase has suffered a dull change, has become coarsened and inept. Yet, it is this translation that must serve.

Mhac an tSaoi introducing a reprint of Hardiman's *Minstrelsy* in 1970 writes that 'Róisín Dubh' 'lends itself far more to Ferguson's acute interpretation that it is the complaint of a clerical lover awaiting release from his vow of celibacy, than to the pious gloss which makes it the hermetic expression of a proscribed patriotism under which guise it has been immortalised by Mangan'.

In 1981 Seán Ó Tuama brought out a seminal anthology, *An Duanaire, 1600–1900 – Poems of the Dispossessed*, with translations by Thomas Kinsella. Mangan isn't mentioned in the introductory essay but I don't think I'm being paranoid in seeing a dig at him in the aside: 'There is a remarkable abundance of Gaelic verse in the nineteenth century; though it is of minor artistic interest it could be argued that it has more vitality on the whole, and more reference to life as lived, than the bulk of nineteenth century Irish verse written in English.'

There is some convergence in these attacks – particularly the dualistic framing that uses Mangan as a whipping boy to make others (O'Rathaille, Ferguson, Gaelic poets of the nineteenth century) look good – but they also diverge to the point of contradiction: Bergin says Mangan's version is inaccurate but has its own merits; Corkery says it is commonplace but still the only translation that can serve; Mhac an tSaoi says his poem is immortal but covered with a pious gloss (sounds like more Victoriana). This scattergun approach suggests a restless, impatient hostility rather than specific concerns.

The strongest accusation is the inaccuracy. No one would argue with Bergin's assessment that Mangan didn't know Irish and worked off inaccurate prose renderings and got details wrong.

The solution that Bergin offers is to judge Mangan's poetry on its own merits, severed from the Irish originals and this is what Mhac an tSaoi is calling for when she says 'Dark Rosaleen' is 'hermetic', i.e. sealed off from 'Róisín Dubh', and it is what Ó Tuama puts into action when he excises Mangan from *An Duanaire*. It may seem the logical solution, but I don't think it's right. I don't think it's possible to sever 'Dark Rosaleen' from 'Róisín Dubh', or 'O'Hussey's Ode' from Eochaidh Ó hEódhusa, or 'The Ruins of Teach Mologa' from Seán Ó Coilleáin's 'Machnamh an Duine Dhoilghíosaigh'. Mangan's versions take their power from the originals and are in dialogue with them and in that sense, they are, I think, translations. If you lose the dialogue, his versions lose power. I think the severing led to the silencing and that is why Kiberd doesn't include Mangan in his *Irish Classics*. As a fluent Irish-speaker, Kiberd was coming from a tradition where Mangan's right to translate the Irish originals had been disputed and then dismissed. Where Corkery was threatened enough by Mangan's versions to launch an attack, Kiberd affably ignores him. In one of his fleeting mentions, he refers to 'Yeats taking over from James Clarence Mangan as the national poet', which is hilariously contradictory: if he was the national poet, then why isn't he included in a book of *Irish Classics*? The title of 'national poet' gets to the crux of the problem: Mangan earned it because he translated Irish poetry during a national catastrophe so if you deny his right to translate, that removes the title. It is a retrospective cancelling, which seems patronising or insulting to all his contemporaries – Young Irelanders, antiquarians, Irish scholars, *The Nation* readers – who bestowed it on him.

I don't like gaslighting the past, and I don't agree that Bergin or Ó Tuama get to speak for the Irish language more than O'Donovan or O'Curry. To try and reinstate Mangan's right to translate from a language he didn't speak, I turned to Ezra Pound, who translated from multiple languages, some of which (French and Italian) he spoke, and many of which (classical Chinese, Greek) he really didn't, but this doesn't prevent him getting pride of place in every world anthology of translation I've ever read.

When I began reading translators and theorists on Pound's right to translate from languages he didn't understand, I had the sensation of moving to a more open, wittier, more imaginative and intellectual space than the hermetic, sticklingly accurate world of the gaeilgóirs. It was bracing to read from the Pound expert, Ira B. Nadel, that Pound 'conceived of translation as an invented turning of previous material' and that he had pronounced 'no need of keeping verbal literality for phrases which sing and run naturally in the original'; and from a Chinese scholar, Ming Xie, that 'the meaning (or essence) of a given work or culture exists for Pound only to the extent that it is accessible and retrievable through the "essential medium" of translation with reference to the needs and concerns of the present. Thus, translation is by necessity disruptive, distorting and transformative.' You could not find three more manganese adjectives and when I read in an erudite blog, going by the manganese name of Mere Pseud Blog Ed, that Pound was 'a quintessentially Benjaminian translator' who understood that the object of translation is to reveal 'the central reciprocal relationship between languages', I recognised this as a great coup for Mangan against the gaeilgóirs. There are certain writers so stylish and intimidating, that they always have the last word and can close an argument. Joyce has this quality and Kafka and Beckett and Barthes (and vanishingly few women, alas, because the culture doesn't give women that power of intellection intimidation) and Walter Benjamin, the high priest of modernist aesthetics, certainly has it, and if he says that 'no translation would be possible if in its ultimate essence [the translation] strove for likeness to the original', and if he can be deployed in defence of Pound translating from languages he didn't know, then the fact that Mangan didn't know

Irish isn't disqualifying and anyone making that argument reveals themselves as gauche and unhip and is doing the Irish language no favours by isolating it from modernist translation theory.

Certainly, I was getting a whiff of isolationism and exclusivity from the Irish scholars I was reading. When Corkery rubbishes Mangan's version but then concludes bathetically that 'it is this translation that must serve', his aim is to attack the English language as intrinsically inferior to Irish, and he deploys the most famous and lyrical translation he can find to make the point that 'this is as good as it gets in English, and it's not good enough, because Irish is incomparable, unique, untranslatable'. I love *Hidden Ireland*, but this is the tedious language of Irish exceptionalism, the language that Joyce heard when he attended Irish lessons in UCD under Patrick Pearse and left because Pearse couldn't lay off disparaging English (apparently the ridiculing of the English word 'thunder' was the limit) and it is the language you still hear intermittently. I recall being at a party where an English girl was poring over a book in Irish trying to figure it out. When she pointed to a word and asked was it a verb, an Irish speaker snapped that she hadn't a hope of understanding, it being like no language she had ever encountered. Admittedly, the girl projected an air of nerdy complacency and her confidence that Irish was within her remit was probably insufferable, but the recourse to uniqueness made me eyeroll. Irish is an Indo-European language, if a peripheral one, and less remote from English than Hungarian, Finnish, Arabic or Mandarin; someone with a grasp of linguistics probably could have a go at figuring out the verbs from the nouns. And in every language, poetry is harder to translate than prose, but I don't see why this should be more true of Irish than of other languages.

Positioning Irish as uniquely untranslatable and like no other language makes it resistant to the Poundian/Benjaminian mission to reveal the 'central reciprocal relationship between languages'. If no 'equivalent' images or rhythms can be found to mediate between English and Irish, then the translator is pushed back to accuracy as the only determinant, and if this stickling accuracy makes a jarring impression in English, so much the better since it underscores the unbridgeable gap between the two languages and the impossibility of reciprocity.

I find this approach a bit defensive, a closing-in rather than an opening-out of Irish, but perhaps it is inevitable with a language so destroyed and besieged; maybe it isn't possible to be witty, generous and imaginative when the language is disappearing like water through a sieve. Still, it is strange to see someone as politically and linguistically radical as Mangan and as indelibly Liberties, being turned into the emblem of everything un-Irish: e.g. Victorian, pious, proscribed in his patriotism, lacking vitality and 'reference to life as it is lived' (why should life in the Liberties be less lived than in the Gaeltacht)? And I'm suspicious that the same tradition that attacks Mangan treats Charlotte Brooke's translations from 1786 with such tender (if patronising) respect. Yes, it's moving that a woman, a Protestant and a unionist was the first to try and mediate between the languages, but her translations are inaccurate and bad poetry. It feels like she is being lauded because her versions are no threat, whereas Mangan is being penalised for turning Irish masterpieces into outstanding English romantic verse.

Reading Benjamin's essay for myself, I found a few gratifyingly Manganese images – 'While content and language form a certain unity in the original, like a fruit and its skin, the language of the translation envelops its content like a royal robe with ample folds' – which suggest that Benjamin would have been very taken by Mangan's draper's approach to translation. And I found one passage which transformed, or rather revealed, my whole relationship to Mangan's Irish translations:

A translation issues from the original – not so much from its life as from its afterlife … Since the important works of world literature never find their chosen translators at the time of their origin, their translation marks their stage of continuous life … No translation would be possible if in its ultimate essence it strove for likeness to the original. For in its afterlife – which could not be called that if it were not a transformation and a renewal of something living – the original undergoes a change. Even words with fixed meaning can undergo a maturing process. The obvious tendency of a writer's literary style may in time wither away, only to give rise to immanent tendencies in the literary creation. What sounded fresh once may sound hackneyed later; what was once current may someday sound quaint.

When I read this, I felt a vast relief. A stress that I hadn't known was weighing on me was lifted. I could come clean about something I had been hiding even from myself. Benjamin is saying that the afterlife of important texts – their continuation long after their author's death – is dynamic. They change! Even when their author knew exactly what they wanted to convey at the time of writing, the text changes and matures according to when it is read and by whom. The language which was amazingly fresh and current when it originated inevitably becomes hackneyed and quaint over the years. This is why Pound insisted 'that the literature of a country should be translated afresh at least once every fifty years since the significance of language changes so rapidly'. The interpreter's job – whether that is a translator translating to another language or an actor or singer performing the text – is to find their way through the datedness of the style to the 'immanent', i.e. inherent, meaning and purpose of the text (what Ming Xie called its 'platonic essence'). The original author used the style of the times to convey something particular, but the interpreter should feel free to say that same thing in new and fresh ways. To suggest that a translator has to slavishly adopt every detail, image and stress of the original is like insisting that Shakespeare can only ever be performed in Tudor costume, without cuts, and that actors and directors have to be deep experts in Elizabethan language and drama and can't rely on dramaturges.

My relief in reading Benjamin's passage allowed me to admit the shameful thing: that I personally struggled to access Mangan's great achievement precisely because of this issue of its now dated language. I knew that what he did was astonishing because his contemporaries said so, including Irish scholars, and so did the next generations, including Yeats and Joyce, and I wasn't going to lecture the nineteenth and early twentieth centuries that they were mistaken and that Mangan's versions weren't marvellous, open-ended interpretations from the Gaelic but rather inaccurate, hermetic, pious Victoriana. I was signed up to Mangan's Famine miracle. But, in truth, I wasn't feeling it. I always loved 'Siberia' and the ambient phrases in 'Dark Rosaleen' – 'I dash'd across unseen', 'I could scale the blue air', 'wasted for you, love' – but I found its refrain, tempo and some of its diction, old-fashioned and frankly off-putting, and more so, in truth, than other Mangan poems; perhaps because fame has deadened their freshness and because the most famous interpreter of 'Dark Rosaleen', John McCormack, sings in what we now consider an old-fashioned way. This inability to get past certain words and phrasing reminds me of my teenage nephews' inability to see past the (for them) impossibly antiquated veneer of black and white to appreciate old films. I could not get past the ageing patina of 'Dark Rosaleen' to its beating heart pumping what Benjamin calls 'continuous life' until I heard Shane MacGowan recite the last verse one night in Chez Max on Baggot Street.

Years after meeting him in McGruders, I had chased Shane down to get more of his take on Mangan and arranged a meeting. He turned up with an entourage, as rock stars do – Dublin liggers I knew from out and about (very tame) and Tipperary men I never saw before or since (very wild). The interview, if that is what it was, went terribly because Shane cannot stand being asked direct questions. I had not at this point worked out Mangan's extreme evasiveness, or I might have recognised Shane's skittishness as manganese. When he howled, in genuine pain, 'Stop interrogating me!' I felt awful and disembodied, as if the me who had gone with the flow in McGruders had been superseded by an uptight nerdy questioner delving impertinently into Shane's mind. Years later, watching Julien Temple's documentary *Crock of Gold*, I felt a little better when I saw that it wasn't just me. Shane has a look of extreme discomfort and wariness as Gerry Adams talks at him and I noticed that Julien avoids doing direct interviews with Shane but keeps to the people around him, which reminded me of my own circling round Mangan through comparisons to Kafka, Macbeth, Cornell, etc.

I left this session with Shane disappointed in myself but bearing away something unforgettable. At the point when our interaction threatened to fail entirely, Shane retreated into himself to recite very quietly the last verse of 'My Dark Rosaleen'. With an instinct that is pure punk, he managed what no one else (that I have heard) has done: to wrest the poem from its lilt and flow. He broke up the metre, removed the stress from its natural placing and disrupted the rhythm. When he gave his signature snarling intonation in his hybrid accent to the line 'Ere YOU shall fade, ere YOU shall die' (nobody else stresses the 'you'), he pulled the poem from nineteenth-century elegy to twentieth-century punk, and the tonal connection, dormant on the page, between 'ere you shall fade' and 'If I should Fall (from grace with God)' fused into life.

*

Armed with Benjamin's argument and Shane's intonation I went back to the two poems rated as Mangan's masterpieces of Irish translation: 'O'Hussey's Ode to the Maguire' and 'Dark Rosaleen', to see if they could be defended as Benjaminian/Poundian translations and if I could get them to speak to me like they spoke to people in 1846.

'O'Hussey's Ode to the Maguire' tells of the hardship suffered by the chieftain Hugh Maguire on campaign with Hugh O'Neill during the severe winter of 1600, which ended in Maguire's death and O'Neill's defeat in the Battle of Kinsale. It was written in the decades after the campaign by Eochaidh Ó hEódhusa [O'Hussey]; for his version, Mangan drew on Ferguson's 1834 translation in the *Dublin University Magazine*.

In the poem, Hugh Maguire wanders in a wilderness of snow, sleet and deluge. Ice that freezes all movement, locks, glazes, paralyses and petrifies him: by the end he's an ice-statue, his fingers gloved by 'white ice-gauntlets' and the freezing, deluging weather has become a metaphor for what's happening to the old Gaelic order. The poem's charge comes from its play of contrasts: an undercurrent of fire begins in the second stanza with the 'red, livid light' of a meteor, and fiery metaphors bubble under the frozen glaze of the poem, bringing the movement of fire (which warms, lights and melts) through to the final line when Hugh sets ablaze the 'limewhite mansions' of his enemies. I have read it in three versions, Ferguson's, Mangan's and Osborn Bergin's, and in all three it is a very bitter poem, as in bitterly cold and bitterly vengeful, and highly successful in its aim: you can't help feeling a surge of gloating savagery when you arrive at the last lines, even as you deplore the arson.

Mangan had proved himself master of cold with 'Siberia' and he clearly relished the challenge of icing over this already frozen poem. In phrase after phrase, he sharpens the tooth of winter: 'the rigor of its showery drops' becomes 'its showery, arrowy, speary sleet'; the 'weather winds of the aerial expanse' achieves acid sibilance as 'the smiting sleetshower', and with a small modification he tightens 'icicle-hung tree' to stalactites as 'icicle-hung thicket'. Not even the fussiest translator could object to Mangan trying to make the English as cold as the Irish. But he makes two striking innovations, which Osborn Bergin does object to: in Ferguson, as in the Irish original, Hugh Maguire is always a warrior among his men, traversing known terrain, but in Mangan, he is 'lorn and lost', 'wandering, houseless, desolate / Alone, without guide or chart'. In Ferguson's final stanza, Hugh marches 'with his host to battle' but in Mangan he 'wanders frozen, rain-drenched, sad, betrayed'.

The other innovation is the insertion of memory and dreaming. In the original and in Ferguson's and Bergin's translations, the poem is taking place in real time but in Mangan the poem is a memory within memory: the narrator, O'Hussey, is remembering the lonely plight of Hugh Maguire, who, in turn, is remembering his warriors charging and the glow of arson (all three versions end with mansions in flames but only in Mangan is it a memory). And Mangan's version is a dream within a dream: O'Hussey is dreaming of Hugh ('Medreams I see just now his face') who is given the romantic hero's sense of wandering into a nightmare ('Darkly, as in a dream, he strays').

Bergin is unimpressed that 'the great captain who is ravaging Desmond is turned into a poor wanderer, lonely, persecuted and betrayed, cheered only by memories, and warmed on by "the lightning of the soul"'. It's true that by stripping Hugh of warriors, military camps and charts, Mangan turns him into the quintessential lost and lonely (peripathetic) manganese protagonist, which is a solipsistic customising of the poem to his own preoccupations, but I believe that Benjamin's argument of 'equivalence' can be made here because, first, the success of all poems, including translations, depends on the poet's personal connection to their material, and second, Mangan turns Hugh into a quintessential Famine figure. The connection is being made between the 'houseless, desolate' chieftain and 'the naked, the unclothed and the unfed poor of Ireland' evoked daily in the news bulletins, 'driven out in hunger and wretchedness, without shelter on the cold road'.

The innovation of memory-dreaming is Mangan at his most paradoxically scrupulous as a translator – reminding the reader that these events didn't happen to him personally but are his version of another poet's translation of a past poet's account of another man's experience – and at his most subtly sophisticated as an interpreter of the Irish literary canon. What Benjamin would call the 'continuous life' of Ó hEódhusa's poem lies not just in its wonderful images and phrasing, but in its status as a memorial of hardship and revenge at a terrible moment in Irish history. By dredging 1601 up in 1846, another terrible year, Mangan is ahead of the 1916 signatories in channelling those 'dead generations from which [Ireland] receives her old tradition of nationhood'. Hugh is not left entirely alone and shivering on the blasted heath; he is warmed by memories of fighting with his warriors and destroying his enemies. In a prefiguring of Freud, Mangan's doubling of memory and dreaming serves to deeply connect the two states: a dream is a wish fulfilment and Hugh's memory of arson stirs the reader's darkest desires. The hot glow, which warms Hugh in his present desolation, is passed down to the reader to keep the flame of rebellion alight. Hugh's memory becomes the national memory and the warmth in his heart becomes the flame for future action. That last line 'But the memory of the limewhite mansions his right hand hath laid / in ashes warms the hero's heart!' looks forward to the Young Ireland Rebellion that would erupt eighteen months later and seems to tremble at the threshold of the War of Independence, when Mangan might have wondered, like Yeats, if that poem of his sent out certain men to conflagrate the Big Houses.

*

The inverse to the icy, bitter laments of the dispossessed are the aislings, the name given to the vision poems 'in which the poet encounters a vision-woman who foretells a Stuart redeemer'. Where the laments are consciously historical and commemorative, recording specific names, places and dates, the aislings bear the same relationship to history as dreams do to waking life. Suffused with momentary light, warmth and splendour, they are the wish fulfilments of a people on its knees. The vision-woman is like the Greek *elpis* or the Romantics' blue flower: the hope that emerges out of, and is inescapable from, darkness.

Mangan translated aislings as well as laments, but in general, he had less success with them. In a typical aisling, a solitary wanderer is overtaken by a vision of a beautiful woman who shows him an ideal of how things once were/should be, before he awakes to the lonely, dreary present. The scenario was familiar to Mangan from Romantic poetry, which should have helped him translate aislings, but in the Irish, the vision-woman always arrives in a glorious burst of light, a transcendent radiant glow, which Mangan can't handle because for him, hope comes as a whisper and a gleam, not in glorious array; it sneaks in, bounded by shadows and hung with protections, refracted and reflected, shimmering at the edge, ungraspable. His flickering images of hope – starlight reflected on water – are another world from the opening resplendence of 'Gile na Gile' ('Brightness of Brightness'). It's not surprising to find Mangan shrinking from the light. What is amazing is that his most famous poem is a radiant allegory of hope.

Why did he decide to translate 'Róisín Dubh'? It came with baggage. The poem is included in Hardiman's *Minstrelsy* with a poor translation by Thomas Furlong. In his introduction, Hardiman explains that: '*Roisin Dubh*, Little Black Rose, is an allegorical ballad, in which strong political feelings are conveyed, as a personal address from a lover to his fair one … By Roisin Dubh, supposed to be a beloved female, is meant Ireland.'

Of all Hardiman's explanations in the *Minstrelsy*, this was the one that got Ferguson going. In his *Dublin University Magazine* review, he fulminates:

> This, says Mr Hardiman, is an allegorical political ballad – it seems to us to be the song of a priest in love, of a priest in love too, who has broken his vow … And why, in the name of holy nature, should the priest not be in love? … and why in the name of divine reason, do the Roman Catholic priesthood of the present day, submit to a prohibition so unnatural, monstrous, antiscriptural and innovatory?

The poem sits on the fault line between Hardiman and Ferguson and their tormenting questions – was Gaelic culture primarily folk or professional bardic? Catholic or pluralist? Is this poem Jacobite allegory or bawdy love-song? Ferguson doesn't have many takers for the lover being a priest (apart from Mhac an tSaoi) – even his biographer thinks this 'a pleasant figment of [Ferguson's] enthusiasm' (I'm not sure 'pleasant' is the right adjective) – but, that detail aside, the answer from later scholars is soothingly balanced: 'Róisín Dubh' is a political allegory grafted onto an older love-lyric, which means that they are both right.

Ferguson's and Furlong's versions read very differently. Ferguson keeps to his 'strict severity of literal translation' with long unrhymed lines and concrete images, while Furlong uses regular, rhyming iambic tetrameter and archetypal, abstract images. Ferguson is arresting and vernacular: 'O Rosebud, let there not be sorrow on you on account of what happened you' where Furlong is vague and twee: 'Oh! My sweet little rose, cease to pine for the past,

/ For the friends that come eastward will see thee at last'. Ferguson is earthy and bawdy: 'And I would make delights behind the fort with my Roiseen dubh' where Furlong is squeamish and vague in imagery: 'I would tell to all around me how my fondness grew'.

But since they come from the same source, there are significant similarities: both end each stanza on the refrain and both are action poems which begin with 'help coming over the sea' and end with nature in turmoil. In between the narrator toils, sails, pleads, ploughs, kisses, etc., and this sense of movement is carried through to the passage of time, with both poems moving from remembrance of the past to the future conditional, and both deploying multiple contrasts of the elements (earth, water, fire), colour (red waves, black rose, white breasts), and the juxtaposition of body and soul (Ferguson has mouth, breast, heart, soul, gospel and Furlong has heart, tongue, blessings).

Mangan helped himself to both versions – reverting to Hardiman/Furlong's interpretation of the poem as political allegory but using Ferguson's images – but what he achieves isn't synthesis but alchemy. He opens the poem out to its fullest expression by an astonishing amplification of the refrain, movement, elements, time, colour and physiology. Here is the poem (try and imagine Shane's hybrid Tipp/Cockney accent dislocating the rhythm):

> O, my Dark Rosaleen,
> Do not sigh, do not weep!
> The priests are on the ocean green,
> They march along the deep.
> There's wine … from the royal Pope,
> Upon the ocean green;
> And Spanish ale shall give you hope,
> My Dark Rosaleen!
> My own Rosaleen!

Shall glad your heart, shall give you hope,
Shall give you health, and help, and hope,
My Dark Rosaleen!

Over hills, and through dales,
Have I roamed for your sake;
All yesterday I sailed with sails
On river and on lake.
The Erne … at its highest flood,
I dashed across unseen,
For there was lightning in my blood,
My Dark Rosaleen!
My own Rosaleen!
Oh! there was lightning in my blood,
Red lighten'd through my blood.
My Dark Rosaleen!

All day long, in unrest,
To and fro, do I move.
The very soul within my breast
Is wasted for you, love!
The heart … in my bosom faints
To think of you, my Queen,
My life of life, my saint of saints,
My Dark Rosaleen!
My own Rosaleen!
To hear your sweet and sad complaints,
My life, my love, my saint of saints,
My Dark Rosaleen!

Woe and pain, pain and woe,
Are my lot, night and noon,

To see your bright face clouded so,
Like to the mournful moon.
But yet … will I rear your throne
Again in golden sheen;
'Tis you shall reign, shall reign alone,
My Dark Rosaleen!
My own Rosaleen!
'Tis you shall have the golden throne,
'Tis you shall reign, and reign alone,
My Dark Rosaleen!

Over dews, over sands,
Will I fly, for your weal;
Your holy delicate white hands
Shall girdle me with steel.
At home … in your emerald bowers,
From morning's dawn till e'en,
You'll pray for me, my flower of flowers,
My Dark Rosaleen!
My fond Rosaleen!
You'll think of me through Daylight's hours,
My virgin flower, my flower of flowers,
My Dark Rosaleen!

I could scale the blue air,
I could plough the high hills,
Oh, I could kneel all night in prayer,
To heal your many ills!
And one … beamy smile from you
Would float like light between
My toils and me, my own, my true,
My Dark Rosaleen!

My fond Rosaleen!
Would give me life and soul anew,
A second life, a soul anew,
My Dark Rosaleen!

O! the Erne shall run red,
With redundance of blood,
The earth shall rock beneath our tread,
And flames wrap hill and wood,
And gun-peal, and slogan cry,
Wake many a glen serene,
Ere you shall fade, ere you shall die,
My Dark Rosaleen!
My own Rosaleen!
The Judgment Hour must first be nigh,
Ere you can fade, ere you can die,
My Dark Rosaleen!

The gestures and hints of the previous versions are given their
full flowering. The suggestion of a refrain becomes the chorus
which turns the poem into a ballad; the elements of earth, fire
and water are completed by the fourth element and time is given
its full arc with the stanzas spinning from 'morning's dawn' till
evening and from 'yesterday' till 'Judgement Hour'; a rainbow arcs
the poem with each stanza allocated a colour; the body is lovingly
itemised, making Mangan's version more corporeal, if less carnal,
than Ferguson's; and the soul is sent into orbit, girdling, praying,
floating like light. The tempo is accelerated from the start – in
Ferguson and Furlong and the Irish original, help is 'coming' but
in Mangan, it 'marches', and the narrator isn't a clinging, pleading,
pining, walking suitor but an aerial, mercurial being who roams
and sails with 'lightning running through his blood' and draws

on magic powers of flight and invisibility – he 'dashes unseen' and 'scales the air' – and at the end the images are explicitly hellish: the earth rocks, the flames wrap, the gun peals, the glens awake, Judgment Hour is nigh.

Without greatly lengthening it, Mangan unfurls the poem to encompass the whole cosmos, the trinity of hell, earth and heaven, with the beloved at its centre. In Furlong's version, Róisín is vague and abstracted, and in Ferguson's, she is carnal and earthy, a girl to kiss and fondle behind the fort; in Mangan, she is the saint of saints, on a golden throne, holy, delicate, the virgin flower, with the narrator's astonishing aerial feats on her behalf gesturing to her assumption into heaven: she is Mary, Queen of Heaven. In a facer to Ferguson and his priest in love, Mangan makes his Dark Rosaleen the Black Madonna or Vierge Noire. More than a 'national apotheosis', the poem is a national Assumption.

In both Furlong and Ferguson, there is disconnect: we don't know why Róisín is troubled at the start and why catastrophe is pending at the end. In Furlong, the calamity in the final stanza seems to come out of nowhere; Ferguson heralds it better with his friars moving purposefully on the ocean, but the portents that open and close the poem don't sit with the seducing and berating of Róisín. We get why the narrator wants to go behind the fort with this excitingly tempestuous girl, but we don't get why the Erne is turning red.

The same disconnect is embedded in the Irish original, presumably because the poem is two poems: Jacobite allegory and folk song. The juxtaposition of national politics and private seduction gives the poem its urgency and intimacy, but Mangan firmly discards the ambiguity. He was too inhibited to handle Ferguson's 'delights behind the fort' but the main reason for blanking the carnality is because he knows that a fleshy, mortal girl hasn't the scope or scale for what he has in mind. What draws him to the poem is its danger and salvation, its motifs of time, colour, movement and the elements. Removing the earthy folksiness enables him to ramp up and round out these motifs and raise the stakes to create a cosmos lofty enough to contain both the hellish threat and the heavenly succour.

'Róisín Dubh' isn't an aisling in the Irish original but Mangan makes his version a kind of radiant aisling. This is the one poem across the whole span of his work where hope arrives resplendent, beaming golden light, in daylight hours, festooned with flowers, and sending the action airborne. And uniquely in the literature of aislings, the vision doesn't fade to a dreary present but instead provokes a great war, calls down Judgement Day, and in the last image, is unfading and undying.

This is the poem that appeared in *The Nation* on 30 May 1846, as the potato crop failed for the third or fourth time that year, and to get a sense of its impact, we have to imagine not only the readers' desperate fears and forebodings about what is happening to the country, but also their knowledge and expectations of Mangan. For fifteen years they have been reading him. They know his melancholy and timidities, his concealments and pathologies. They know they can count on him to make black jokes and articulate their rage and document their pain and, if they are perceptive, they have picked up on the glimmers of hope released in fugitive phrases. But nothing has prepared them for this: in the midst of horror, to find themselves sailing through dazzling golden light. Intrinsic to the poem's amazing grace is that it came from a wretch like Mangan.

The only modern comparison I can think of is to Philip Larkin's readers coming to the end of his 1964 collection, *The Whitsun Weddings*: for a decade, they have been reading in wry admiration his sharply cynical take on human relations – 'When I see a couple of kids / And guess he's fucking her and she's / Taking pills or wearing a diaphragm / I know this is paradise' – to be suddenly brought up short by the last line in the last poem in the book: 'What will survive of us is love.' The fame of this line comes from our sense of Larkin breaking through his own misanthropy and cynicism. In a poet who had made a profession of love like Yeats or Neruda, the sentiment might seem banal or routine, but Larkin arrives at it through struggle and disbelief.

Just as it took a misanthrope to tell us the truth about love, it took a furtive, paranoid and over-protective pessimist to shine out radiant hope. Larkin and Mangan's most famous lines are the exceptions that prove their rules.

*

If, as Benjamin says, the 'task of the translator' is to find 'equivalence' and 'reciprocity' between languages and to perpetuate the 'continuous life' of the original by 'transforming' and 'renewing' it, then Mangan, like Pound, is a quintessential Benjaminian translator and when Ó Tuama fails to mention him in an anthology of laments and aislings, he is not only denying Mangan's versions, he is denying these poems the 'continuous life' that Mangan gave them during the Famine. By contrast, when Shane wrenched 'ere you can fade / ere you can die' into 'If I should fall (from Grace with God)', he was saving Mangan, and through Mangan, 'Róisín Dubh' from fading and dying out. Where most Irish poets have preferred to riff on the heroic myths and legends of pre-conquest Ireland, Mangan sought the entropy and dissolution of plantation. The Famine was the greatest disaster to ever hit Ireland in terms of death and emigration, but it was also just more of the same – the apex of the food shortages, epidemics, evictions, internal migration and emigration that had been ongoing since the plantations. It was Mangan's genius to realise that the past could describe the present. He understood the power of these poems that were transmitted orally for generations so that they hung like shadows in people's minds.

In the quarrel that has been going on for two hundred years and longer over what constitutes Irish identity, and does Irish by necessity mean un-English, and should translation be accurate or reciprocal, Joyce came down on Mangan's side. Already, as an undergraduate, he grasped that the exceptionalism and isolationism he was being taught by Pearse was narrow, exclusivist, reductionist. He gave that world view to the Citizen in *Ulysses* – one-eyed like James Hardiman, whose *Minstrelsy* insisted that Irish meant Catholic, Jacobite, Gaelic-speaking – and he gave to Molly Bloom motifs from Mangan's great poem, the rose and the flower of flowers and waves turning red and flames and the arc of the rainbow, but mixed in – because mixing is the point; why should one exclude the other? – with Ferguson's earthier version:

> and O that awful deepdown torrent O and the sea the sea crimson sometimes like fire and the glorious sunsets and the figtrees in the Alameda gardens yes and all the queer little streets and pink and blue and yellow houses and the rosegardens and the jessamine and geraniums and cactuses and Gibraltar as a girl where I was a Flower of the mountain yes when I put the rose in my hair like the Andalusian girls used or shall I wear a red yes and how he kissed me under the Moorish wall

Of all the things I should like to tell Frank, this comes high. Other people might think these old poems and arguments don't matter, that what's past is past, let the dead bury the dead, whatever that means, but for Frank – who loved his quarrels ('I wish him ill') as much as he loved his food and his friends, and for whom there is no past as in done and dusted, but only a dialogue of continuous unflagging energy between the then and now, who had a poster of Haughey on the inside door of his bedroom cupboard to my amazement till he explained that the slogan 'Down to the Last Man

Standing' was Parnellite, and who remarked gnomically that the French project (by which he meant the French nation) would have failed but for Proust – for Frank, these cultural arguments could hardly be more consequential, and nations stand and fall, or at least progress and decline, on the question of whether a translation should be allowed the licence to roam.

I hear you talking in my head

I was glad when I was able to settle, or so I believed, the question which had preoccupied me, of what kind of book I was writing. It was, I decided, a detective or true-crime book (missing-person rather than murder). There was nothing original in this positioning: biographers are always casting themselves as investigators patiently assembling evidence from interviews, archives, press cuttings, site visits, ever mindful that the record is partial, biased, falsified. Typically, the detective-biographer signals this intention through the title, e.g. Fiona Sampson *In Search of Mary Shelley*, James Pope Hennessey *The Quest for Queen Mary*, Richard Holmes *Shelley: The Pursuit*. When I felt exhausted and disbelieving over how long it was all taking me, I would cast myself as one of those dogged detectives who give up years of their lives to crack the case. This was a self-serving analogy, and an alarming one because there is always a moment in these scenarios when the viewer realises that the price is too high – the moment the detective defers getting married or loses her badge because she is over-identifying with the case – and it was false to put myself in this mould because I don't have that kind of steely dedication. When I was defending Mangan from his past biographers or attacks from Irish-speakers I liked to see myself as an avenging crusader but in my less self-glorifying moments I had an uneasy sense that neither defensive valour nor thirst for discovery explained why I was giving quite so much to this quixotic project which, after all, no one was demanding of me, Mangan being wholly obscure and also a poet, which is to say a turn-off. (Tell a dream, lose a reader … Quote a poem, lose ten readers … I was doing both.)

The point I continually found myself circling back to is the moment on his deathbed when he fixes his enormous eyes on his confessor and threatens to become a ghost. This is the vanishing point of the whole tale: 'the point at which receding parallel lines viewed in perspective appear to converge' – the parallel lines in this case being his lives and afterlives. From the deathbed prophesy you move forward to the hauntings recorded by later writers and backwards to his 'walking corpse' syndrome, the delusion that he was a ghost.

He doesn't overplay this delusion. The first time I spot him at it is when he is nineteen years old, sitting in a graveyard 'musing deeply, unseen and alone / On the trophies of death spread around us'. The spooky words here are 'unseen' and 'trophies' for tombstones: this is not your average Romantic/emo youth. My favourite of all his lines 'I have wearied with my plaints, the unending wastes of air' sounds like a banshee lamenting and the uncanny line 'So meagre am I, no lath is like me / Death for my shadowy stillness cannot see me' could be a description of the hungry ghosts in Tibetan Buddhism who are described as having necks as thin as needles. Such ghosts are said to arise from people whose deaths have been violent or unhappy, or who have been neglected in death by their relatives and so return to the world of the living, hungry to take what they can, in compensation for the insufficient prayers and offerings of their relatives. Denis Plunkett, whose father put up the tombstone, would have indignantly denied that Mangan was neglected by his relatives, but the addiction specialist Gabor Maté uses the hungry ghost as a metaphor for the insatiable cravings of the addict, and Mangan's line seems to channel this brilliant image, with its suggestion that the reason why these ghosts are hanging round earth instead of being packed off to heaven, hell or purgatory like other dead souls, is because they are so wasted that Death looks through them, the way we look through junkies begging on the street.

Then there is the strange moment in the impersonal memoir when he is left almost blind following a drenching, 'in the twilight alone could he attempt to open his eyes'. This turns him into a bat which, then as now, had supernatural and sinister connotations because of their liminal, hybrid nature as winged mammals that come out at twilight – in Homer, Ovid, Dante and Shakespeare, bats signify the souls of the dead, metamorphosis, the Devil, witchcraft. In 1810 the French zoologist Geoffroy Saint-Hilaire had given the name 'vampire bat' to a species of bloodsucking bat from South America and it is this species of bat which flits through Mangan's first short story, 'An Extraordinary Adventure in the Shades', when the increasingly unhinged narrator foresees 'the destiny whereunto I was reserved':

I saw the black marble dome, the interminable suites of chambers, the wizard scrolls, the shaft and quiver, and in dim but dreadful perspective, the bloody cage, in which incarcerated under the figure of a bat I should be doomed to flap my leathern wings dolefully through the sunless day.

This bat must be vampiric because why else is the cage bloody? In none of the vampire tales available to Mangan – Ossenfelder's 'Der Vampyr' (1748), Byron's 'The Giaour' (1813), Poldari's 'The Vampyre' (1819) – do vampires take the form of bats. Bram Stoker is usually credited with conflating the myth with the bloodsucking mammal named by Saint-Hilaire, to create his shape-changing vampires who flit between bat and human forms, but this passage reads like a description of Dracula's castle and was perhaps an influence on Stoker.

With these elliptical metamorphoses into bats and ghosts, Mangan seems to be hovering, like the bat at twilight, in liminal spaces, neither alive nor dead, but undead, to use the very manganese phrase for vampires, and he must have carried this atmosphere beyond his work to his person because acquaintances were always recalling him in ghostly terms: 'moving with noiseless step'; 'the man without a shadow … like an anatomy new risen from the dead'; 'gliding, even as a shadow on the wall'; 'an unearthly and ghostly creature'. These descriptions, recorded in the decade after his death, slip imperceptibly into accounts of hauntings which could be gathered into an anthology as testimony to Mangan's strange lurking presence in Irish literature.

The anthology could start with Mitchel and John Savage in the 1850s since their 'memories' have the quality of sightings. and continue up until David Wheatley's sonnet sequence 'Misery Hill' (2000), which recounts the poet's Dantesque descent into hell through modern Dublin, accompanied by a guide called Nemo, who introduces him to Mangan's ghost who asks to be called 'The Nameless One' … Between Mitchel's 'ghostly and unearthly creature' in the nineteenth century and Wheatley's 'skinny wreck' in the twenty-first, the anthology would include all the hauntings, including Yeats who places Mangan among 'the elemental things that go / about my table to and fro', and David Lloyd who described his sense of being 'summoned' as Mangan's 'long bony arm reached up from the grave to grasp me', and Brian Moore who put his haunting into a novel, *The Mangan Inheritance* (1979) and – to prove that it isn't only writers that Mangan haunts – it might also include the story recounted to me by a friend:

In the 1960s, my dad lived in a spooky tenement on Charles Street, just off Mountjoy Square. One night as he was rushing home over Summerhill, he saw a strange man in a long black cloak and tall hat walking/floating towards him with eyes red like burning coals. My father lashed home as fast as he could … and yes … the same man was standing opposite his house, on the other side of the street, staring over with eyes of fire. My dad almost kicked the hall door in. His mother went out with a bottle of holy water and doused the door and steps, and made the whole family get up and kneel to say the rosary. They called him 'the man in the cloak'.

(I note that Petrie's house, where Mangan worked for three years, was 21 Charles Street.)

Shane MacGowan's haunting would be there, of course: he was on holiday in Thailand, on an epic binge, when a strange, cloaked figure appeared, whom he couldn't identify till he got back to Ireland, and then he wrote a song 'The Snake with Eyes of Garnet':

> Last night as I lay dreaming
> My way across the sea
> James Mangan brought me comfort
> With Laudanum and Poitín

The snake recalls Mangan's depiction of his father as a boa constrictor, but since Shane never answers direct questions, I can't say if he'd read the memoir or if the snake appeared in his vision. I did manage to get out of him that when he was a boy in Tipperary his uncles would recite Mangan poems, so we could take his Thai vision as a buried memory, but that isn't the way Shane saw it. He took the ancient Greek rather than the Freudian view of dreams and visions – he thought they are how the dead talk to the living; for years after his Thai vision, he continued to contact Mangan on an Ouija board.

I would include in the anthology the lyrics of two earlier Pogues songs: 'The Sick Bed of Cuchulainn' because I think Mangan, dreaming of foreign lands, is among the ghosts/devils crowding the sick bed:

> McCormack and Richard Tauber are singing by the bed
> There's a glass of punch below your feet and an angel at your head
> There's devils on each side of you with bottles in their hands
> You need one more drop of poison and you'll dream of foreign lands.

And 'Rainy Night in Soho' for these lines which need no explanation:

> Sometimes I wake up in the morning
> The ginger lady by my bed
> Covered in a cloak of silence
> I hear you talking in my head

But the most amazing of all the hauntings is Joyce's and if it were the only one, you would still claim for Mangan his outsize role as the ghost of Irish literature. As an undergraduate, addressing the L&H, Joyce was already positioning Mangan as 'a feeble-bodied figure departing the earth' and, a quarter of a century later, he layers Manganalia into the ghostly echoing voices in the *Wake* – 'he had flickered up and flinnered down into a drug and drunkery addict, growing megalomane of a loose past.' And he fed Mangan into the most enigmatic figure in Irish and maybe in all twentieth-century literature: the man in the brown mackintosh who flits spectrally through *Ulysses*: he appears first by the graveside to turn the number of mourners into thirteen ('death's number') and he 'loves a lady who is dead' and he 'springs up through a trapdoor' in the phantasmagoria of 'Circe' to point 'an elongated finger' at Bloom and declare him an imposter. This mysterious figure is catnip to critic-detectives who have unmasked him as, variously, Christ, the Devil, Hermes, Theoclymenus in the *Odyssey*, the Wandering Jew, Lazarus, Parnell, the ghost of Leopold's father Rudolph … Nabokov thought it was Joyce himself; the Catalan novelist Enrique Vila-Matas thinks it is Beckett. Joyce leaves the identity open, but the Mangan motifs are unmistakeable: the 'Man in the Cloak', the brown coat, the imposter-ing, the lady who is dead (Mangan's student, Catherine, to whom he wrote affecting poems). That Joyce should feed Mangan into this flitting figure who draws together day and night, the living and the dead, the waking and the dreaming, the sober and the hallucinating, is an astonishing gesture to the significance he accords Mangan's continuing ghostly presence on Dublin streets and in its literature.

These amazing tales of haunting became my model of how Mangan might contact me. I guess I was expecting him to manifest in a cloak, or beside a grave, or to spring from a trapdoor, or float down the street, and the almost cartoonish Scooby-Doo nature of these apparitions prevented me from grasping what now seems obvious: I had been 'summoned' from the outset.

*

Mangan claimed to see ghosts 'in the normal half-waking state [when] the soul continues lingering about the Dream-sphere'. In the course of an essay on 'Madame Hauffe, the celebrated Wirtemberg ghost-seeress', he drops one of his lightning insights:

> the Seeress (who had herself the information from one of her grey visitants) [informs us] that ghosts make noises, not from any abstract love of noise, but simply for the purpose of *drawing attention upon themselves*, as, whenever they succeed in doing

so, their condition becomes 'more tolerable'. … If it be, as it is, the fact, that a certain class of suffering ghosts derive the greatest benefit from being *prayed for*, is it unreasonable to suppose that the same ghosts may experience a proportionate relief, however slight it may be in degree, from being *thought on*.

If I pounced on these lines like a mosquito scenting blood, it's because I was primed by my sense of the parasitical transactional Mangan who uses the texts of dead authors as 'hosts' to bring his own writing alive. It was a small leap from this to grasping that Mangan in this passage is positioning ghosts as parasites subsisting on human attention. Like all great insights, this is less his invention than the uncovering of something inherent: we talk about haunted people being 'possessed' much like fleas possess dogs or hookworm possess our intestines. Once he has pointed it out, you realise that intercessory prayer has much in common with manipulative parasitism, which is when one species uses another to gain its ends, not so different to the souls in purgatory invading the conscience of the living and manipulating them into prayer.

But, unlike hookworm and toxoplasma, the dead are not, in general, very successful parasites. Their generic methods of 'possession' – creaking, chain-rattling, pushing letters around a Ouija board – are so weak and pallid that they are easily ignored. After his father's death, Mangan complained to Father Meehan that 'the miserable old man will not let me sleep o' nights but comes to the side of my bed and enters into conversation'. He has turned his father's ghost into another parasite, a kind of mosquito preventing sleep, that he clearly wants to swat away.

Oblivion is the likely fate for most ghosts, but this is not the fate that Mangan expects for himself. He is quietly confident of doing much better than other ghosts, including his father's. He expects to be 'thought on' and is not reliant for this on friends and associates, but on future generations. He has a super-power: his deathless words.

If the dead in purgatory are ghosts seeking to be prayed on, then writers are vampires seeking to *prey on*. A vampire is an evolved ghost that has progressed from trying to rouse the attention of the living, to feeding directly off them, growing stronger with each bite. Words and narrative are the vampiric writer's fangs. The reader who opens a book, like the poor innocent opening a coffin lid, delivers herself to the beast. If the words are powerful enough, she is hooked and unable to escape the text. Compelled to read on till the end, she is left exhilarated, drained, altered, even destroyed by the experience: 'Dr Weiss, at forty, knew that her life had been ruined by literature' is how Anita Brookner opens her first novel, and I shivered when I read this, aged fifteen, like someone just walked over my grave ... but I kept on reading; it was too late for warnings.

A constant supply of readers, such as Shakespeare receives, is optimal but not essential since unread writers can lie dormant, for centuries if necessary, waiting for the next victim to lift the cover. In this way, the vampiric writer's deathless prose can keep going for ever, as long as there are readers to feed off. And once a writer finds one victim/reader, they generally find more since they are pathogenic: the infected reader passes on the contagion to new readers through book reviews or 'word of mouth'.

Not all writers make the successful transition to vampirism. Many, perhaps most, remain as hapless ghosts, their unread words not much more effective than table-turning. What marks out the successful? Mangan has that worked out as well. Three years after he positioned himself as a vampire bat in 'An Extraordinary Adventure', he wrote an essay on Goethe, which contains this startling passage:

Goethe probably wrote more for an undeveloped Future than for our own era. He wrote less with a view to the wants of the age he lived in than in the anticipation of an era when much that is now abstruse and clouded, as well in ethics and in metaphysics, shall become the subject of familiar inspection and analysis … Throughout his works we frequently stumble upon skeletons of thought whose gigantic and foreign aspect startles us, but which, we have no doubt, hands competent to the task will hereafter fill up with the flesh-and-blood essentials of its vitality.

In his own indirect way – he is using Goethe to talk about himself – Mangan is saying the same thing as Joyce in his famous boast: 'I've put in so many enigmas and puzzles that it will keep the professors busy for centuries arguing over what I meant.' Like Joyce, Mangan understands that the future is mainly interested in what the past passes up. A writer who wants to stay read needs to leave something 'abstruse', 'clouded' and 'foreign' for future readers to sharpen their wits on. Writers with the instinct and discipline to set enigmas and bury treasure create the conditions for their long-term survival, whereas writers who are slick, expedient and showy had better make money in their lifetimes because they aren't going to be revived.*

Mangan's prophesy is more striking than Joyce's boast because Joyce was witness to literary criticism and biography becoming a profession whereas Mangan had no such security and the idea of people being paid to spend years excavating and elucidating difficult texts would have seemed brilliantly bizarre in the early nineteenth century. Joyce's boast is also rather anaemic and academic – university professors arguing the toss – where Mangan's mise en scène is startlingly visceral. He depicts an actual resuscitation involving real blood and organ transfusions, with the

---

*This is obviously true – see, for instance, Joyce's *Dubliners*, published in 1914 to few reviews and fewer readers; the bestseller that year was *The Eyes of the World* by Harold Wright Bell, apparently 'the first novelist to make a million from his writing and the first to sell over a million copies of his novel' … No, me neither.

future critics/biographers cast as skilled surgeons whose 'competent hands' will bring the dead writer's skeletal works back to life. The issue of where the 'flesh-and-blood essentials' for the transfusion come from is not spelled out but the inference is unmistakeable: in this strange masochistic operation, they are the surgeons' own.

There is something charmingly complicit in Mangan's wink and nod across the centuries to us, his current readers and critics – I guess it's preferable to be recognised as a surgeon in the resuscitation process, even a weird masochistic vampiric operation, than to be a puppet dancing on Joyce's string. And for such an oblique and secretive person, he is being disarmingly frank about his open interest in posthumous survival. Writers today won't admit to giving this a thought. The Guardian runs a regular questionnaire in which they ask authors which book 'they most want to be remembered for'. Almost all react defensively, recoiling at the whole idea of being remembered – e.g. Jonathan Franzen 'I'd rather be alive than remembered'; Sally Rooney 'I don't think I care much about being remembered, really. I never think about it'; Nick Hornby 'I'd settle for any of [my books] staying in print for the rest of my life'; Richard Flanagan 'Writers start with dreams of greatness and end grateful for news of payment. Pondering any future beyond that for even a moment is the path to insanity.'

All this seems disingenuous. Unless you're getting very rich producing bestsellers, why do something as difficult and unlucrative as writing except in a brave bid for immortality? Why, if you love the words of the dead, would you not want to gift your words to the future? Why limit your readership to your contemporaries, when reading and writing is the main conduit between past and future, the living and the dead?

Because he was so obsessed with death and its threat of oblivion, Mangan grasped that the whole point of writing is transmission and to confine that transmission to your own lifespan is reductive. With this insight, he subverts the well-worn cliché which positions biographers and critics as parasites and scavengers on the writer's creativity. Writers are always finding dismissive and self-serving metaphors to convey this: 'A fly may sting a stately horse and make him wince, but one is but an insect and the other a horse still' (Samuel Johnson); 'Like the fleas who rush to jump on white linen' (Flaubert); 'The dogs are eating your mother' (Ted Hughes on Sylvia Plath's biographers).

It is a measure of the lowly status of critics and biographers, and their lack of confidence and skill with metaphor, that they (*we!*) accept this so meekly, but our submerged sense that this is the wrong way round comes out in our phrasing – we talk about being 'possessed' or 'haunted' or 'drained' by our subject, the writer. This language reveals our latent sense of victimhood: in the quest for life-giving readers, the vampiric writer seeks in particular critics and biographers who will act as super-influencers, spreading the word until it goes viral. A new biography is a massive transfusion of blood to the writer, and the blood is the biographer's.

A few years before Mangan died, a contributor to the *Dublin University Magazine* wrote fancifully of being introduced to Mangan and 'held by his "glittering eye" like the wedding guest by the Ancient Mariner'. This is a trope and it was only after I grasped the concept of ghostly parasitism did I start to think about what is really going on in Coleridge's poem – the Wedding Guest is the Mariner's prey, and the tale is contagion. At this realisation, I got a sudden vision of myself back that night in McGruders at the witching hour, and Mangan rearing out of the shiny book of poems to speak through Shane, his avatar. It was only then I realised what now seems so obvious: I had been 'summoned' from the start, just like every other Manganista, and the genre this book belongs to isn't detective/true crime but the ghost story. During all the years I was complaining of being passed over by Mangan's ghost, I was in fact possessed; this didn't make me feel triumphant, but chilled.

*

On 12 December 2021, which was a Sunday, I was at my desk early to work on the chapter on the Famine. Frank was downstairs on a Zoom call with his sister and the priest who would be officiating at their father's funeral the next day. At 9.50 a.m. Frank's brother called 'Bridget' from downstairs in his habitually calm and deliberative way and I jumped from my desk in blind panic and ran downstairs.

Two weeks earlier, I had walked out the morning after Frank had been taken suddenly into hospital the night before and had dropped a large note into the hat of a beggar on Baggot Street. He took it and secreted it without looking at me or thanking me so that I understood that my propitiation had been rebuffed, but when Frank emerged a few days later with a diagnosis that seemed eminently treatable, I allowed myself to dismiss this thought as superstition while, at the same time I was beside myself with worry since he would not take to his bed and rest and I had begun phoning his friends to beg them to help me persuade him. One of them said 'yes, we do not want him to be Parnell', which put the heart across me because I knew – you could not know Frank without knowing – that Parnell went from pillar to post in autumn 1891, traversing Ireland 'wretchedly ill' to support his doomed candidates in elections, finally arriving back to Katherine in Brighton to die. From this, Joyce got his image of the hunted stag and the line that Frank loved best 'but hunt me the journeyon, iteritinerant, the kal his course, amid the semitary of Somnionia. Even unto Heliotropolis, the castellated, the enchanting'. The mention of Parnell was a frightening omen, and it was frightening too, when in the days after Frank came out of hospital, his father, who lay ill and dying, suddenly asked another of his children had Frank died – but we did not how to read these omens.

In the terrible days and weeks and months after, people told me he was still with me, which I didn't feel, though neither did I feel that he was gone because how could someone so much here be so suddenly not here. I would beg him to come to me in dreams but he came seldom which tormented me, as if I were failing him, or he me, until a friend, who had lost her partner a few years earlier, told me that it was the same for her, and that her psychiatrist had told her, with some impatience, that of course he wasn't coming in dreams because he was on her mind throughout the day, firing her consciousness, and dreams dredge the unconscious. It gave me some comfort to think that the dead who are always on our minds do not have to prey on us parasitically through dreams and visitations. In the journal I kept that year, the only sustained period I have ever kept a journal, I find an entry for 12 September, when I was in Greece: 'Sometimes I imagine I feel him walking here beside me. But I don't want to think of him hovering and yearning. I want him to be somewhere free and complete.' It is a stray line which I didn't return to or explicate but reading it now it seems to capture my unease at the idea of the hungry ghost hovering anxiously and greedily around the living, which has always seemed to me the most terrifying of all the images and scenarios we have for the afterlife, which is why I find films like *The Sixth Sense* and *The Others* so chilling, with their anxious ghosts who do not know that they are dead but imagine they are still interacting with the living, and what terrifies me is not the idea of being haunted when alive, but of hanging around when dead and not crossing over to suffer death's sea-change into something rich and strange.

I knew Frank wasn't a hungry ghost in the Tibetan sense of being 'deserted or neglected' by his relatives and this wasn't just thanks to me and his siblings and nephews and nieces, but to the vast collective effort of his friends, colleagues, clients and associates whose number was unending or so it seemed to me in the days and weeks after when I would hang like a hungry ghost in the hall each morning waiting for the white envelopes that would arrive from all over the country from people whom I had never met, and I understood from their heartfelt outpourings that went beyond conventional expressions of sympathy, that I was the conduit for them to comfort themselves, the means by which they could reach and articulate their sense of loss. After a while I began to discern a theme or pattern to these letters: many referred obliquely to something he had done for them, the details of which they did not wish to burden me with, but which they felt compelled to mention so to mark his extraordinary kindness and efficacy, the way he had got them out of some issue and never referred to it again, brushing aside both payment and thanks, and I had no idea what any of these issues might be since he had never mentioned them to me, but I supposed they might be legal matters, and I guessed that I was not to be burdened with the details because they were abstruse and difficult and personal, and now no one would ever know what they were, but the proliferation of these white envelopes on the mat each morning with this same theme running through became in my mind like so many white wings winging him up to what I hesitate to call heaven or nirvana, because I have no real sense of such a place, but winging him away from Earth.

I could not in those first months read anything except poetry, my attention span being too poor for prose. That poetry did not include Mangan's, which I had reached for during the break-up, craving his sly irony which acknowledged the faint absurdity of the situation. If a break-up is a rehearsal, a kind of petit mort, for the final separation, it is a reversal of Marx's maxim on history: it is the first time as farce and the second as tragedy. I could find no absurdity in the separation of death. We use poetry as a mirror to reflect back to us our own feelings. In a book of poems for bereavement given to me by Frank's sister, I found my mirror in an urgently haunting poem by Leanne O'Sullivan:

> If we become separated from each other
> this evening try to remember the last time
> you saw me and go back and wait for me there.
> I promise I won't be very long,
> though I am haunted by the feeling
> that I might keep missing you,
> with the noise of the city growing too
> loud and the day burning out so quickly.
> But let's just say it's as good a plan as any.
> Just once let's imagine a word for the memory
> that lives beyond the body, that circles
> and sets all things alight. For I have
> singled you out from the whole world,
> and I would – even as this darkness
> is falling, even when the night comes
> where there are no more words, and the day
> comes when there is no more light.

The line 'I have singled you out from the whole world' broke me – and reminds me, writing it out now, that there is no such intimacy in Mangan, God help him, since he singled no one out from the whole world, which is perhaps why his poetry has nothing to impart to my grief – and the poem seems to me to be happening in the afterlife, or at death's door: it is the urgent instruction, as the light fades from the poet to her lover of where to meet, 'confusion of the deathbed over' as Yeats has it, and I took it that the place she was referring to 'the last time you saw me' was in Dublin – although there are no Dublin markers in the poem and the poet is from the Beara peninsula – because the lines seem to me to start up where 'Raglan Road' lays off 'on a quiet street where old ghosts meet'.

It was when cycling past certain street corners, houses, bars and restaurants in Dublin that the pain would come at me like a knife and seemed more than I could bear, except that I could not seem to help returning to twist the knife. I realised that I was the hungry ghost and that, in the poem, it is the poet rather than her lover who is the hungry ghost, which makes me wonder if the Tibetan tradition makes too much of neglectful relatives and not enough of the over-possessive who will not let our loved ones go.

It was in film, rather that poetry, that I found the clearest mirror of my grief. The first film in Kieślowski's triptych, *Three Colours Blue*, has an image of bereavement which has stayed with me since I saw it almost thirty years ago: Juliette Binoche doing lengths in an empty swimming pool at night, after the death of her husband and child in a car crash. It is the blue of the pool that signifies grief – a cold, sustained colour, not a passionate spurt like red – and also the repetitive routine, the monotonous lengths up and down the pool. I found that numbing routine myself, not in swimming but at barre pilates classes, which became my reflection of grief: girls in a mirrored room, hands on barre, the quick words, plié, repassé, chassé, élevé and the small, tightly controlled repetitive movements, which hold off the moment I have to go back out to the street at twilight, once my favourite moment of the day because it was when he would call to see did I want to eat in town or did I want for him to pick something up, but what is waiting for me now, as my foot goes forward, to the right, and back, and forward, to the right and back, this nicely mindless routine which stops my thoughts, is the exit to the cold night air, the blank phone screen, the cycle back to the empty house.

Working at my desk, I would hear like the angel melodies that perhaps come down to the souls in purgatory, the sounds of hurrying feet and quick laughter as Frank's niece and her friend and their boyfriends flew up and down the stairs to the apartment above, pursuing the busy idle lives of humanities students with what Henry James called 'the hungry *futurity* of youth'. One evening, when I encountered them on the stairs, the niece and her boyfriend began speaking enthusiastically of a lecture I had given on Mangan years ago in the Little Museum of Dublin. I was bemused that the lecture was still online and that these kids, barely twenty years old, should have seen it and not from any exaggerated sense of what was owing to me, but because they had quite independently conceived a passion for Mangan. 'We have a Mangan appreciation society upstairs,' his niece announced cheerfully, explaining that she was the latest recruit, drawn in by the other three.

It had come about during the summer, her boyfriend explained, when they were interrailing round Europe and had brought with them an anthology of romantic poetry, which they would open randomly every time they piled, half-washed and part-slept, into the compartment of the latest train taking them to a new city and would read aloud from whatever page they alighted on. Among all the Byron and Shelley and Keats, Mangan was a rare Irish romantic, which aroused their interest, and then they became entranced by his misery – 'such an *orgy* of misery, it was like a *joke*' they remarked with great perceptiveness – and finally, they found to their surprise that it was his lines that stayed with them when all the knights and nightingales and damsels with dulcimers had departed. 'Sleep! – no more the dupe of hopes or schemes / Soon thou sleepest where the thistles blow – / Curious anti-climax to thy dreams / Twenty golden years ago!'

I was amazed by the coincidence or destiny that had brought these callow Manganistas to live on the floor above me. Since I knew, from years of blank stares, into what obscurity Mangan had fallen, it was hard not to read some deeper significance into this, and I was charmed until the niece's boyfriend approached one day with enthusiasm and diffidence to say that he had written a monograph on Mangan, which he would be delighted if I would read. I gazed speechless upon this pale and slender young man with his dark hair flopping over his forehead. It was amazing to me that, with all the competition from social media and streaming platforms, Dublin was still producing the type of bookish young man whom I had encountered in college in the 1990s, and my parents in the 60s, and Joyce had put into the pages of *Portrait.* I was moved by the unlikely survival of this type, which seems to me quintessentially Dublin, and had he been waving a pamphlet on Joyce or Yeats or Beckett, my enthusiasm would have been unconstrained but, as it was, I was filled with a sense of disquiet, which only deepened when I read his monograph, which was, I thought, stunningly good, coming from someone so young, but the way it echoed themes in my book, which he had not then read, was unnerving. When I came upon this line: 'By this point, Mangan has vanished, a fleeing shade seeking shadier corners' I was spooked since it could be a line from my passage on the 'Man who Wasn't There' and this is not a generic trope in Mangan studies, at least not in the two major biographies that are the usual starting points – although it is a leitmotif in Joyce's essay and since that was a framing device for the monograph, I should not perhaps have been so unnerved, but the phrase 'a fleeing shade', which is to say, a ghost, left me frightened for this young man. I realised that Mangan had seized him by the same means – an anthology of poetry – as he had me. It was terrible that he should be possessing someone so young. No part of me wished this youth to give up his lifeblood to 'fleshing out' Mangan's 'skeletons of thought' although I could not but admire Mangan for secreting himself into the anthology to be taken on a whistle-stop tour of Europe, ready to pounce … I pictured the scene in the compartment of the train like the last scene in the Swedish vampire film *Let the Right One In*, where the boy, Oskar, is seen seated on a train with the trunk beside him containing the vampire girl, Eli, who has just routed his bullies in bloody slaughter, and whom, we infer, will now go with him everywhere until he ends up like the ruined old man glimpsed earlier in the film, and she moves on to possess the next child …

To prevent this terrible eventuality, I gave my niece's boyfriend this book in draft and asked for his editorial assistance (which I did need) in the hope that the narrative of my obsession, at times so mad, if also at times I hope exhilarating, would deter him, although, in truth, I have absolutely no idea if this book is a prophylactic against Mangan or its opposite, a stimulant and inducement. While I cannot imagine a sane person wishing to hurl themselves down the rabbit hole after me, I have too much respect for Mangan's talent for survival to think that he would have recruited me if I was going to prove a dead-end or, worse, a deterrent.

And now, writing this, it occurs to me that perhaps my pious reason for passing my book on to this young man – to save him from possession – is an instance of what the existentialists call *mauvaise foi*, the bad faith that makes us cast our bad deeds in a positive light. Perhaps I gave him this book for the same reason that the Ancient Mariner related his tale to the Wedding Guest, and that Shane opened 'The Vision of Connaught' for me: to pass on the spell and free myself. It has been a long haunting. I think it is over. I remain in awe of Mangan but also in sadness. I'm not sure that his kind of immortality is worth it. Perhaps, after all, it is better not to plan to be a vampire feeding on each new generation of the living. Perhaps it is better to let go.

It was the summer after Frank had gone, in or around Bloomsday, that his brother came into the kitchen where I was dining with friends to say that the previous evening, he had seen bats in the square, and we should check it out now because twilight was approaching. It seemed of such exotic-ness to see bats in Dublin city centre that we put down our plates and went out to the square and lay down on the grass without a blanket since it was dry as dust, there having been no rain in weeks, and gazed up at the sky now shading to grey, and I couldn't believe we would see anything, but then someone cried 'There's one!' and someone else 'I see it!'

But I couldn't see anything; I had never seen a bat, though in a place called Trancoso in Bahia state in Brazil, a dusky magical place by the sea and the darkest place I have ever been because unilluminated by street lights, Frank saw, emerging from a dense tree at twilight, crowds of bats, and he stood there transfixed, watching them swoop, but I, having come out without my glasses, could make out nothing, so I watched him watching them until the light was gone, and now remembering this, I thought it would be same again in the square, even though this time I had my glasses, and that I would never see a bat, just as I have never seen a ghost, and I knew time was against me since twilight was fading, but then from the corner of my eye I saw a kind of flicker or whoosh, like the shooting stars that fall in Kerry every year in August around the time of my father's anniversary, and then another, and another, whooshing all around like blanched fireworks, as if every bat in the square were on the move or as if my eyes, finally attuned to what they were looking for, had speeded up to crowd everything into the final seconds before darkness fell.

Thanks

to Shane MacGowan for introducing me to Mangan, and to Trevor, John, Sinéad and Cillian for being there that night,

to Ciaran Brady and Patrick Geoghegan for suggesting I do a biography for the UCD *Life and Times* series and endorsing Mangan as a good choice (I'm sorry it got out of hand),

to Jacques Chuto for his immense expertise and generosity in sharing it, to the other Manganistas – David Lloyd for his insight and enigma, James McCabe for his aperçus and David Wheatley for suggesting a psychogeography approach – and to the impromptu fans whose enthusiasm confirmed that Mangan is still undead, Paddy McCarthy, Patrick Prendergast, Gary Coyle and Seamus Moran,

to the staff in Pearse Street Library for their kind support and for bringing me journals in hard copy,

to my writing group, Maggie, Luke, Simon, Dillon and Donal, for keeping me on my toes, and to Nadia Whiston Battersby, Regan Hutchins, Sharon Beatty, Brian Lynch, Eoin MacNally, Trevor White and Margaret O'Callaghan, amazing readers who made wonderful suggestions, to my brother Francis for his marvellous sketch,

to Ivan Mulcahy, prince among agents, to Seán Hayes, for his élan in taking the text in a new direction, commissioning it and doing a brilliant edit, and to my publishers, Margaret Farrelly for pin-sharp editing and Teresa Daly, Iollann Ó Murchú, Fiona Murphy and all the team at Gill for their talent, enthusiasm and professionalism and for putting up with my delays and demurrals,

finally, to my family and Frank's, my mother, siblings, in-laws, nephews and nieces. Thank you for being so great and seeing me through.

Picture Credits

Notes

Abbreviations:

AG	Mangan, James Clarence. *Anthologia Germanica*. William Curry, 1845.
CW	Chuto, Jacques, R.P. Holzapfel, P. Mac Mahon, Augustine Martin, P. Ó Snodaigh, Ellen Shannon-Mangan, Peter van de Kamp, editors. *The Collected Works of James Clarence Mangan*. Irish Academic Press, 2002.
DUM	*Dublin University Magazine*
Lloyd	Lloyd, David. *Nationalism and Minor Literature: James Clarence Mangan and the Emergence of Irish Cultural Nationalism*. University of California Press, 1987.
Mitchel	Mitchel, John. *Poems by James Clarence Mangan*. New York: P.M. Haverty, 1859.
O'Donoghue	O'Donoghue, D.J. *The Life and Writings of James Clarence Mangan*. Dublin: M.H. Gill & Son and T.G. O'Donoghue, 1897.
Shannon-Mangan	Shannon-Mangan, Ellen. *James Clarence Mangan, a Biography*. Dublin: Irish Academic Press, 1996.

11   **I cannot do so if I would … laying bare [his] own delinquencies** 'Autobiography', *CW, Prose 1840–1882*, p. 227.

15–16   **[Mangan] was invited to a social party** O'Donoghue, p. 191.

18   **fathering upon other authors the offspring of my own brain** *CW, Prose 1840–1882*, p. 224.

23   **a miserable back room destitute** Meehan, C.P. *Poets and Poetry of Munster* (1883), preface, p. xx.

23   **Oh! the luxury of clean sheets** Atkinson, Sara. *Mary Aikenhead, her life, work and her friends*. Gill, 1879, p. 259.

23   **bruised and disfigured** Meehan, op. cit., p. xxiv.

24–5   **habitually as a huntsman would treat refractory hounds** All quotes from 'Autobiography', *CW, Prose 1840–1882*, pp. 227–39.

27   **did not think it a faithful picture** Meehan, op. cit., p. xli, footnote.

27   **destroy the performance … leave it as a souvenir** Editorial note prefixed to Mangan's 'Fragment of an Unpublished Autobiography', *Irish Monthly*, Vol. X, No. 113, November 1882, p. 675.

28   **My mother and father held me by chains** Letter to James McGlashun, May 1845/April 1846, *CW, Prose 1840–1882*, p. 277.

29   **hair-brained [*sic*] girl** *The Irishman*, 17 August 1850; *CW, Prose 1840–1882*, p. 222.

29   **A kind friend** *Irish Monthly*, November 1882, op. cit.

29   **full of terrible, untrue things** Yeats, W.B. 'Clarence Mangan's love affair', *United Ireland*, 22 August 1891.

30   **the merest rêve d'une vie** Meehan, op. cit.

30   **of course, purely imaginary … esteemed him highly** O'Donoghue, p. 20.

31 **In a moment of frenzy [Mangan] breaks silence** Joyce, James. 'James Clarence Mangan', *St Stephen's*, vol. 1, no. 6 (May 1902), pp. 116–18.

32 **a fiction … a representation of psychosis** Lloyd, p. 167.

33 **courageous witness to the abuse he suffered** Shannon-Mangan, p. 393.

38 **had no recollection of a sister** McCall Papers, op. cit.

39 **Terence Brown's essay** Brown, Terence. 'Mangan and the Worst of Woes', *Borderlands: Essays on Literature and Medicine in Honour of J.B. Lyons*, Royal College of Surgeons in Ireland, 2002, pp. 60–9.

40 **the adamantine barrier that levered me from a communion with mankind** Quoted in obituary article by Price, James. *Evening Packet* 11 October 1849.

41 The quotes in this chapter from the Smith relatives are from the John McCall papers, National Archives, MS 7959, p. 271; McCall, John. *Life of James Clarence Mangan*. T.D. Sullivan 90 Middle Abbey Street, 1882.

44 **said to be a cousin** *Denis Mangan*, www.humphrysfamilytree. com/Mangan/denis.sr.html. Accessed 20 March 2024; Bourke, Marcus. *The O'Rahilly*. Anvil Books, 1967.

44 **quarter of the Catholic population** Lewis, Samuel. *A Topographical Dictionary of Ireland.* Printed for Clearfield Co. by Genealogical Pub. Co., 2004, p. 550.

46 **wouldn't have had to sleep in Dublin's doorways** *Irish Press*, 21 June 1949.

47 **For some days and nights** *CW, Prose 1840–1882*, pp. 270–1.

54–5 **To the rere of the house extended** 'My Transformation, A Wonderful Tale', *CW, Prose 1832–1839*, p. 42.

61 **The most remarkable feature to be noticed** Wakeman, W.F. 'Old Dublin, No. XVIII', *Evening Telegraph*, 7 May 1887, p. 2.

63 **repeatedly devoured stupendous quantities** *CW, Prose 1832–1839*, p. 113.

74 **unduly fortified by the long wait** Dickson, David. *Dublin: The Making of a Capital City.* Profile Books Ltd, 2015, p. 267.

75 **a military look throughout** Viscount Palmerston, cited Dickson, p. 271.

75 **each window [with] a sloping cover** Grimes, Seamus. *Ireland in 1804.* Four Courts Press, 1980, p. 20.

76 **The streets are generally narrow** Whitelaw, James. *An essay on the population of Dublin, being the result of an actual survey taken in 1798.* Graisberry and Campbell, no. 10, Back-Lane, 1805.

77 **hollowed out** Dickson, p. 281.

78 For conditions in Ireland after Battle of Waterloo in 1815, see Tuathaigh, Gearóid Ó. *Ireland before the Famine: 1798–1848.* Gill and Macmillan, 1987, pp. 135–40; Cullen, Louis Michael. *An Economic History of Ireland since 1660.* B.T. Batsford, 1972.

79 **some dreadful fever may be the consequence** Costello, Kevin. 'Imprisonment for Debt in early Nineteenth Century Ireland, 1810–1848'. *UCD Working Papers in Law, Criminology & Socio-Legal Studies Research Paper No. 09/2013.*

79 **30 per cent in parts of Dublin** 'Hibernicus', *A Letter to the Right Honourable Sir John Newport*, published Dublin 1821, cited Maxwell, Constantia. *Dublin under the Georges, 1714–1830.* Faber and Faber, 1956, p. 285.

79 **3,100 looms were idle** *Dublin Evening Post and Saunders Newsletter.* 25 April 1826, p. 128.

79 **for the distressed weavers in the Liberties** Hansard, House of Commons 1826, xxix, p. 206, cited Milne, Kenneth. *The Dublin Liberties, 1600–1850.* Four Courts Press Ltd, 2009, p. 16.

79 **dreadful visitation of fever and other malignant disorders** Milne, op. cit., p. 16.

81 **He never startles us by saying beautiful things** Yeats, W.B. 'Clarence Mangan (1803–1849)', *Irish Fireside*, 12 March 1887, p. 170.

83–5 **I saw Maturin but on three occasions** *CW, Prose 1840–1882*, pp. 192–3.

86 **'demolished towers' etc.** The quoted lines are from 'To the Ruins of Donegal Castle', 'Melancholy', 'Lament over the Ruins of Teach Malaga', 'Verses to a Friend', 'The Kiosk of Moonstanzar-Billah'.

90 **using the novelist's art of arrangement** Woolf, Virginia. *Granite and Rainbow: Essays*. Harcourt Brace Jovanovich, 1958.

90 **barren period** O'Donoghue, op. cit., p. 22.

90 **a gap that painstaking biography** Mitchel, op. cit., p. 11.

92 **'abominable' joking** *The Nation*, 28 March 1846; **Fescennine buffoonery** Mitchel, op. cit., p. 23.

92 **a bright-haired youth** Mitchel, op. cit., p. 11.

93–4 **In Mangan's juvenile days** McCall, op. cit., p. 7.

94 **the greatest source of information** *Irish Book Lover*, vol. 3, 1912, p. 129.

94 **never in all my life knew business so bad … Printing of books is comparatively nothing in Ireland** Benson, Charles. 'Printers and Booksellers in Dublin 1800–1850', *Spreading the Word: The Distribution Networks of Print 1550–1850*, St. Paul's Bibliographies, 1990, pp. 47–59.

94–5 **from £21,000 in 1813 to below £15,000** Inglis, Brian. *The Freedom of the Press in Ireland*. Greenwood Press, 1954, p. 190.

95 **By 1830 the average number of advertisements** Inglis, p. 193.

95–6   **The conflict of Catholic-Whig-Irish Nationalist versus** Hayley, Barbara. 'Irish Periodicals from the Union to the Nation.' *Anglo-Irish Studies*, vol. 2, 1976, pp. 83–108.

97   **never deigning to attorn to English criticism** Mitchel, op. cit., p. 85.

105   **another, in fact better explanation** Shannon-Mangan, op. cit., p. 85.

106   **a Miss Stackpoole of Mount Pleasant-square** Yeats, W.B. 'Clarence Mangan (1803–1849)', *Irish Fireside*, 12 March 1887, p. 169.

106   **a dozen or more unpublished letters of Mangan's … a very handsome girl** Yeats, W.B. 'Clarence Mangan's love affair', *United Ireland*, 22 August 1891.

107   **[Mangan] once, with unusual bitterness of manner, alluded** *Evening Packet*, 22 September 1849.

108–9   **In one at least of the great branches of education** Mitchel, op. cit., p. 11.

110–11   **Shortly after our acquaintance commenced** Duffy, C.G. 'Personal Memories of James C. Mangan', *Dublin Review*, April 1908, no. 285, pp. 278–94.

111   **Shannon-Mangan, declaring herself 'almost certain'** Shannon-Mangan, op. cit., p. 170.

113   **Mangan's affair with a cold enchantress** He reprinted the poem 'To xxxxx xxxxx', slightly amended, in *DUM* in April 1839, retitling it 'To Laura', having recycled the two sonnets into the earlier January issue. *The Collected Works* follow the *DUM* positioning rather than the *Comet*'s so that the sonnets precede 'To Laura'. This messes up the sequence of the 'love affair', and the *DUM* version 'To Laura' is not as good as the *Comet*'s.

122   **seized on and decoded** Ehrlich, Heyward. '"Araby" in Context: The "Splendid Bazaar," Irish Orientalism, and

James Clarence Mangan.' *James Joyce Quarterly*, vol. 35, no. 2/3, 1998, pp. 309–31.

122   **a brilliant essay entitled** Van de Kemp, Peter. 'Hands Off! Joyce and the Mangan in the Mac.' *Configuring Romanticism: Essays Offered* to C.C. Barfoot, BRILL, 2003, pp. 183–214; Chuto, Jacques. *James Joyce Quarterly*, Winter 2017.

124–5   The 'hand' lines are from 'The Four Idiot Brothers', 'The Knight of Toggenburg', 'Bleak was the Night', 'To Marianne', 'Faust', 'The Glove', 'Hundred-Leafed Rose', 'Dark Rosaleen', 'Lament over the Ruins of Teach Mologa'.

126   **we are sexual from the moment** McGahern, John. *Love of the World: Essays.* Faber & Faber, 2013, p. 3.

128   **oh! that was a glorious moment** AG VII, *CW, Prose 1832–1839.* p. 113–14

131   **notable journalistic venture** Moody, T.W. *Thomas Davis, 1814–45: A Centenary Address Delivered in Trinity College, Dublin, on 12 June 1945 at a Public Meeting of the College Historical Society.* Hodges, Figgis & Co., Ltd, 1945, p. 27.

133   **all the founders of *The Nation* agreed** Wallis, Thomas, editor. *The Poems of Thomas Davis.* D. & J. Sadlier & Co., 1866, p. xiii.

135   **when our acquaintance was still new** Duffy, C.G. 'Personal Memories', op. cit., p. 283.

135   **He was about five feet six or seven** Meehan, op. cit., p. xv.

136   **He possessed very weak eyes** Wakeman, op. cit.

136   **coxcomb** *DUM*, vol. 46, June–December 1855, p. 448.

137   **I have had no experience in that genre** Letter to Duffy, 1840, *CW, Prose 1840–1882*, p. 254.

139   **regarding the Asiatics as a subordinate** *DUM* 1837; *CW, Prose 1832–1839*, p. 254.

140   **O'Connell sneered publicly at 'the poor rhymed dullness'** Brown, Malcolm. *The Politics of Irish Literature.* University of Washington Press, 1972, p. 63.

143   **My poor mother lies dangerously ill** Letter, 14 December 1844, *CW, Prose 1840–1882*, p. 256.

150   **Late last Summer** McCabe, James. 'The Desert and the Solitude', *Metre*, vol. 10, 2010, pp. 115–25.

151   **a new confusion** Letter Jacques Chuto to David Wheatley, 7 March 2002.

157   **The disposition and temper** *CW, Prose 1840–1882*, p. 205.

157   **words of encouragement and gentle attentions** Meehan, op. cit., p. xvii.

158   **in the lowest and obscurest taverns** Mitchel, op. cit., p. 18.

160   **Mangan must have been very hurt** Shannon-Mangan, op. cit., p. 394.

160   **full of terrible untrue things** Yeats, W.B. 'Clarence Mangan's love affair', *United Ireland,* 22 August 1891.

160–1   **there was nothing unusual in a fifteen-year-old** Shannon-Mangan, op. cit., pp. 21–2.

163   **There are more sources for his death and burial** James Price, Fr Meehan, Joseph Brenan, Hercules Ellis and Sir Fredrick Burton left written accounts; a 'literary friend' of John McCall and Dr William Stokes left verbal reminiscences. Unless otherwise specified, the quotes describing Mangan's death are from James Price's articles in the *Evening Packet*, 22 September 1849, 11 October 1849, 3 November 1849.

163   **Our fears proportionately increase** *Belfast News Letter*, 8 June 1849.

164   **two thirds of Dublin's cholera cases are among vagrants** *The Freeman's Journal*, 15 May 1849.

164   **Over a hundred people this week** *Kerry Evening Post*, 16 June 1849.

164   **The Board of Health has begged people** Descriptions of cholera from Cholera Board Proclamations, cited

Duffy, Patricia. 'Cholera in County Louth, 1832–39', *Journal of the County Louth Archaeological and Historical Society*, vol. 20, no. 2, 1982, p. 117, https://doi.org/10.2307/27729546; O'Neill, Timothy P. 'Fever and Public Health in Pre-Famine Ireland.' *The Journal of the Royal Society of Antiquaries of Ireland*, vol. 103, 1973, pp. 1–34.

165 **presentiment that he was doomed … maintaining that there was no such thing in rerum natura as contagion** Meehan, op. cit., p. xxv.

166 **You are the first man who has spoken** O'Donoghue, op. cit., p. 219.

166–7 **without having the sufferer's suspicions aroused** McCall, op. cit., pp. 29–30 (McCall attributed this anecdote to a 'literary friend').

167 **I feel that I am going** All quotes in this para from Meehan, op. cit.

168 **his first inquiry naturally** McCall, John, op. cit.

169 **sultry day … you never saw anything so beautiful in your entire life** letter Frederick Burton to O'Donoghue, cited O'Donoghue, p. 222.

171 ***Five* friends who knew the man** Brenan, Joseph. 'James Clarence Mangan', *The Irishman*, 23 June 1849, p. 393.

172 **moving with noiseless step** Brenan, Joseph, op. cit.; **the man without a shadow … like an anatomy new risen from the dead** D'Arcy McGee, Thomas. 'Reminiscences of an Exiled Confederate, Clarence Mangan', *The Nation*, 25 September 1852, p. 58; **gliding, even as a shadow on the wall** Savage, John. *The United States Magazine and Democratic Review,* 1851; 'an unearthly and ghostly creature', Mitchel, p. 13.

177 **it is a curious fact** *The Nation*, 20 October 1849.

181   **common belief stems from a misinterpretation** Wilde, Robert. 'Why Mozart Wasn't Buried in a Pauper's Grave.' *ThoughtCo*, 25 March 2019, www.thoughtco.com/where-was-mozart-buried-1221267.

186   **blistering, anglophobic rhetoric** Quinn, James. 'Mitchel, John', *Dictionary of Irish Biography*, 1 October 2012, https://doi.org/10.3318/dib.005834.v2.

192   **not the least powerful talisman** Savage, John, op. cit.

195   **air of discovering Mangan, a little pretentious** Ellmann, Richard. *James Joyce: New and Revised Edition.* Oxford University Press, 1982, p. 94.

196   **he read quietly and distinctly, involving** Joyce, James. *Stephen Hero: Part of the First Draft of a Portrait of the Artist as a Young Man.* Paladin, 1991, p. 105.

196   **Joyce's delivery remains in my memory** Curran, C.P. *James Joyce Remembered.* Oxford University Press, 1969, p. 13.

196   **the structure of a symphony** Hackett, Felix. 'The society restored', *Centenary History of the Literary and Historical Society of University College Dublin 1855–1955.* Tralee: Kerryman, 1956, p. 64.

199   **rallied with 'timid courage' … in magnificent and sympathetic style** Hackett, op. cit., p. 66.

202   **Jacques Chuto's excavations of the 'manganese' elements** Chuto, Jacques. 'Mangan at the Wake', *Dublin James Joyce Journal*, vol. 11, July 2022, pp. 189–204.

202   **disperse by their wizard art the mists** *AG V, CW Prose 1833–1839*, p. 88.

207   **the empty room from which Lucy sets out** Muldoon, Paul. *To Ireland, I.* Faber & Faber, 2011, p. 76.

212   **presented Irish criticism with a challenge that has not yet** Denis Donoghue, jacket endorsement for Lloyd, David.

Anomalous States: Irish Writing and the Post-Colonial Moment. Duke University Press, 1995.

216 **Whether from an absence of sympathy with the unmitigated elements of the Ideal** *AG II, CW, Prose 1832–1839,* p. 73.

216 **The veils that his perverted translations** Lloyd, p. 128.

217 **providing a survey of German romanticism** Lloyd, p. 181.

222 **Writing on JCM in the late 1970s and early 1980s** Lloyd, David. 'Crossing over, On Mangan's "Spirits Everywhere" *Essays on James Clarence Mangan,* edited Sturgeon, Sinéad. Palgrave Macmillan, 2014, p. 14.

233 **Indeed the very circumstance** 'My Bugle, and How I Blow It', *CW, Prose 1840–1882.* p. 62.

235 **The subject is by no means easy** Berlin, Isaiah. *The Roots of Romanticism.* Edited by Henry Hardy, Princeton University Press, 2014, p. 14.

237 **The melodrama and morbidity of this fragment** Boland, Eavan. 'The Mangan Mystery', *The Irish Times,* 19 October 1968.

237 **Mangan's writing being read as a falling off from the romanticism it seeks to continue** Lloyd, p. 20.

237 **where all the most unbridled desires** Andrews, Jean.'James Clarence Mangan and the Romantic Stereotypes: "Old and Hoary at Thirty-Nine"', *Irish University Review,* vol. 19, no. 2, Autumn 1989, pp. 240–63.

246 **Mangan's sartorial eccentricity is thus doubled** Lloyd, op. cit., p. 197.

246-7 Lines are taken from 'The Separation', 'Curiosity', 'Saying from Djelim', 'To Marianne', 'The Wrongs and Woes of Erin', 'Kathleen Ny Houlahan', 'A Voice of Encouragement, New Year's Lay'.

249 **Only when you read the annotations to the** *Collected Works* CW *Poems vol 1*, Notes, p. 404

250 **not very 'eingehend'** Beers, Henry A. *A History of English Romanticism in the Nineteenth Century*. Henry Holt & Co, New York, 1901, p. 95.

250 **his oblique message to remain oblique** I was alerted to Schlegel's allusive instructions through an essay by Gerald McNiece, beginning: 'Friedrich Schlegel obviously enjoyed being ironic and allusive about irony, offering glances and indirections in the form of aphorisms and Delphic fragments calculated to quicken the imagination but never making altogether clear exactly what he meant by the "schillernde Phänomen" of his new irony.' McNiece, Gerald. 'Friedrich Schlegel and Romantic Irony', *The Knowledge that Endures*. Palgrave Macmillan, London, 1992, p. 109.

252 **Alcoholics frequently begin to experience** 'Mental Health Facility in Houston: Mental Health Services.' *New Dimensions Day Treatment Centers*, accessed on 4 January 2024, nddtreatment.com/.

254 **bristling with beauties, charm, sublime** Amis, Martin. *The War on Cliché*. London: Jonathan Cape, 2001, p. 427.

255 **a shot of espresso** *The Guardian*, 17 January 2015.

255–6 **by no means as coherent as the world of fiction** Malcolm, Janet. 'The Morality of Journalism', *The New York Review*, 1 March 1990.

260 **Farrell is clearly equating Ireland with the courtesan** *Irish Times*, 7 September 2013.

273–4 **As a man in a dream** *CW, Prose 1832–1839*, p. 147.

277 **The company was chiefly composed** Hudson, Joseph. 'An hour with James Clarance [*sic*] Mangan', *The Shamrock*, 27 February 1875, pp. 343–4.

280 **From the opening of the year** O'Donoghue, p. 159.

280   **He had the misfortune to live through one of the most chilling periods of Irish history** Welch, Robert. *Irish Poetry from Moore to Yeats.* Smythe, 1980. p. 105.

280–1   **Mangan was now forty years old** Shannon-Mangan, p. 266.

281   **It was at this moment** Boland, op. cit.

282   **I had a singular dream a few nights back** *CW, Prose 1840–1882,* p. 278.

286   **There was a rapid deterioration** Dickson, David. *Dublin: The Making of a Capital City.* Profile Books Ltd, 2015, p. 317.

297   **rotten potatoes and seaweed** *Cork Examiner,* 21 January 1846.

307   **deadbeat odysseys** Ransley, Lettie. 'Review of Two Serious Ladies', *The Guardian,* 14 November 2010.

307   **a mere quarryman digging** John O'Donovan, correspondence, NLI MS 132, No. 173, dated 6 June 1857, cited Boyne, Patricia. *John O'Donovan (1806–1861): A Biography.* Boethius, 1987, p. 128.

309–10   **all Irish men of learning before the advent** Mhac an tSaoi, Máire. 'Introduction', *Irish Minstrelsy.* Irish University Press, Dublin, 1971, p. xi.

311   **I felt a keen deprivation** Mantel, Hilary. *The Guardian,* 4 April 2009.

313   **fought and spoke and wrote in Irish** Mhac an tSaoi, Máire. 'Introduction', *Irish Minstrelsy.* Irish University Press, Dublin, 1971, p. xxv.

314   **our penal laws or of their own savage customs** Ferguson, Samuel. 'Hardiman's Irish Minstrelsy', *DUM,* Vol. III (January–June 1834), pp. 465–78, Vol. IV (July–December 1834), pp. 152–67, pp. 447–67, pp. 514–42.

316   **so far in advance of the taste** Mhac an tSaoi, ibid, p. vi.

317   **a clamor from landowners** Parsons, Ciln. *The Ordnance Survey and Modern Irish Literature*. Oxford University Press, 2016, pp. 10, 12.

318   **a mission 'to collect every possible information'** Wakeman, William Frederick. 'Aran – Pagan and Christian, Part 1', *Duffy's Hibernian Six Penny Magazine*, 1, n. 5 (1862), p. 460.

318   **hung with mahogany cases** Wakeman, op. cit., p. 461.

319   **it 'preserved on paper'** Parsons, op. cit., p. 84.

319   **carried their bigotry and politics to all parts of the kingdom** whistleblower letter, October 1842, cited Andrews, John Harwood. *A Paper Landscape*. Clarendon Press, 1975, p. 167.

320   **I verily believe the composition did not occupy [Mangan] half an hour** Wakeman, op. cit., p. 461.

321   **Duffy eulogised Mangan's 'power …'** *The Nation*, 16 November 1844.

321   **Mr Mangan has no knowledge of the Irish language** O'Curry to Thomas Davis, cited O'Donoghue, pp. 120–1.

322   **Mr P is working, on Mangan's back, for the life, on the P.J.** Cited Shannon-Mangan, op. cit., p. 241.

324–5   **The authentic chill of winter** Heaney, Seamus. 'The God in the Tree: Early Irish Nature Poetry', *Preoccupations: Selected Prose, 1968–1978*. Faber & Faber. 1980. p. 182.

326–7   **fills him with 'horror victorianorum'** Email Sean Haldane to Bridget Hourican, 1 April 2012.

327   **Mangan did not know Irish** Bergin, Osborn. *Bardic Poetry*. Dublin Institute for Advanced Studies, 1970, p. 124.

328   **There is a remarkable abundance of Gaelic verse** Ó Tuama, Seán, and Kinsella, Thomas. *An Duanaire 1600–1900: Poems of the Dispossessed*. The Dolmen Press, 1981, p. 68.

329 **Yeats taking over from James Clarence Mangan** Kiberd, Declan. *Irish Classics*. Granta, 2000, p. 278.

330 **It was bracing to read from the Pound expert** Nadel, Ira B. 'Understanding Pound', *The Cambridge Companion to Ezra Pound*. Cambridge University Press, 2008, p. 18.

330 **the meaning (or essence) of a given work or culture exists for Pound** Xie, Ming. 'Pound as translator', *The Cambridge Companion to Ezra Pound*, op. cit., pp. 204–23.

330 **a quintessentially Benjaminian translator** '[From the Vault] Ezra Pound's The Seafarer, Rhythmic Translation, and the Modernist Uses of Old English.' *MERE PSEUD BLOG ED.*, merepseudbloged.wordpress.com/2016/03/27. Accessed 21 March 2024.

330 **no translation would be possible if in its ultimate essence** Benjamin, Walter. 'The Task of the Translator', *Walter Benjamin: Selected Writings 1913–1926*, vol. 1. The Belknap Press of Harvard University Press, 2004, p. 253.

332 **such tender (if patronising) respect** see for instance Ó Mórdha, Séamus P. 'Charlotte Brooke – her background and achievement', *Breifne*, vol. 24, 1986, pp. 320–41; Brooke, Charlotte. *Charlotte Brooke's Reliques of Irish Poetry*. Edited by Lesa Ní Mhunghaile, Irish Manuscripts Commission, 2009.

333 **A translation issues from the original** Benjamin, Walter, op. cit.

337 **the great captain who is ravaging Desmond** Bergin, Osborn, op. cit., p. 124.

340 **pleasant figment of [Ferguson's] enthusiasm** Denman, Peter. *Samuel Ferguson: The Literary Achievement*. Barnes & Noble, 1990, p. 25.

356–7 **The Seeress (who had herself the information from one of her grey visitants)** *CW, Prose 1840–1882*, p. 90.

358–9 **Goethe probably wrote more for an undeveloped** *CW, AG V, CW, Prose 1832–1839*. p. 95.